GOD WITHOUT LIMITS:

Escape From the Matrix of Lies

By Bri Griffen-Moss

GOD WITHOUT LIMITS: Escape From the Matrix of Lies

1st Edition, 2024

Copyright © 2024 by Bri Griffen-Moss

Published by Amazon Kindle Direct Publishing

ISBN: 979-8-218-26537-3

For more information about the book and the author, please visit:

GodWithoutLimitsMinistry.com

Email: GodWithoutLimitsBook@Gmail.com

Printed in the United States of America

Contents

Preface

This book holds a journey awaiting your embarkation. It's no accident you hold it now. It represents a path I once scoffed at, a realm of understanding I arrogantly dismissed, until life itself unraveled the fabric of my certainty and laid bare a profound truth. It wasn't until a life crisis brought me to my knees, and destroyed my house of certainty, that I could begin to grasp a truth worth knowing. My tale is one of dramatic spiritual awakening.

Ensnared by the immense matrix of lies that entangles our existence, my series of supernatural encounters with the Creator of this world broke me free from a prison of darkness I didn't even know existed. From the despair and rubble of my shattered reality blossomed a new understanding of who our Maker truly is.

It was only in my sincere longing and humility to know the truth about God and this world that I was able to escape the lie I was living in. Arrogance, pride, and faulty assertions bound me to a world of delusion and deception of such magnitude that I could not see what had been in front of me my whole life.

Through my intense desire for a genuine relationship with my Creator and the relentless pursuit of truth, this book came to be. As I embraced more fully an unyielding surrender in my journey towards the Comforter, I experienced the miraculous healing of sicknesses, witnessed the restoration of broken hearts, and saw remarkable displays of the Giver of Life's mighty power.

I always knew I was going to write a book, yet the content I'm about to present in these pages was something I could never have predicted. My entire mental framework of reality before my encounters, my firmly held perceptions of the world and spirituality, had become an impenetrable concrete wall that cemented me into an illusion where truth remained elusive. In the quarry of my challenging life circumstance, my humility created a crack in the world I was living, allowing the radiant light of the Spirit of Truth to illuminate the most shadowed areas of my understanding.

In the chapters that await you, I reveal how the Spirit of God uncovered hidden chains of bondage within me, chains I never knew existed. As you turn these pages, I challenge you to look beyond the veil of your own perceptions, to question, to seek, and to leave no stone unturned in your search for truth.

I extend to you an invitation: join me in this exploration of the unknown. This book isn't just a recounting of events; it's a doorway to a new realm of unparalleled freedom, understanding and experiences. Though it may challenge the worldview of some, it nonetheless is an exploration worth pursuing. In this personal story, I will share the vivid and sometimes surreal encounters that profoundly altered my perceptions of God, reality, and my own self.

It is my aspiration that this book will lead you in humility to ask the right questions and uncover profound truths. For those bound in hidden bondage as I once was, may this narrative serve as a key to unlock unseen confines and shed light into the deepest corridors of your soul. For those who have already found the freedom I have, may this account be a testament to unparallelled power of our Maker as well as an inspiration and reminder of just how great the Restorer is.

God the Creator asked me to be a vessel through which this message can be shared, and I give it to you in deep humility, love, and devotion in service to God, and for the freedom some might not know they have yet to gain. If the supernatural intrigues you as it does me, you will find within this book a wealth of stories that reveal the extraordinary and unrivaled power of God. For all the unsolvable sufferings and conundrums of your life, there is an answer. You may discover that answer within these pages, which have been enlivened with the life-giving Spirit of God, whom I now serve.

The decision now lies with you. I'm on the brink of sharing insights, that once I uncovered them, I could never return to the matrix of lies I once lived in. I can't unsee what I have seen or deny the unveiling of this world's mysteries by God. Now, like Neo in *The Matrix*, you face a choice: will you take the red pill, venturing beyond the veil to discover what lies beyond, or choose the blue pill, leaving the insights within these pages unexplored? (This analogy references the 1999 movie *The Matrix*.)

Choosing the red pill symbolizes a readiness to embrace truths that might be disruptive or transformative, while opting for the blue pill means continuing to live within the comfortable bounds of conventional reality. Regardless of one's awareness, there are phenomena occurring beyond the scope of our ordinary perception, in realms most aren't aware of. My experiences have taught me that ignorance is not bliss; rather, it's a facade that gradually frays the fabric of our souls.

If you've been endlessly seeking in various spiritual practices like meditation, Buddhism, Yoga, Reiki healing, following gurus, studying Shiva, delving into chakra healing, Vipassana, and other paths in search of a connection with the divine and a remedy for persistent issues, then this book is for you. Continue reading.

If you have sought God by attending church your whole life but have yet to witness the supernatural aspects of God described in the Bible, may this book serve as an inspiration to your firm faith. For those yearning to experience miracles, herein these pages are insights into accessing the extraordinary, supernatural abilities of our Creator.

This book is not just for the spiritually or religiously inclined; if you are someone who appreciates a good suspenseful story, regardless of your spiritual beliefs or lack thereof, you'll at the least find it engaging. This narrative was authored under the influence and inspiration of the Spirit of Truth, and it carries a unique message for every reader it reaches.

In the coming pages, I share revelations bestowed upon me through numerous supernatural interactions with the Giver of Life. Through my story, you will be introduced to a presence that surpasses all things in our world; a power that defies ordinary constraints of reality, produces miracles, and is the very essence that all souls long for. Should this book come into your possession, I encourage you to read it through to its conclusion.

While certain aspects of this book contain the potential to push you out of your comfort zone, remember, it's often in that place that the greatest change and transformation can occur. By reading it with an open and objective perspective, you may discover valuable insights uniquely meant for you. Above all, my deepest hope is for you to encounter the awe-inspiring magnificence of God, who reigns over all the heavens and Earth. Within God, there lies an unmatchable power and grace, ready to be revealed on the other side of the escape from the matrix of lies.

Part 1

My Search for Spirituality

1

Leaving Religion for Spirituality

The hunger for God has ached in me for most of my life. I have always considered myself to be a spiritual person. Life, to me, seems meaningless, without a connection to something holy, something sacred. Having a connection to the divine has given me a reason to rise every morning, to strive to be a better person, and provided me with the compassion necessary to help and serve others.

For many years before my supernatural encounters with God, I held the conviction that all paths lead to God, and that God can be found in anything and through any kind of spiritual worship. I traveled around the world, praying in Catholic churches in Peru, worshiping in Hindu temples in India, and perspiring prayers in the sweat lodges of Mexico. At the time, I fully believed any spiritual act I did, I could do for and with God, whether sitting in all the Cacao circles in my hometown, calling on the Hindu god Ganesha to remove obstacles, or drinking ayahuasca in the jungles of Peru to learn from the Spirit World.

I lived and operated my life under a New Age philosophy, holding the assertion that God is everywhere and in everything. It is because of those strongly held beliefs that I explored many paths of spirituality on my spiritual journey. The more ways to touch God, the merrier, I believed, exploring a wide range of saints, spiritual teachers, and traditions, enjoying the novelty of a diverse spiritual path.

Through my adolescence, I occasionally attended Christian churches, coming in and out of the youth groups, but was always inconclusive about how much of the Christian religion I actually believed. One night at church, when I was a teenager, they did an altar call, saying, "You must let Jesus into your heart, so you don't go to hell." I felt fearful and skeptical, but despite my hesitation, I heeded the call.

I walked shyly to the altar, and a youth leader came and placed his hand on my back. I prayed as earnestly as I could at the time, inviting Jesus into my heart. Much to my dismay, nothing noticeable happened. I could sense no change, no magic feeling, and I felt no different. In the weeks and months to follow, I continued to experience the same emotional pain and struggles, and still was unclear whether I was going to heaven or hell, or if either even existed.

Though I didn't realize then, I was longing for an encounter with the Spirit of God, and the church I was attending then was not the right setting for such an experience. Despite my courage in answering the altar call, I still lacked an experience of God.

When I was seventeen, I watched one of my best friends die. It was a strange incident where the reality of what was happening didn't sink in until it was too late. Deep into the midnight hour one night, my friends and I sat upon rocks at the top of a waterfall that dropped suddenly into a cascading river below.

At one point, I wandered away from my group of friends. As I was walking back, I glimpsed my friend Thomas removing his sweatshirt as he walked towards me and down the side of the cliff. He unexpectedly tossed his crumpled sweatshirt into my hands and walked swiftly past me to the edge of the waterfall. When the reality of what was happening hit me, I was so caught off guard and horrified that I could barely choke out, "No, stop!"

It was too late; my voice was drowned out by the sound of the pounding waterfall. He leapt and disappeared into the darkness and swirling water. I ran frantically down the cliff towards the water below. When he didn't come up, I ordered my friends to go get help. We were in a remote area, and I knew every moment counted. When they left, I ran along the banks of the river, wildly searching for him, straining my eyes to try to see through the blackness of the night. The water was moving so rapidly, it being the winter months; I was afraid if I dove in after him, I may not survive.

I screamed to God for a miracle—my desperate prayers echoed through the cold darkness. With every minute that ticked by, I began losing hope of Thomas surviving. I wondered in my frenzied desperation if there even was a God. My mind grappling to accept the life of my beloved friend may have come to a bitter end.

Time stretched on, and my friends had not returned with help. I was alone, cold, and in shock. I told God I would give anything to bring Thomas back. When those words passed over my lips, I felt the recoil of that offer. At the time, I was a drinker and smoker; some selfish, destructive part of me wasn't ready to give up the habits I thought God wouldn't approve of.

I was distraught and losing all hope for my friend's life. My heart was breaking. The only thing I had to lean on at that moment was my distorted interpretation of religion. I was a sinner because of my habits, making the assumption God would help save my friend only if I would give up the guilty pleasures of my life.

In my young mind, I was distressed and confused by the fragmented perception of God that I held. I knew nothing of the deep well of truth that can be accessed through our personal, direct, and intimate relationship with God. I was clueless about God's laws that govern the Earth and how they can affect our quality of life. What I did know deep down was that the choices I was making then, were outside of God's plan for me.

As I anxiously watched the water's surface and shoreline, I came into agreement with the notion that it was my fault God did not save Thomas. The question plagued me: if I had been willing to give up everything unholy in that moment, would God have produced a miracle to save my friend's life? I heard stories of people being raised from the dead in the Bible, but never imagined they were actually true. Even if the power of God could resurrect, I didn't feel I had the strength or willpower to renounce the things I was participating in that were out of alignment with God's principles. I had little or no faith.

All through the night, I howled and screamed and begged for the life of my dear friend. I was still out there alone, waiting for the others to return with help. After running around and searching for him for an excruciatingly long time, eventually, I stopped and fell to my knees at the shore. I wrestled with my inner demons, feeling deep guilt and shame for not risking my life to save him; for not being willing to give up everything in my pleas to God.

Night turned into dawn on that wretched day, and in the early morning light, I finally saw an emergency response team arrive with my friends. I clung on to a thin thread of hope until I saw the EMTs recovering my friend's lifeless body. He was so unnaturally stiff and blue, his life lost forever.

A dark shadow fell over me after that awful morning, and I was tormented in the days following his death. I could not sleep. Instead, I began to have out-of-body experiences, where my body became frozen and immovable in terrifying bouts of body paralysis. When my spirit lifted out of my body, I heard the voice of my deceased friend calling to me over and over again. When I would hear my friend's voice calling out to me, my spirit was tugged in astral travel towards the sound of his voice. As my spirit approached his, I was assaulted by cold, dark evil spirits that were very demonic in nature. This happened several times, and I felt as if my friend was trying to tell me something and the evil spirits were preventing me from reaching him. I had never had an experience like this before, and I was deeply disturbed. I got so freaked out by the dark entities that I resolved to calling the church of my youth and set up a meeting with my former pastor.

I will never forget the meeting that day with the pastor. As I walked from my car to where he was standing out front, I moved slowly and deliberately, my breathing shallow under the tremendous weight of grief in my chest. I clung to the hope that somehow, he could help me in my darkest hour and chase away the hell that had been set loose against me.

I shared the events that occurred—my friend's traumatic death, and his desperate cries from the spirit world to me ever since. The pastor looked me in the eye, cold and distant, and said, "What you're experiencing isn't real. There is only heaven and hell and no in-between worlds." What I heard was, "You're not hearing his voice. I don't know what you're hearing, or you're just making it up for attention, but you aren't hearing your dead friend's voice." His statement landed on my chest, further constricting my already labored breath. Did he just completely invalidate the intense and distressing experience I was having?

Here I came in my deepest suffering, and this supposed "man of God" was inadvertently suggesting I was a liar? Like I was just making it all up? A fury ignited deep within me, fueling my burden of pain, confusion, and loneliness. When I walked away from that exchange with the pastor, I not only walked away from him, but I also walked away from the church, rejecting Christianity and everything that went with it. I felt so let down, betrayed, and fooled by a church that could not help me in my most delicate and unique circumstance.

My youth pastor became the face of Christianity for me in that pivotal moment of my adolescence, painfully imprinting my young and impressionable mind with a memory of grave disappointment and betrayal in the midst of my greatest suffering. After that unfortunate experience, I became convinced that I could not find God in such a place as the church. I was so emotionally wounded, that for years after that exchange with my pastor, any mention of Christianity or organized religion brought up a bitter, repulsive, unsettled feeling in me.

After that day, I thought it wise to scratch religion and church off my list. I set course to search for God outside of religion and outside a church that seemed to stifle the Spirit of God more than to host it. I was determined to stay away from lists of rules and doctrines and far away from the fear-producing teachings that felt oppressive to me. I turned away and was set on not looking back. I came to the conclusion the churchgoers I knew were caught in a web of lies, so I set my sails for a new horizon in my pursuit of God.

The next year after my eighteenth birthday, my dad hired a Yoga teacher to come to our house and teach us. Although it was a bit difficult at first, over time, I found deep peace and restoration through the poses, called asanas. It calmed my mind and emotions and helped me feel closer to strong and comforting spiritual energy. It also had physical benefits, and I enjoyed the growing strength in my body. This experience in my young adulthood planted a seed in me that grew over the years, and eventually led to me becoming a certified yoga teacher.

Soon after my exploration with yoga began, I went on a hike with my father and his friend. After climbing down a steep embankment, we nestled in on a sand-covered beach, the majestic river before us, listening quietly to water spilling over endless rocks. His friend picked up her drum and began to play a melodic rhythm, steady...like a heartbeat.

Suddenly, my spirit was lifted away from my body, and I found myself in another body and life. I experienced myself as a Native American man, staring at a hawk in the sky. Later in life, I often referred to and interpreted this to be my first "spontaneous past life regression." It was this incident that led me to develop a firmly held belief in reincarnation.

As I grew older, I had numerous experiences in addition to the one I mentioned, where I would find my spirit experiencing a different life, through a different body. When my encounters with God happened years afterward and God pulled back the veil on the underbelly of the world to expose His design, I was completely shocked to discover a radical new perspective on this.

After that night down at the river, a new door to the spirit world opened up for me, and over the next few years, the occurrence of psychic impressions and visions I was experiencing increased significantly. These impressions were dream-like visions of either myself or others in what seemed to be past lives.

Since few people I knew were having such experiences, I felt compelled to find others who could validate and support what I believed to be a meaningful gift. In my early twenties, my dad went to work and live at Esalen in Big Sur, a holistic healing and training mecca for meditation, yoga, and various New Age spirituality practices. He extended an invitation for me to come stay with him and try one of their month-long work-study programs. Intrigued by the opportunity, I agreed.

My time at Esalen was a whirlwind of magic and mystery, captivating my young and curious mind. During my stay, I struggled with a stomach issue. As if it were meant to be, I embarked on a journey led by my shamanism teacher, who guided us into the underworld to discover our spirit animals. When I entered the spirit world, I was immediately met by a mysterious wolf, as if he had been waiting for me. The wolf extended an invitation for me to join him, and when I agreed, he led me into a desert. In the midst of the arid terrain, the wolf pointed out a cactus, telling me that if I were to eat it, my stomach pain and discomfort would subside. When I emerged from the journey into the spiritual realm, I excitedly told my teacher what I had seen in the spirit world.

Upon hearing the details, she said, "I'll bet you can find that cactus right here on the property. I believe I may have seen something similar to what you described near the art barn. Go and see if you can find it after class."

As soon as class was over, I skipped my way down the well-trodden path that runs parallel to the Pacific Ocean. I was enthusiastic about the possibility of potentially finding the cactus from my vision. As I neared the art barn, I peered through the ocean-side foliage, and spotted a cactus, just where my teacher had said it would be.

I carefully removed what looked like a fruit of the cactus and pierced it with a stick I found in the dirt below. Delighted by my discovery, I carried my newfound treasure on the stick, and headed towards the cafeteria. I happened upon my father on the path, and he said, "What do you have there?" I cheerfully recounted the story of my journey into the spirit world and how I thought that the cactus could be a cure to my stomach issue.

Then my father replied, "I believe that is a prickly pear, which is known to help with digestive problems." I was astounded! How awesome that I was able to find what the wolf had shown me. I was fascinated by my new relationship with the spirit world and excited about the possibility of acquiring information in the spiritual realm to assist and guide myself and others in the physical world. Something I learned more recently is that there are many sources in the spirit world that offer access, insight, and helpful information, but what I didn't know at the time, is that the source I began using that day came with a hidden contract and unknown consequences.

In addition to studying shamanism, I also studied astrology while living at Esalen. It amazed me how accurate the information in astrology was in identifying people's personalities and significant life events. It fascinated me that perhaps our destiny could be found in the stars. For the first time in my life, I felt a sense of purpose and meaning, something that I had been longing for, and I was elated about my new "superpowers." I developed a deep hunger and desire to help and serve people with the insightful tools I was discovering. In the churches of my youth, such insights or connections to the spirit world were unheard of, and I was intrigued to see where my new path would lead me. My inspiration swelled, and I sought to learn all that I could about the world of magic, mysticism, and the occult.

While living at Esalen, I dove deeper into the practice of yoga and began using it as a spiritual practice to worship and surrender into my budding relationship with spirituality. One day, I was wandering along the path that winds along the ocean cliff at Esalen and happened to stumble across the meditation hall. Though I had walked past it many times, this time I felt drawn to go inside. I peeked through the dusty window and saw that it was empty; I slipped off my shoes and tip-toed inside.

I made my way around the curved wall and sat down on one of the meditation cushions. It was a silent, still atmosphere, and I could hear the coastal winds in the trees outside. As I stared out into the greenery, a soft and gentle voice entered my mind and said, *The only way you can be close to God is through deep meditation.* I pondered the great many people that meditated their whole lives, and the power and abilities that I observed came from a devout, disciplined practice. I was eager for spiritual power and longed for a deeper connection to God. Motivated to be closer to God, I made a vow to start meditating every day.

What is a life without God? I wanted more from life, and I felt like God whispered in my ear, instructing me on how to find Him. After I left Esalen, I felt as if I was finally finding footing in my pursuit of the divine. I was searching for something to do with my life at the time and ended up landing a job working on cruise ships. It all came together rather quickly, and my new employer set a date for me to take my first cruise. Before my departure, I had begun to explore the use of psychedelics. My experimentation stemmed from a deep desire to be closer to the divine presence I perceived and enhance my understanding of the spirit world.

Consuming these substances unlocked portals to realms filled with mystery and mysticism. During a psychedelic experience before I left, I had a vision of a desert landscape with red rocks, accompanied by a guiding voice instructing me to journey to the land where the red rocks could be found. At the time, I was committed to beginning my new job abroad, so I chose not to heed the call of the vision.

While working overseas, I fell ill with a mysterious sickness that consisted of extreme and undiagnosable abdominal pain. I was sent home and endured months of doctors' appointments that left me feeling exasperated. One evening, in desperation, I dropped to my knees and prayed to the full moon; at the time, I believed that the Spirit of God resided in the moon. The practice of praying to the moon is found in various cultures such as Egyptian, Norse, and Native American traditions. Although I am unsure where I obtained the practice, I would often pray to the moon. When I closed my eyes, the same vision I had before my departure resurfaced. Once more, I beheld crimson rocks in the desert, and a voice instructed me to journey in that direction.

At this stage of my journey, I believed all the quiet, persistent voices of guidance that I heard, were indeed the voice of God, and I sought to obey them. An intuition led me to believe the place of the red rocks was Sedona, Arizona, so I took a leap of faith, packed up my life, and headed into the unknown.

That year in Sedona was an exhilarating spiritual exploration that led me deep into the world of the occult. Upon my arrival, I had a consultation with a spiritual psychic to see if she could help me solve my mysterious illness. I called to set up the appointment, and she asked me for my birthday information over the phone.

The day I went to her house was a pivotal moment in that chapter of my spiritual journey. I walked into her office and sat down. When I looked up, she was staring at me. She kept her gaze fixed on me for so long that I started feeling anxious and uncomfortable.

After what felt like an eternity of waiting, she finally broke the silence and said, "I've been studying your chart, and I don't understand why you are here. You have great power in your chart. All the great magicians, healers, and wizards I know have charts like yours. Why are you here? You are supposed to be doing what I am doing—and more—with the potential power you have. I can do a session if you would like, but you need to start awakening your own power and destiny."

Her words landed with a thud. *Wow*, I thought. *Maybe she's right. I better get my act together.* A sense of self-significance and purpose started to swell in me, along with a burning motivation to become a great healer. Now I had a mission to fulfill and was ready to take it seriously.

In the coming months, while living in Sedona, I explored various types of spirituality, magic, rituals, and metaphysical teachings. I was introduced to Drunvalo Melchizedeck's work and read two of his books, *The Ancient Secret of the Flower of Life* and *The Serpent of Light*. When I learned about his "Merkaba" meditation, I began to practice it daily. As I continued with the meditation practice, I noticed a significant increase of spiritual power and a substantial enhancement in my connection to other dimensions and realms.

As my connection to the spirit world grew stronger, I communicated daily with spirits and guides. They led me to different "energy vortices" in the land of the red rocks, teaching me about dimensional doorways. Through extended meditations in these concentrated areas of energy, I gained psychic power and sight, and began to see energy and auras for the first time in my life. Through these explorations, I opened numerous doorways in the spiritual realm, oblivious to the peril that drew me further into unknown captivity. Under what I termed as the Spirit of Sedona, I received instruction in the art of white magic. The spirit guides that I listened to at that time informed me of an ongoing conflict between light and darkness in that land, and they summoned me to serve in blocking the use of black magic and defeating dark agendas being pursued in that region. Me being a person devoted to the pursuit of light, good, and righteousness, I agreed.

If a battle between dark and light ensued, I was prepared to do whatever it took to serve the light. Back then, I remained oblivious that I had been deceived into choosing from two sides of the same coin, unaware of the existence of a realm and power beyond my perception at the time.

After I accepted the invitation to combat on the side of what I believed to be the forces of light, additional gateways to the spirit world unlocked, and my spiritual power and capacity increased. During my hikes in the desert, I began to receive psychic messages from ravens and coyotes, guiding me to specific locations where I was to practice white magic. There, I was instructed to open and close various energetic gateways or portals. My guides provided me with specific directions on how to harness the energy from these power points and influence the spirit realm and consciousness of those contained within particular spheres of Earth's energetic grid.

I believed with all of my heart and soul that I was valiantly serving the greater good and restoring light to areas of darkness. However, unbeknownst to me, there was a malevolent force at work in the shadows that I could not perceive, that was using me to fulfill an agenda not of God.

Towards the end of my time living in Sedona, I was so enraptured in the spirit realm that the lines of reality began to blur. One day, I climbed a treacherous trail up the tallest mountain in Sedona, Thunder Mountain. Upon reaching the top of the summit, I sat down and instantly perceived a potent and piercing energy flowing through my body and the area beneath me.

My eyes fluttered open and closed as my vision alternated between the realms of the physical and the spiritual. I found myself being drawn in the spirit towards a doorway; the hair on my arms stood up as I approached it. It appeared to be ancient, and I intuited and sensed that behind it lay great power and knowledge.

Deep in the pit of my stomach, I knew that if I opened that door, my life would be forever changed, and that I may never return to the world as I knew it. I wasn't sure if God resided behind that door, but I was certain that it held potent knowledge that had the potential to profoundly alter my life.

When the moment came for me to make the decision on whether to open the door, fear gripped me. I got spooked by the power and gravity of what lay beyond the door and pulled my spirit back into my body. Even though my spirit guides had urged me to open that door, I was too afraid to find out what was on the other side.

For many years after, I always wondered what would have happened if I had opened that doorway. Thoughts of that doorway taunted my mind for years to come, an unseen force always tugging and whispering to me to come back and see what was behind the door. For so long, I felt I had missed the opportunity of a lifetime. It was only after my supernatural encounters with God that I came to understand that I had been spared from accepting a dark invitation from a false light, one that would have inevitably led to my downfall.

I decided to leave Sedona soon after the unsettling vision of the ancient doorway. I desired to continue the spiritual work I had begun in the land of red rocks but did not feel ready to face the doorway that had opened to me in those lands. The only question was, where to next?

I had a good sense of where my next calling lay. During my time working on cruise ships, I found myself frequently ported in Cozumel, Mexico. While exploring the local area, a knowledgeable tour guide shared with me the fascinating history of ancient civilizations and pyramids in Mexico, sparking a deep interest within me. During my residency in Sedona, I obtained and read *The Serpent of Light* by Drunvalo Melchizedek, which further fueled my curiosity to venture into the realms of Mayan ruins and explore other power centers with dimensional gateways.

In reading *The Serpent of Light*, I discovered that each of the pyramids was erected on specific power points in the energetic ley lines of the Earth. I felt inspired to visit these ancient places to meditate, bask, and commune in the energies contained within the archeological sites. I was driven by a calling to persist in the work I had been initiated in while living in Sedona. I sought to obediently follow the spiritual guidance instructing me to pursue my mission in bringing a balance of light to places where the veil between worlds was thin and oppressed by darkness.

Filled with the inspiration and magic I captured in Sedona, I settled my affairs and commenced my unforgettable journey through southern Mexico. I believed I had a spiritual path that resonated with me, enlivened me, and was guiding me toward spiritual growth. I remained clueless that the path I was walking was leading me into a well-lit tunnel of a lower realm and ultimately, would keep me from what I longed for the most—union with God.

2

Spiritual Pilgrimages

I wandered the southern states of Mexico for five months, exploring pyramids and ruins of ancient Mayan civilization. I found myself captivated by the archaeological sites and fascinated by the energies and spirits that inhabited them. Often, as I would meditate in these places, I found myself filled with an exhilarating spiritual energy, as I immersed myself in a world of magic and well-kept secrets.

A curiosity and craving for the mystical had been planted in me from a young age, likely due to the way magic and mystery are often revered in children's movies and media. I delighted in the mysteriousness of the path I was on and found my exploration of spirituality significantly more exciting than the seemingly dead-end churches of my youth.

As I explored the spirit world within these ancient archeological grounds, I heard telepathic messages from spirit guides along the way. At this juncture in my spiritual sojourn, I ignorantly assumed that all the spirits that I encountered were good-natured. When spirits manifested in my inner vison, or as a voice, I innocently followed their guidance. They guided me to open energetic doorways in the ancient archeological sites, claiming that by doing so, I could help to illuminate areas of darkness. I relied on their guidance, convinced that the noble cause they pointed me towards was in alignment with the call of God and the greater good.

There are others similar to me, who call themselves lightworkers, and have been beckoned by guides or "spirit helpers" to tend the energetic gateways within the Earth's grid. They believe that this work helps bring light and consciousness onto the planet. Gateway tending is a concept that is familiar within the New Age community, where lightworkers tend portals and dimensional doorways between worlds. The peculiar yet seemingly sacred tasks I was called upon to perform at these ancient, holy sites of civilizations long past aligned with my spiritual perspective at the time, so I did not question them.

I was oblivious to the complex web of deception my life was becoming entangled with, unaware that I had become a pawn in a game I didn't even know I was playing, with an enemy I didn't know I had. Several months into my journey, I was meditating in my hostel one morning and received a psychic message.

At the time, I held the belief that all the messages I received originated from a divine source, so I listened intently and followed obediently, as my innermost desire was to serve the divine. In this specific message, I was directed to go downstairs to the plaza, where I would find someone waiting for me.

I slipped on my shoes and strolled down the busy street. It was a typical Mexican plaza, full of hustle and bustle, with vendors selling a myriad of goods. The sunlight streamed through the trees, and I spotted a park bench ahead. I sat down, letting my eyelids slide partially closed, returning to a state of connection with the spiritual world. I quieted my mind, slowed my breathing, and listened for guidance. I heard the guiding voice in my mind whisper, *ahead.* My eyes gently fluttered open, revealing a man of short stature whose eyes were fixed on me. I stood up from my spot on the bench, and in silence, we slowly approached each other.

After we stood looking at each other for a while, he said, "Hola, what are you doing here in the plaza today?"

"Waiting for someone," I replied, followed by a long pause.

20

"So am I," he said. A few moments passed, as we studied each other intensely.

"I wonder if we are looking for each other," I said after some time.

He paused, not taking his gaze from me, and finally said, "I thought you were going to be a man. I've never given initiation to a woman before. Let's go. I have a home down the street from here," he replied. I hesitated. Should I go to a stranger's home in Mexico?

I pondered for a moment and reached for the voice that had been guiding me. When I checked in with my guidance, it confirmed that this was the man I was waiting for. I aspired to live a life fully surrendered to faith, placing my trust in the divine guidance I received. Despite feeling uneasy, I went to his home with him, driven by my deep desire to trust in "God" and obediently follow the divine guidance I received.

We sat swinging in hammocks in his backyard for hours. He told me about his heritage and about his mother, who came from a Mayan village. He showed me pictures and told stories about hidden powers and magic that could be found through his heritage, elaborating on how these could be transmitted through an initiation.

He said that over the years, there had been only two others he had been instructed to do the ancient Mayan initiation with, and that I would be the third. His voice trailed off in the distance, as my mind pressed into deep contemplation.

Everything that was happening seemed so synchronistic. I felt as if God had called me to meet this man, to arrive at this moment. Who would I be to turn away from this opportunity and not listen to the divine calling I had received in my meditation that morning? With all my heart, I yearned to wholly surrender my life to the divine and faithfully follow the guidance that whispered to me in moments of profound stillness.

I looked him in the eyes, and finally said, "Ok, I will do it."

He replied, "Ok, we will start first thing tomorrow morning."

I left his home and walked slowly and sulkily back to my hostel. I felt unsettled, even if I wasn't aware of it at the time. I had convinced myself that I had to do what I believe the divine was calling me to do, even if I was uncomfortable.

I spent three days with the Mayan man until the initiation was complete. During the initiation, he transferred ancient Mayan energies to me in a series of rituals. I endured many long hours of concentration, focus, and Mayan prayer, sitting with him in his modest Mexican home. I kept thinking that I should be excited about what was happening, about being obedient to the divine call, but I only felt uneasy.

Once it was complete, I felt shaken up but didn't understand why. Wasn't I supposed to feel honored and uplifted to receive the sacred gift of ancient Mayan energies? I continued to rationalize with myself, convincing myself that I had done what was necessary to follow the highest guidance I knew at the time. However, the feeling of uneasiness persisted.

Before we parted ways, the Mayan man told me there would come a time when I would have to choose to be a good witch, or a bad witch. Certainly, when faced with the decision between light and dark, I would always choose to do what I believed to be good and right. Once again, I was misled into thinking that my only options were to become a good witch or a bad witch, unaware at the time that there existed an even greater and higher realm where I could align myself and fight for a greater cause. After that day, I buried the peculiar experience for a while, pushing it out of my mind and memory.

Following my recent encounter with God, I discovered chains of bondage that were forged during that initiation, intended to imprison me within a dark realm of power. Because of my lack of discernment at the time, I unwittingly opened a gateway to a sinister realm, believing I was answering a divine calling but ultimately being led astray. As I reflect upon the New Age and occult communities, I see there is a fascination with and a pursuit of receiving various initiations from ancient traditions in shamanism, Native American culture, and other indigenous societies. In their sincere quest for connecting with God through these spiritual practices, they often find themselves unknowingly bound to forces that are not aligned with God.

Despite the profound spiritual experiences I had during my six-month journey through Mexico, my spirit still yearned for something I had not yet attained. Now twenty-three years old, I was brimming with passion in my unrelenting pursuit of the divine, and I was willing to do whatever it took to find what I was searching for.

Upon returning to the United States and replenishing my travel funds, I made the decision to embark on yet another spiritual pilgrimage abroad. My yearning to discover God and live a life of spiritual surrender and fulfillment led me to an unexpected and abrupt decision to travel to India. Everything happened so quickly, and before I knew it, I was departing on a flight to Delhi.

During my twenty-hour plane journey, I had plenty of time to contemplate what I was getting myself into and whether it was a fantastic or dreadful idea. The many stories of India I had heard depicted it as a spiritual mecca, full of gurus and saints with powers called Siddhis. I was drawn to India because it seemed as if their culture offered a deeper level of spirituality beyond what I could see available in America, which ultimately felt spiritually devoid to me, much like the churches I had been to. My mother's allegiance to Jesus meant that my sister and I were regularly taken to churches and Bible studies when we were young girls. This early exposure left a lingering impression of what churches were like.

I hungered for the power of God to manifest through me, my soul yearning for union and stature with the divine. This insatiable drive was the very reason I spontaneously boarded that plane with a plan in my pocket to go to Rishikesh and get certified as a Yoga instructor. It was an auspicious time in India during Maha Kumbh Mela, the world's largest spiritual gathering that only happens every twelve years.

India was the only place I traveled where I experienced extreme culture shock. I will always remember the night when I arrived, driving through the darkness, witnessing the slums, and wondering when we would reach the "actual city" with the "real buildings." The realization that would never happen came upon me with the sudden halt of the rickshaw and my driver shouting at me to get out.

No way in hell am I getting out here, I thought as I clung to my seat. I peered through the darkest part of the night, at what he swore was my hotel. From the perspective of my American upbringing, this looked like a drug-infested ghetto. We argued about it for a while until he grabbed my bag and started heading toward the building. Not wanting to get left alone, I ran after him, protesting. My driver quickly abandoned me in the lobby, where I checked in, and made my way to my makeshift room for what was left of the night.

The coming days were filled with me desperately trying to find my way as a woman alone in India. Whenever I ventured outside, I drew a great deal of unwanted attention; people on the street would reach out and pull at my arms and legs for various reasons. I had the urge to board a plane and head back home, but I held my ground and stuck it out. After all, I had come all that way to find God, to find my purpose, and to do something meaningful with my life. Eventually, I made my way to a town called Rishikesh, where I settled for two months.

Those days were filled with a wide array of supernatural experiences, and India offered a spiritual sustenance I craved. My early mornings and late afternoons were filled with long transcendental meditations where my consciousness seemed to expand over the city and fill with "divine" messages from some of the more prominent Indian gods. The place buzzed with spiritual energy, and the land itself seemed alive.

One night while lying in bed, the spirit of the Ganges River came to me in a vision, beckoning me into its waters in the spirt realm. When my spirit entered the etheric water, I was overcome with cosmic bliss and euphoria. *This must be God,* I thought to myself. The spirit told me to go to Kumbh Mela, the spiritual gathering happening a half day's journey away. I asked my yoga teacher for special permission and commenced my pilgrimage the following day.

I hoped to meet Babaji there, who some claimed to be an incarnation of God himself. I called out to him in my meditations, hoping he would come in visions and dreams like others had reported, wishing I would see him manifest in physical form at the gathering. Although I didn't meet him that day, years later, he visited me in a potent vision.

Arriving and finding my way at the Kumbh Mela was one of the most extreme experiences of my life. I couldn't keep my head from spinning or my body from being shoved around in a crowd of ten million people, all in a hot and sweaty pursuit of spirituality. I found a place to stay in a tent with a guru, a teacher of some friends of mine from Mexico. I can't recall the guru's name, but his stature and presence remain vivid in my memory.

The guru was kind and had a powerful presence about him. He took me and another woman under his wing and walked us through the streets of the Mela, taking us to sit at the feet of many gurus. He strode with confidence, wielding a serpent-head staff in his right hand. I was in awe of his commanding presence; when he raised his staff and shouted, the seemingly impenetrable crowds would instantly part to create a path for our passage. I wanted what he had, spiritual authority, power, and devotion to a higher power.

In India, there is a belief that on a special day, called Shivaratri, the river receives a divine blessing directly from Lord Shiva, and numerous people report miracles during this time. Intrigued by these accounts, I decided to try the "holy bath" in the Ganges River that day, hoping for my own miracle.

We gathered at the river's edge, filled with anticipation as we prepared to enter the spiritually charged waters of the Ganges. We lined up one by one as a woman praying in Hindu submerged each woman into the water. Then, it was my turn.

When the Indian woman prayed over me and dipped me into the water, time itself stood still. It was as if my soul stretched into the cosmos, and suddenly, I found myself soaring in the spirit realm through stars, nebulas, and entire universes in one silent and still explosion of consciousness. When I surfaced from the water, it felt like I was emerging from another dimension. I was altered and deeply changed.

During that time, I was elated by this extraordinary spiritual encounter, blissfully ignorant of the fact that I had just unknowingly entered into a covenant with Lord Shiva by being bathed in his energy on the auspicious day of Shivaratri. I began building a relationship with Lord Shiva after that day, also known as the Lord of snakes. His power is often symbolized in various images by serpents; this serpent power was depicted in my guru's staff that he used to part seas of people.

Over the coming years, I continuously chanted and recited mantras, keeping my mind focused on Lord Shiva. I recall attending a puja, a ceremonial fire offering to Shiva, and as the ghee (clarified butter) poured from the spoon into the fire, I had a vision of a serpent undulating and consuming the worship and offerings. I was mesmerized by these types of visions and supernatural displays of power, assuming them holy due to their otherworldly nature.

There are many tales of Shiva in the Bhagavad Gita where he is depicted holding his trident and wearing a live, coiled snake around his neck. He is said to be the Lord of Destruction and master of snakes. The snake-god coiled around his neck three times represents the past, present, and future—time in cycles. Many images of Shiva also depict a fanned cobra above his head, representing what people believe to be kundalini or spiritual energy that rises up the spine.

Many years after my time in India, in the depth of extreme and unfathomable suffering in my battle against neurological Lyme disease, I cried out in distress, and Shiva answered my call. He appeared in my mind's eye and revealed a doorway in my third eye. He broke it open, and he showed me how to use his three-pronged trident to penetrate through the different levels of consciousness.

Additionally, he showed me the use of the Sri Yantra (geometric pattern) as a portal between realms. I astral traveled with him through various dimensions and vast cosmic realms, believing that we were exploring what I thought to be the universe of our Creator. I believed I was being shown some of the most majestic and powerful realms one could travel to, unaware they were upper rooms of a lower dimension below God's Kingdom.

Amidst this period of intense suffering and numerous medical interventions for Lyme disease, I eventually experienced the encounter with Babaji that I had yearned for and been praying about for many years. In India, Babaji is perceived to be God himself, and to have had two separate incarnations. One night, I was lying in bed in excruciating agony and pain due to my illness. I reached a point where I contemplated that I would prefer death to continuing in such suffering.

As soon as that thought crossed my mind, Babaji appeared, and I found myself in a pool of water with him. He reached out and touched my third eye, which propelled me backward in slow motion, as if falling into a strange time warp. I was completely overtaken with intense electric energy that surged through my body, my consciousness catapulted into cosmic expanses of interstellar space, all the while saturated in a feeling of deep oneness with the world. I recall how deeply I cherished that experience. During that phase of my life, it was the closest I had come to feeling a profound spiritual presence that I believed to be God. I've come to learn now that experiences of oneness with the world are not oneness with God.

Through all these mystical experiences, I improperly concluded that many paths led to God, and that God could appear in many forms. I asserted that all these paths must eventually lead back to God, even though some were more direct than others.

Nevertheless, I still had many unanswered questions about God, and intricacies of existence. Questions like, why were there so many gods? Were we meant to be our own mini version of God, like many of these paths taught? I reluctantly confess that, at that juncture, I was intrigued by the notion of being my own god and possessing supernatural abilities. I felt special, chosen by these gods and deities, yet remained unaware of the intricate web of deception being woven around me in order to distort my perception of reality.

My belief systems and framework for understanding reality, God, and the way the universe works were built on the foundation of these early-life spiritual encounters with gods and deities. I found many sojourners in my spiritual walk who agreed with these fundamental principles of "God is in everything," "all things are one," "man is God," and our "mind creates reality." I arrogantly looked down on and felt sorry for those still trapped in the dogma of organized religion, placing myself above them, convincing myself my path was superior.

I learned how to control and manipulate my experience of reality with principles such as those found in *The Secret*, that teach manifestation through concentrated focus and intention. I believed in the acquired spiritual power and strength that I had obtained through my numerous spiritual practices. As a spiritualist, I sought higher consciousness through meditation, breathing exercises, yoga, diet, crystals, channeling, and spirit guides. I did not believe in traditional biblical concepts of good, bad, or evil.

A year after my journey to India, I embarked on yet another spiritual pilgrimage. Even though I had undergone a new level of profound spiritual experiences, I yearned for something I had yet to encounter. My spiritual pursuit brought me to the jungles of Peru, where I found myself participating in late-night ceremonies with shamans, ingesting ayahuasca (a psychedelic plant referred to locally as plant medicine). The indigenous people believe this plant has healing power and use it for spiritual sight and in treating both physical and psychological ailments. I needed healing; I still felt broken and lost, searching for purpose and true meaning in my life.

During my explorations with this jungle plant concoction, I had many intense visions and otherworldly spiritual experiences. The following is an excerpt from my journal, describing in detail the experience:

As the ayahuasca took effect, I started to feel a shift in my conscious state and watched as the room filled with sparkles of purple energy. My body began to feel very heavy, and it was if I was sinking deeper into the cushion beneath me and the wooden post behind me. I became very fond of that post behind me, the solid wood that at times was the only thing supporting me and anchoring me to reality.

I began to see channels of energy, purple and blue light. I saw the same thing whether my eyes were open or closed. It was like my eyelids didn't exist or that what was being projected had nothing to do with the "normal" vision that we use. The channels of energy began to swirl together in a perfect spiral. The spiral flipped and then turned into a torus. The center of the torus was aligned with the center of the room, and I could see everyone's energy flowing into the center of the torus.

A dark tunnel opened beneath the torus, and I entered, feeling a sensation of falling down. I found myself in a profoundly dark place. My body and consciousness were adjusting to this new state, and I became dizzy and disoriented. I found it difficult to concentrate. I experienced a complete loss of control, as if I had no other choice than to remain an observer the journey I was on. I glimpsed flashes of strange, indescribable sights, enveloped in an atmosphere of gloom and darkness.

A sensation of energy, like streams of water, tingled all throughout my body. I began to notice areas of my energetic body where I felt blocked, places where I often experienced physical pain. I took deep breaths, attempting to break up these areas of my body where energy felt stuck. My stomach was wadded into a tight knot. Pressure bore down on my chest and heart. My eyes were fluttering, and a persistent force pressed into my forehead between my eyes, what I believed was my third eye. I saw incredible light coming from this area.

Memories arose, consisting of times of sorrow, regret, fear, shame, guilt, sadness, insecurity, and other heavy emotions. The memories began to manifest even quicker, flashing before me as if someone were rapidly flipping through the pages of a book.

31

My emotional and energetic reaction to the stimuli intensified, the sensation becoming increasingly overwhelming.

I sat up on my knees and placed my forehead on the ground. This is a pose of surrender, and it was my way of saying to the spirit of the plant that I was ready, ready to go where I needed to go in order to be free from suffering.

It was so surprising to see how much of my past I had forgotten, to see how much I had overlooked. The bird's-eye perception showed me things about myself that I could not see at the time that it was happening. It is very similar to a near-death experience, when one's whole life passes before them, and eyes are opened anew.

In the spirit, I was outside of myself and watched vines made of energy enter my body and infuse my veins. I understood this to be "the plant medicine," the vine of ayahuasca entering me. My head rocked back and forth, gently but rapidly, supported by that unbreakable solid wood post behind me. I couldn't tell if my eyes were open or closed.

My vision transformed into a world of energy again, lines and channels of energy. I saw the torus at the center of the room. I saw the way the shaman was guiding everyone's energy into it. It was as if we were all on some crazy ride, like a merry-go-round. Though we began our journey on the platform of the merry-go-round, we would fall back into the void of our individual experience, held by energy cords that secured us to the platform.

I was resting on this "platform," and I had a sensation like I was being lifted out of my body. The songs being sung by the Shaman were inviting me to go higher. Then suddenly I was flying towards the stars, journeying through the cosmos. I found myself in some sort of spaceship and looking out large glass windows. It reminded me of a scene out of the TV series Star Trek; the beings around me were not all humans.

In a flash, the scene disintegrated, and I felt I was falling, gently, slowly. I became aware of my body and the puffing sounds of the maestro blowing smoke from his tobacco pipe. When I closed my eyes, I heard the voice of ayahuasca spirt telling me about the vast universe of possible worlds I could visit. I saw scenes of beautiful places, of space and stars, and of brilliant white lights. The spirit explained that these are places of visions that I would see in time, but that I must return to the lower world to continue the cleansing of heavy energies and memories.

I understood that I must return to the world below, and I saw what seemed to be a trapdoor open. The chains connected to the door lowered, and I walked inside the opening.

Many individuals who venture into the realm of plant medicine can empathize with the sense of seeking and longing that I experienced, the profound yearning for deep healing that compelled me to journey to the jungles of Peru. I desired to delve deeper into the realm of the spirit world and to explore the profound depths of my soul. With the assistance of the psychedelic vine and the shaman, I gained access to other dimensions, and insights that I didn't have on my own. What I didn't realize at the time, was that these explorations were part of a deceptive veil I was becoming enmeshed in. My consent to participate gave legal rights to the spirit of ayahuasca to indwell my bodily vessel. Until my encounters with our Creator, I was unaware that the spirt of ayahuasca is a serpent spirit that uses serpent power to produce supernatural experiences.

One of things I learned in my recent encounters with God is that there are both legal and illegal ways to enter the spirit world. God has constructed His kingdom with specific divine laws and principles, many of which people like me have very little understanding of. I had no idea that by entering these realms in the manner I did, I was being led deeper into a maze of deception and distancing myself further from the profound union with God that I desired above anything else.

I concluded my stay in Peru with an eleven-day silent Vipassana retreat. At Vipassana retreats, participants meditate for approximately twelve hours each day. Attending the retreat was an impactful experience in my life, mainly because of the sense of control I felt I gained over my life and my emotions. The Vipassana technique had a unique way of numbing the mind and its response to the often unpleasant and challenging stimuli of this world.

Based on my understanding at the time, I believed that the only genuine and reliable way to connect with God was through extended periods of meditation. Having witnessed numerous examples of connection to the divine through Buddhism, Hinduism, and other spiritual lineages, I continued to pursue God through transcendental meditation. When I sought God through meditation practice, I entered realms of profound peace and serenity, experiencing a sense of oneness with the world around me.

Throughout my mid to late twenties, I held the belief that I was making substantial spiritual advancements. I regarded the deepening of my meditative experiences as proof of this progress, and much of my spiritual journey had been captivating, shrouded in mystery. However, as I felt I was ascending higher, I was actually descending deeper into a deceptive realm, a dimension intentionally crafted to thwart my efforts of being close to my Creator. In the upcoming pages, I will describe how, when God opened my eyes, I gained the ability to perceive things that were previously beyond my comprehension.

3

The Healing Arts

Following my journey to Peru, I settled back into my home state of California. At the time, I was severely afflicted with nerve pain from a herniated disk in my spine. I made numerous efforts to find relief, including acupuncture, yoga, and herbal remedies, but the torment of pain continued to afflict me.

After trying every possible avenue for alleviating my pain, I found myself at a crossroads, faced with the choice of surgery or taking prescribed pain medication daily for the rest of my life. Unsettled with those options, I reasoned there had to be another way. Despite what the doctors told me, I had a hard time believing invasive surgery or taking medication for the rest of my life were the only two options I had to get relief.

My search for a better way led me to Pranic Healing, an ancient science and art that claims to use prana, or energy, to aid the body in its natural healing process. After studying and applying the method, I witnessed what seemed to be a miraculous result. Within six months of using the technique, my back and sciatic pain had completely subsided!

It was the first time in my life I had experienced something miraculous physically. Observing the supernatural or encountering phenomena that defy ordinary reality has a tendency to strengthen one's conviction. In this case, I was convinced of the power the technique had to generate results. No medication necessary. No surgery required. With just a wave of my hand and the projection of energy using this simple technique, my pain would diminish.

Motivated by newfound inspiration and a burning desire to assist others, I dedicated many years to studying the art of Pranic Healing and eventually obtained certification as a Pranic healer. In addition to healing techniques, Pranic Healing offered a spiritual system called Arhatic Yoga, which consists of meditations, character building, breathing exercises, and other spiritual practices. After being drawn in by what I experienced with the healing techniques of Pranic Healing, I began a deep and serious study of Arhatic Yoga as a spiritual practice.

During the intense mediations of Arhatic Yoga, I achieved altered states of consciousness that overflowed with intense spiritual energy, immersing me in euphoric states. At times, I felt as if I had been transported into entirely different spiritual realms. I believed that what I was experiencing was the divine—was God. Within this system, there are levels of practice that progressively introduce the practitioner to greater amounts of spiritual energy, power, and capabilities as a healer.

As I continued to practice the meditations, my spiritual abilities continued to expand and strengthen. Excited by the results I was seeing, I opened a healing arts office in my town, quickly gaining a following of clients. Individuals sought me out for Pranic Healing sessions, which were administered in a series and varied in length, based on the seriousness of their symptoms. After working with my clients for some time, there was more often than not a clear remission or marked improvement of their symptoms. Each ailment had specific protocols that would often provide the results they were seeking. I treated women with menopause, people with severe anxiety, watched back pain symptoms disappear, and even helped failing marriages amend.

There were endless protocols for all types of ailments, and the stronger I grew in the Arhatic spiritual practice, the easier and more miraculous the healings that took place appeared to be. On the surface, everything seemed wonderful. People were experiencing healing, and I felt a profound sense of purpose in my life, with a career that allowed me the daily opportunity to assist and serve others.

Following the teachings, I genuinely believed I was making continuous spiritual progress, interpreting the increasingly intense states of altered consciousness as a confirmation. Although my experiences at the time seemed positive, shadows loomed in the background, concealed by the matrix of deception in which I was bound by. In the soon-to-come intimate encounters with God, I shockingly uncovered an unsettling truth about the source of power I had been instructed to utilize for healing.

As advanced practitioners of the healing technique, we were encouraged to do Kundalini meditation regularly, due to its potential to yield great power. In the practice, energy is cultivated up the spine, and then wound around and stored in the navel. The more energy that is stored, the more powerful a healer can become. The Kundalini meditation is often depicted with a snake coiled at the base of the practitioner, known as the sleeping serpent, another source of serpent power that slithered its way into my life.

In the coming chapters, I unveil what God taught me about serpent power and the danger associated with using it. Serpent power subtly infiltrates numerous New Age and occult practices, camouflaging itself as a divine source of power. It mimics and counterfeits God's power to entice unsuspecting spiritual seekers, but its connection to the dark realm brings unfortunate consequences to the person using it.

Pranic Healers and Arhatic practitioners are trained to cultivate this type of Kundalini or serpent energy, to utilize it in assisting people with their healing. Helping others to heal was just the right noble cause to distract me from questioning things, such as the source of power that the system uses to obtain its objectives.

In the domain of New Age and the occult, spirituality itself is frequently glamorized, often inadvertently intertwined with self-glorification, and a deep desire to fulfill a purpose in life. Many people get lured into these types of systems because they observe more miracles and signs than what is seen in the majority of churches today. My colleagues in Pranic Healing were filled with compassion, kind and devoutly living spiritually disciplined lives. If God did not give me eyes to see, I would have probably spent the rest of my life serving in that community, thinking I was doing the right thing and believing it to be a virtuous path.

I was continuously impressed by the results I saw while practicing Pranic Healing. There is a technique in this system called rapid healing of fresh wounds, that when applied, can fuse together broken skin. If an asthmatic is having an asthma attack, another technique dilates the lungs, enabling the sufferer to breathe. Witnessing people get "healed" in sessions ignited a powerful drive in me to help people in the way I believed I had been helped.

During my study of Arhatic Yoga, the teachings focused intensely on character building, in which we developed positive virtues such as loving kindness and generosity, harmlessness, and servitude. With years of practice, I watched myself transforming into a better version of myself, cultivating greater patience, increasing my generosity, and developing a deeper sense of compassion for others. The essence of these teachings, filled with virtuous aspirations, wasn't the source of my undisclosed bondage; it was the hidden aspects which were secretly attached to the teachings that proved so perilous.

I was enchanted by Pranic Healing and Arhatic Yoga because the systems inspired incredible spiritual growth within me, and there existed a solution to pain and illness that I had not found elsewhere. I thrived in the community of deeply seeking spiritual aspirants, thinking that this was the way to grow closer to God and be the best human I could be while on Earth.

I began to host evening clinics with another Pranic healer to introduce interested persons to Pranic Healing. In the clinics, we provided guidance to participants on how to sense energy, educated them about chakras, and demonstrated live healing. For instance, if someone had a backache, I would invite them to the front, apply the technique, and then their pain would vanish. All I perceived in Pranic Healing was the goodness it seemed to provide, and how honorable a life path I believed it to be.

In addition to spending years as an energy healer, I also studied Rebirthing Breathwork, massage, and taught Yoga. I had a strong drive and passion for serving others in their healing processes and sought many ways to do so. I have always felt motivated to help people, and the world of healing arts delivered magic, results, and rich spiritual experiences.

During my late twenties and early thirties, my psychic and intuitive abilities blossomed, allowing me to perceive and comprehend details about my clients, their lives, and their ailments. I had the ability to sense what part of their body was afflicted, or what emotions or patterns were causing their suffering. I regularly engaged with the spirit world, spirit guides, and what I called my "healing angels." Every time I performed a healing session, I would invoke the name of the guru known to have given the whole system of Pranic Healing and Arhatic Yoga and call upon "healing angels" for assistance.

One of the things I realized very quickly after my encounters with God, was that what I saw in the spiritual terrain as a psychic and clairvoyant New Age healing arts practitioner in the spirit realm, is *very different* from what I began to see when God opened my eyes with new spiritual sight. Since the source of power in the world of psychics and clairvoyants I was involved with is not of God, the power behind it controls what the person sees and doesn't see. For those who find themselves in a similar trap, I want to convey that God is eager to restore rightful spiritual sight to His people, should you be willing.

In ten years of being a healing arts practitioner, I witnessed the deep sufferings of many. People with all types of physical ailments and psychological and emotional disturbances came through my office door. The practice I was involved with seemed to provide great results and give reprieve from unfavorable symptoms. However, something I noticed over time was that my clients seemed to be caught in a recurring cycle of complaints and suffering. If one problem improved, another would emerge. Even if their issue showed improvement, it would often resurface years later.

I longed to help my clients obtain whole and complete healing. I sought to address the root of people's deep pain, ailments, and sufferings. I started searching for answers that would solve some of life's most pressing conundrums. At the time, I believed that true transformation originated from within, and that if I genuinely wanted to help people, that I needed to help them change. I began developing a coaching program based on project management principles, aiming to systematically enhance the lives and situations of my clients.

I dedicated years to exploring various types of spiritualism and alternative healing techniques. However, it wasn't until I had a supernatural encounter with God that I realized everything I was involved with at that time was merely a counterfeit for the real thing. One single, genuine touch from God, completely transformed my perception of what I had previously considered divine.

In the spiritual systems I studied, attaining spiritual power demanded arduous effort. The systems were overly complicated, requiring hours of meditation and years of practice to reach the supposed "divine." I have since come to believe God's path is simple, inviting us to embrace humble surrender and unwavering faith.

Thanks to the boundless mercy and grace of God, I was freed from the delusion that kept me from the intimacy with God that I longed for. In order to escape my unseen prison, my life required a catalyst for change. Often, our most challenging life circumstances can serve as the most profound opportunities for redemption.

4

The Catalyst

In the year 2020, I met my partner, Gabriel. We were both in our mid-thirties at the time. He was also a practitioner in the healing arts, using a system known as Functional Symmetry to aid individuals in their healing processes. We shared a common aspiration in our deep desire to help and serve others, alongside our personal quests to lead a spiritual way of life.

With care and attentiveness, we built a deep, meaningful, and spiritually focused relationship. When I prayed for a partner, I compiled a list of qualities I desired in my future husband, and he met the criteria. Over the next couple of years, our union blossomed, and we began the journey of building a shared life.

By this point in my life, I had arrived at a stage where I felt settled in my chosen spiritual path. I had faith in the perceived progress of the spiritual system I followed. I found great fulfillment from my service of assisting others in their healing processes. My relationship with my partner was thriving, and it seemed at the time that I was leading a good life.

The catalyst I needed in order for God to make a jailbreak on my life came crashing down unexpectedly one day when I returned from a trip. My son and I had just returned from a yoga retreat at an ashram in the Bahamas. The day following our return, I dedicated hours to preparing a nice dinner for my partner and I while he was at work.

That day, Gabriel was working at the Psychic Fair in Nevada City, sharing his life's work in the healing arts with attendees looking for answers to their sufferings. I had suggested to him that he should set up a table there to promote his healing arts business, referencing the success I had working as an energy healer at the Psychic Fair on numerous occasions in previous years.

When he arrived home that evening, Gabriel appeared despondent and gloomy. Despite his beautiful soul and charismatic personality, there were some things he was struggling with. In every relationship, there are things to work on, and I was willing to be there for him through his challenges. His often and sometimes drastic changes in moods were something I had become accustomed to.

Gabriel was withdrawn and avoiding eye contact. I assumed it to be one of his "moods," silently reminding myself to be patient and loving. A few bites into the dinner, I broke the tense silence, asking him what was on his mind. I could sense there was something he was not saying. With hesitation, he looked up, paused, then finally said, "When I am quiet, surrendered and reaching for God, I am interpreting that God says it is best for me to end our relationship."

His words went like an arrow to my heart, and my body began to tremble. It made no sense to me. We had an amazing relationship, a family, and had even bought a home together. We lived harmoniously and had a fulfilling, spiritually focused life together. We had great communication and similar life paths. I knew I had treated him well throughout our relationship, and I could think of no valid reason why we shouldn't be together.

He went on to explain why he thought we shouldn't be together, taking it to the extent of claiming that he had never loved me and that I was merely a friend to him. It left me bewildered. Could this be the same man who had previously declared that I was the only woman he had ever desired to be with? Who had professed that I was the sole partner he had ever loved? Who had, on many occasions, gazed into my eyes and asked me to spend my life with him?

I challenged him in disbelief, but he seemed to be quite serious. Overwhelmed by the ludicrousness of it all, I stormed out of the house on foot, pacing around our neighborhood. I made my way to my sister's house, which was not far from my own. After I tearfully recounted what had transpired, she regarded me with disbelief and suggested, "This doesn't seem to make sense; you might want to consider the possibility of a mental health issue."

Perhaps she has a point, I contemplated silently. On my journey home, I took slow, deep, trembling breaths, reaching out to God and fervently asking for help. Amidst the chaos, God's wisdom broke through, instructing me to stick by Gabriel's side no matter what happens. I was to grow in my love for him until my love for him became a godly love. *Okay,* I thought, *I will strive to be the embodiment of divine, unconditional love.*

When I came home, I sat on the couch with my partner and looked him over. When my gaze reached above his head, I noticed something bizarre. There, on the left side of his head, I glimpsed a blurred shadow. I was seeing in the spirit, sensing something I had not noticed before. As I continued to study Gabriel, I also saw an eclipse of the light around his body. *What on Earth is that?* I wondered.

Recently, I had been listening to a YouTube channel where a man spoke about over-cloaking spirits. The presenter in the video explained that spirits can gain access to influence us through our emotional wounds. From what it looked like, it appeared my beloved had a spirit or shadow directly obstructing the entrance of light into his body. Could it be a spirit that was pretending to be the voice of God?

That thought slipped abruptly from my mind as I recalled what my sister had said. My partner had a history of mental illness, and I wanted to explore the possibility of his state being caused by a mental breakdown. As I sat quietly looking at him, I could tell he was in a dissociated state, distant, and lacking in emotions.

Often, he fell into what we referred to as his "numb" states, where there was disconnect from his ability to feel. I pressed into God, searched my heart, and pondered what I could say to get through to him. Godly love. That is the wisdom that God gave me to face what was ahead. *Ok God, I will attempt what you have asked of me,* I affirmed to myself.

I said to Gabriel, "You seem dissociated. I'm not going to leave you when you need me the most. You have stood by me through some of my hardest times when I was in the hospital and getting treated for neurological Lyme disease in Mexico. If this is your moment of breaking down, I'm going to stand by your side. I won't let you push me away."

Suddenly, he burst into tears, and I gathered him tenderly in my arms. I felt him start coming back from the mentally distant land he had been in and settle into a more genuine state. "I can't believe that I forgot my love for you," he said, confused about what had caused him to do and say the things that he had. I expressed great concern over his behavior. At the end of our discussion, he agreed to seek therapy and support from a professional.

In the morning, he returned to his normal upbeat self, albeit he was quite tender. The next night, he asked, "Will you spend your life with me?" something he had asked many times before. I looked into his eyes and said, "Yes, of course my love." I so loved this man and would eagerly walk through life hand-in-hand in a divine union for the rest of our lives.

The next day, I was deeply disturbed when I noticed Gabriel's unusual behavior return. He was again dissociated, devoid of emotion, and distant from me. When he was walking around our house, I again glimpsed a shadow, this time around his eyes.

At one point, we passed each other in the hallway, and when our eyes met, he said, "I'm sorry, God is telling me to leave you, and I can't stay." I tried to protest and get through to him, but this time his certainty was impenetrable. He was convinced God was telling him to leave. That night, he left, declaring the end of our relationship.

This was one of those devastating moments in life, when everything I had been working towards, everything I loved and treasured, crumbled into nothing. That agonizing moment, of grieving in the rubble of what once was, desperately trying to cling onto everything that has moved just out of reach. All those memories, only still frames in time, fleeting, never to be had again. That moment when attachments are revealed, pain clutching relentlessly at my chest, each laborious breath fighting for space in the tightened muscles of my broken heart.

Losing my partner was the loss of something so sacred and special to me. My love for him woven deeply into my dreams of a family, and my vision of our life together. How could I stop believing in a dream that I was so deeply invested in? The tragic loss of my partnership weighed heavily upon me; my world now darkened.

None of what was happening made any sense to me. During our time together, Gabriel and I both lovingly referred to our relationship as the best one we ever had. He had frequently told me that he wanted to spend his life with me.

To me, our relationship was precious, its foundation deeply rooted in our spirituality. How could a relationship founded in God fail?

Confused, I cried out to God, "If I am a woman of God, and he is a man of God, why can't we walk together? Why was our sacred relationship broken? Why couldn't we bind and sanctify our holy union?" Through tears and clenched fists, I demanded an answer. God's response to my cry came in the coming weeks.

5

My Crushed House of Certainty

The day after Gabriel left our home, I sent him a distraught text, begging for him to explain why he ended our relationship. I needed resolution, I needed to know what I could have done better, and if there existed an underlying cause of the breakup. I could not understand why he would leave what I considered to be a healthy, deeply spiritual, and fulfilling relationship.

His answer to my query came in the form of a thirty-minute voice memo. I eagerly opened it up and listened as he said, "Over the course of our relationship, I spiritually evolved to a place beyond your capacity to join me, and if I were to stay with you, I would be trapped in lower realms of consciousness." He then pointed out, "You are too certain about everything, and don't have the humility necessary to truly understand me or where I am going."

Astonished, I set my phone down, struck by his words. I was greatly humbled. Was he really more evolved than me and headed to a place beyond my spiritual capacity to reach him?

I began searching myself for answers, reviewing past actions to determine if there was truth in what he said. *He's right*, I thought. The more I looked, the more I became aware of an all-permeating arrogance in who I was. My firmly held beliefs, fixed and unshakable, were suddenly exposed. The perceptions I held about him, about myself, about life in general, and about spirituality as a whole, were bound in place by my unwavering certitude.

Towards the end of the voice note, he said, "Bri, you just need to let go; let it all crumble." In this perfect culmination of timing, events, and surging anguish, his message penetrated to the depth of my being. His words reverberated in my soul as my world collapsed like a house of cards. As my pride tumbled to the wayside, fresh humility cracked open deep-seated convictions. Ways in which I was egotistically puffed up deflated as the winds of change rushed into my life.

With new eyes, I suddenly saw all the ways my pride and arrogance had led to a lack of open-mindedness and narrow worldview. The reality of my foolishness set in, my allegiance to sure-set convictions now unmasked. I could see the moat I had built around the castle of certainty in my mind, that nothing could penetrate through. All my assumptions and assertions about everything that I felt so convinced of, were now under immediate scrutiny. My high-built castle of unwarranted confidence began to crumble, its faulty structure now uncovered.

Instead of fighting it, or resisting what was being revealed, I let go. My world was shaking, and for the first time, I was willing to let all my belief systems be challenged. With my sureness now unbridled, I was empowered to ask important questions that I had ceased asking long ago.

What if I am wrong about everything I think I know? What if the world is nothing like I imagined it to be? What if Gabriel has evolved beyond me, and I am stuck in a world of delusion?

Then, I asked the most important question of my life: WHO IS GOD? Did Gabriel and I have different gods? Why was the God of my world telling me to stand beside him and love him through this, while the god of his mind was telling him to leave me? A new, burning need to know the truth sprung up within me. I was overtaken by an urgent necessity to get to the bottom of all my pressing questions. I was desperate. I needed answers.

That's the moment I did one of the most important things I have ever done. I got down on my knees and cried out to God, "Who are You, God? Are there many gods? Is there a God of the Most High? Who is my Creator? Who made humans? Who made this world? Who is in charge of Earth?"

These questions are common to ask as a child, but how often do people ask them as an adult? Usually, by the late thirties, as in my case, most people have settled beliefs about these questions. Having the humbleness to ask these questions with child-like wonder unleashed a bounty of treasure I would have completely missed had I been stubbornly attached to my certainty for the rest of my days.

These big questions required big answers, and I was determined to maximize my chances of acquiring them. That's when a brilliant idea struck me—I decided to make a proposition to God. I surmised that if I truly wanted to capture the attention of God, that I needed to go all in. In that pivotal moment, I offered God everything I had to give, "God, if You reveal yourself to me, I will give my life to You, like I never have before. If You make Your presence known in an undeniable way, I'll be yours for the rest of my life."

When I said what I said, I meant it. Not half-heartedly. Not on my conditions. I sincerely meant what I was offering. I put all my cards on the table. I offered God my life and everything in it, with the full intention of keeping my word till death. My yearning for the truth of God was so great that I was willing to give my life up for it. I wasn't sure what that would look like, but I did know that it meant giving up my preferences, and living life God's way, not my way.

As an affirmation of my conviction, I spoke these words aloud in declaration: "Lord of the Most High, God of the universe, I want You to take spiritual authority over my life. Take spiritual authority over my life, my home, and my relationship. Show me who You truly are, and I will give myself to You fully."

Over the next couple of days, I took a new approach to my life, treating it as a spiritual science experiment. I tore down the remnants of my house of certainty and made the decision to leave no stone unturned in my pursuit of truth. I diligently sifted through my beliefs, my assertions, and challenged every assumption about my life, God, and the universe.

I laid out my beliefs and convictions on a table in my mind for sorting, labeled: "I don't know." I imagined myself as a spiritual scientist in an objective exploration of what the truth about life and God could possibly be. My entire framework for understanding reality and the world around me was placed on the observation table for analysis. I started life over. I pretended I knew nothing about anything, aspiring to new understanding by collecting data and developing hypotheses about God and life.

If you have never done this, I would argue this is perhaps one of the most powerful exercises one could do from a place of absolute humility. Not only that, but when you offer your life to God on the results of that research, it is a potent fuel to travel far into uncharted realms and territories that hindrances in our minds can keep us from experiencing.

Until I performed this exercise, I never truly made space in my perception to allow a greater truth to enter my awareness. I was so sure of my lofty New Age, spiritual perception being the truth of reality and this world. I thought I had found a higher path, and that I was on my way to enlightenment through mediation.

Even though I perceived myself as a humble seeker of God and truth, I was so deeply entrenched in the matrix of lies that there was no way for the truth to get in. Yet this perfect storm of circumstance shook me to my core, creating a deep crack in my understanding of the world. Fueled by a potent combination of grief and willingness to question, the veil of deception began to unravel, making way for what God was about to reveal to me.

One day, when my suffering felt too great to bear, I took a walk along the creek near my house. I watched the water stream over mossy rocks and took in the lush greenery. Sadness burned in my chest as my shaky legs tried to find stability on the forest floor beneath me. I kept asking God, "Why, why this, why now?" My soul cried out to God, yearning to understand the reason for my challenges.

I stopped at the end of the creek path and stared into the water. There before me, was an old concrete bridge that had cracked and fallen into the water. I sat down on the edge of the broken bridge and let the sounds of the water passing over rocks soothe the ache in my heart. I put my hands in prayer position and bowed my head slightly, keeping my eyes open and fixed on the creek. It was then that God graced me with a revelation.

With my soft gaze resting on the broken concrete bridge, God gave me the insight that this bridge was like my life, broken open, the cracks making space for the water of the Spirit to pour forth in deep places within me, otherwise inaccessible. My mental framework, my pride, my arrogance, all had to be shattered and brought to destruction, so that the fullness of the Spirit of God could enter me. Such a deep crack in my world, such an intense life breakdown, created an opportunity for God to penetrate to new depths in me. For the first time since my partner had left, I felt peace and understanding with this realization.

It is often in our greatest trials and tribulations that our hunger for God becomes necessary and irresistible. When life has broken us, in our most desperate moments, humility arises to open the door to strengthening our connection to God. In a world that can be so superficial and distracting, it is no wonder that a great humbling is needed for some of us to come home to God.

I had no idea what was going to happen after I shouted into the sky to God and pleaded for him (or her, or it) to reveal themself. I was surprisingly open to finding out who God is, and ready to consider whatever response I was to receive.

God heard my prayer...and delivered! The supernatural reply I received in response to my inquiry was wildly beyond anything I imagined it would be. Belief systems can blanket the ability to think outside of what we have already decided we know. They are the wool over our eyes. By being willing to let my beliefs shatter into pieces, it made room for the light of truth to radiate into my life.

So often we miss a greater truth in front of us, because of how uncomfortable it can be to explore what is beyond our firmly held assertions. Whether you walk a path similar to the one I was on, in the world of spirituality, or you are someone who has been inside a church your whole life, inaccurate assumptions and assertions we hold can prevent us from fully experiencing the truth God longs to reveal to us. As you will see in the coming chapters, adopting humility and the earnest willingness to investigate outside what is familiar and comfortable can lead to groundbreaking discoveries and unprecedented glory.

Part 2

Deliverance

6

The Stirring Shadows

After my partner left, I sought support, counsel, and insight into my situation from sources I trusted at the time. I consulted several great healers and psychics to evaluate the situation with Gabriel. All three of them confirmed there was indeed an entity attached to my partner, but what was I to do about it?

In the first few crushing days after Gabriel left, my mother came to stay with my son and me. My mother and I had differing spiritual views most of my life, my mother being a devout Christian and me being a new age spiritual seeker. Despite our differences, we both believed fervently in God. I was grateful to have her support for my son and I, during that difficult time.

During my mother's stay, we decided to attend a local Evangelical Christian church. It was a place not far from my house that came recommended by people in my neighborhood. I desired to be in a house of God and was open to trying a church my mother would like. It didn't matter much to me where we went, as long as I could feel His presence. I sat through the service curled up next to my mother in the back row, not feeling much besides my grief.

I closed my eyes and leaned my spirit into God, praying fervently for something—anything—that could restore my family, my home, and my broken relationship. As my heavy eyes lifted, I saw the pastor walking out into the crowd. His eyes were fixed steadily upon me, as he made his way to the back row where we were seated. He stopped right in front of my mother and me, and said, "The Lord has a word for you."

Then he prophesied, "Hope deferred makes the heart sick. So many things try to come between us, but LOVE conquers all. God is going to immerse you in His love and His Word. Daughter, my hand is upon you, and has been. Those of you who strayed away, God says, 'Come home.' God says, 'There is a time coming that I am going to use you to go where angels fear to tread. I'm going to use you in ways that are different. I never send you out alone. I always send you in twos or threes.' The Lord says, 'I'm going to give you things to share, and it will be in your testimony.' The Lord says, 'By the blood of the Lamb and the word of my testimony, you are saved.' The Lord says, 'Call upon me, and I will show you great and mighty things, things for good and not evil.' The Lord says, 'I got a word for you, and it's going to be buried deep inside your spirit.' Let it arise, and let God arise and His enemies be scattered."

At the time, I wasn't quite sure what to make of what the pastor said. God was going to use me to go where angels fear to tread? What did that even mean? That didn't sound like something I wanted to do.

Though the word released over me that day didn't make sense at the time, it quickly began to make sense as the veil was lifted from my eyes. Good and evil were not strong concepts in the New Age doctrine I followed at the time. I knew of dark influences in our world, but I was clueless to the extent of their influence over the land of the living.

The next day, I called my dear friend Kathy to talk to her about the concerns I had about Gabriel. She excitedly mentioned a Pentecostal church in Yuba City that she had been attending for the last year. She said, "The church is well known for its background in exorcism and deliverance ministry." When I asked her what deliverance was, she explained that it is the casting out of evil spirits or demons, like Jesus does in the Bible.

How interesting, I thought, *this might be worth checking out.*

"Have you ever heard about an internationally famous satanist named Anton LaVey, who founded the Church of Satan?" she continued.

"Definitely not," I replied.

She then shared the story of Dave and Cheryl Bryan, pastors of the Church of Glad Tidings. Kathy explained, "They came head-to-head in a spiritual battle against Anton LaVey, founder of the Church of Satan. The Bryans' epic battle began when the daughter of Anton LaVey, Deborah Joy, sought refuge from her father and the world of Satanism at their church. Under the Bryans' protection, Deborah encountered the light of Christ and underwent radical deliverance from demonic possession."

"Wow," I said, "that sounds pretty wild."

"Yes," Kathy replied, "It was. Protecting Deborah put Dave, Cheryl, and the congregation of the Church of Glad Tidings at the forefront of supernatural spiritual warfare in an unimaginable battle between light and dark. The church was thrust into the onslaught of spiritual attacks, defending against ongoing curses from witch covens and the Church of Satan."

"Crazy…" I said, trying to imagine what it was like when the Church of Satan was throwing down with a church of Christians.

"Yes, and in the end, they defeated Anton LaVey," Kathy said.

"Like how?" I asked.

"They asked God to cut his silver cord," she said mysteriously.

"Well, if there is anyone that could help me with the suspected demonic possession of Gabriel, Glad Tidings sure seems like a great place to start," I declared, intrigued by the story.

I later read that the Bryans and other church leaders relied on the supernatural power and protection of Christ to thwart these attacks and strengthen their faith as spirit-filled believers. The spiritual warfare reached its zenith with the death of Anton LaVey on October 31, 1997, marking a pivotal victory in the spiritual realm for the Bryans and the Church of Glad Tidings. The Church of Glad Tidings then gained international recognition for its potent spiritual warfare and deliverance ministries, becoming a haven for those afflicted by dark forces.

After listening to Kathy's story about the history of the church, I was compelled to check the church out. Despite my reservations in attending a Christian church because of my experiences with other churches, I had to admit, any church able to win a spiritual battle against the founder of Satanism could likely help with my unusual predicament.

Kathy was someone whom I had spent over eight years practicing energy healing and attending countless spiritual classes with, and I trusted her recommendation. I was desperate for help, and willing to do anything to help my beloved, estranged partner.

Not only that, from the time I was young, I was captivated by the supernatural. That fascination inspired a steadfast pursuit of finding the places and ways in which the spiritual and supernatural collide. Since the churches of my youth lacked supernatural spiritual occurrences, I read countless books on spirituality, Indian saints with Siddhis (supernatural powers), magic, levitation, and out-of-body experiences. I longed to be where the action was and participate in it. My friend's mention of a church operating in supernatural gifts such as the casting out of demons, prophetic word, and other supernatural phenomena, was just the bait I needed.

I could not erase from my mind the shadow I had seen on my boyfriend before he left, nor shake the suspicion of spirit possession. If some dark entity had fooled Gabriel into thinking it was God's voice he was hearing, I had to do something to intervene. I was the only person in the world who suspected this possibility. If I didn't help him, who would? Would he go his whole life thinking he is surrendering his life to God, when actually it was an imposter evil entity? I could not bear the blasphemy of it!

Impassioned by the drive to put an end to this plausible abomination, I made the bold decision to attend a service at Church of Glad Tidings, eager to enlist help in my dilemma. I generally avoided most church settings, but the idea of a church that teaches about the supernatural was too enticing to pass up.

That evening, the church service was led by a speaker named Jess Parker. My friend Kathy informed me that he was the head of the deliverance team at Glad Tidings Church, with over 30 years of experience in casting out demons. *Now this is the guy I need to talk to,* I thought to myself.

His talk that evening was on the impartation of speaking in tongues. Speaking in tongues was not something I had previously experienced in church. I sat quietly, listening with an open mind, committed to leaving no stone unturned in my search for truth. His thought-provoking talk captured my attention, as he explained how speaking in tongues is a prayer language that connects you to the Spirit of God and heavenly realms.

I like the sound of that, I thought, *a secret prayer language to connect with heavenly realms.* As his sermon neared completion, he invited anyone who hadn't yet received their prayer language to come to the front of the room.

Inescapably curious, I stood up and walked to the front. *Why not? Might as well give it a try,* I reassured myself as I approached. I saw around ten people gathered at the front of the room, as I made my way to stand beside them.

Jess Parker walked down the line of people, touching their shoulders, and praying in tongues over them, one-by-one. After about thirty seconds of prayer with a person, I watched awestruck as all of sudden their prayer language emerged from their mouths. He stepped in front of me, his hand resting gently upon my shoulder.

"Pray with me," he said, and began speaking in tongues. I was skeptical. Unsure. I opened my mouth to see what might happen, and to my astonishment, a flood of sound came out. As my mouth poured out strange words, a surge of pleasant energy passed through my body. I was humbled, taken aback by my unexpected experience in church that evening.

Upon reflection, I recalled Jess Parker saying that our prayer language is something to practice, and that we can learn it like any other language. I took his suggestion to heart and practiced in the morning and night for several days. By the third day of practicing speaking in tongues, I was discouraged by judgmental thoughts that crept into my mind. I began to doubt the authenticity of speaking in tongues and stopped practicing.

One week later, I attended a class at Glad Tidings on prophetic visions and dreams. Being someone who has frequent visions and dreams, the class aroused my interest.

I was keen to the idea of inviting God to be the director of my dreams and visions. I delighted in the material covered in class that day, feeling inspired to invite the Spirit of God to guide my visions and dreams in a new way.

As the class came to a close, I approached the teacher, Lee, to request prayer for my estranged boyfriend. In two days, I was to have a meeting with Gabriel and a therapist to begin our separation process. I was desperate to find a way to get through to Gabriel and put a halt to what felt like a big mistake. After sharing the details about my situation, Lee responded by asking, "Have you been given the power of speaking in tongues?"

"Yes," I said timidly, still feeling unsure about it.

He replied, "Have you ever tried praying in tongues for three hours?"

"Uhh, no. Definitely not," I said, feeling slightly ashamed about giving up so easily the week before.

"Try praying in tongues for three hours for your partner, prior to your arranged meeting," he suggested.

I paused for a moment, thinking, Well I did ask for help, and this is the answer I received, whether I liked it or not. I'm just going to trust that God is leading me and give Lee's suggestion a try. "Okay, I am up for the challenge," I said, feeling resolved. I thanked him for his wisdom and went to gather my things. I was willing to try anything in my relentless determination to help Gabriel, even if it meant trying new things.

◊ ◊ ◊

The next day happened to be Wesak, a Buddhist holiday celebrating the birth, enlightenment, and death of Buddha on the full moon of May. In the spiritual lineage I pursued for seven years, it was considered a significant day in which participants go to great lengths to fast and prepare. Through my spiritual teachers, I was told it was a day in which one could draw a great amount of spiritual energy as fuel for the year ahead.

I looked forward to this day as a day of spiritual purification; however, this year was destined to be an entirely different experience of Wesak. After fasting and taking a ritual bath, I joined an online Zoom conference to meditate and pray with the spiritual community of Arhatic Yoga practitioners.

When the meditation began, the leaders instructed participants to connect their "third eye" and forehead chakra (energy point) with those of everybody else, intending to unify our collective power as a group. Although I had performed this exercise numerous times before, this year I found myself hesitating; something deep within me was holding me back.

As I searched for guidance from God, it became very clear that I was being cautioned to not take part in the practice that day. *How strange,* I thought, *something in me is shifting.* For the first time in seven years, participating in Wesak didn't sit right with me.

I quieted myself, connecting to God with deep humility in my heart. In the stillness, I received clear instructions to only pray in tongues. Lee's suggestion to pray in my prayer language for three hours came to mind, and I decided to follow through on my commitment. I surrendered my mind and sunk into deep prayer. A surge of incredible energy washed over me.

At first, my prayer language came out awkward and clunky, but I kept at it, determined to go as deep into prayer as possible. After about 20 minutes of focused prayer, the words of my prayer language smoothed out, becoming seamless. I sensed an inexplicable shift in the atmosphere as I prayed continuously in tongues.

All of a sudden, a flicker of white light flashed in my inner vision, and I became subtly aware of a sacred presence descending from above. A wash of all-permeating holiness flooded into the room as a spirit in the shape of a translucent white dove drew near to me. My body trembled as the weight of His presence fell upon my body like a heavy downpour of rain.

I bowed my head to the floor in deep reverence, the only thing that made sense to do in a moment such as this. A powerful current of energy coursed through me, sending shivers through my spine. The profound spiritual experiences of my life that prefaced this encounter, could never compare to the exquisite beauty of that intimate moment when I realized that it was the Spirit of God that had descended on me that fateful day.

Only God could wield such a commanding and striking presence. It was all I could manage to lay awe-struck, reverent, and fearful of His eminence. His all-knowing presence pierced into the depth of me. I sensed Him examining the innermost parts of me, my life history, and the desires and intentions of my heart.

I was utterly exposed; completely witnessed by God's Spirit, as He searched out every hidden part of me. I felt deeply seen, known, and understood. This presence knew *everything* about me. Never before had I encountered anything or anyone that knew me with such depth.

In that moment of union with God, He began to teach and reveal things to me about myself, about the world, and what His desires were for my life. In an instant, I gained understanding that there are certain laws and principles that govern us in God's Kingdom. Under God's firm and compassionate guidance, my attention was brought to the ways I was living out of alignment with God's laws and principles. It suddenly became clear to me that there are consequences to breaking God's divine laws, even when one is unaware of their existence.

What was interesting about being perceived in this manner was that God was not reading off my offenses one by one; instead, it was a profound knowing that came upon me in an instant, a spontaneous download that took no time to process. In that single moment, God showed me that there are both legal and illegal ways to access the spirit world, and that I had been breaking spiritual laws by opening doorways between realms, astral traveling, and accessing information sources used in my healing arts practice.

He had a surprisingly long and detailed list of the infractions I had made on God's laws, which I had unknowingly been breaking for much of my life. In this intimate moment of divine revelation, I perceived and clearly understood God's goodness; he instilled within me that day, a deep desire to follow His ways, convicting me to live a life of righteousness.

In that soul-shattering realization of how much of my life had been against God's wishes, unbeknownst to me, I was suddenly overcome with an inescapable sadness. I cringed in realization of my own ignorance and arrogance as God flooded my mind with memories of how belligerent I had been in my assuredness, which ultimately had drowned out the subtle whispers of the Lord. As God pulled back the veil on the inner workings of His creation, the matrix of lies I had been living broke open, spilling out layers and layers of deception.

In my life review, God even declared that I was a *wanted felon in the spirit world*, for all the spiritual laws I had broken. God's humor in this is laughable now, but at the time it was a great shock. My beloved Creator God educated me about the illegal nature in which I was accessing the spirit world, and how it was harmful to myself and others.

I later found an interesting definition for the word felon in the online etymology dictionary, which says "one who deceives or commits treason; one who is wicked or evil; evildoer," used of Lucifer and Herod, from Old French felon "evildoer, scoundrel, traitor, rebel, oath-breaker, the Devil." I had been unknowingly committing treason against God. The weight of that realization pressed heavily upon me.

Had I really been that fooled? The surprise I felt was overwhelming. It would take time for me to process the fact that I had been cunningly swindled by the well-disguised trickery of the matrix of lies. I felt so betrayed, by myself, by the spiritual teachings and teachers I had diligently followed. My mind was spinning out of control as I grappled with coming face to face with the truth. Sensing my distress, God then lovingly and reassuringly said to me that people can do good things with illegal power, like when I performed energy healing to help relieve pain or emotional turmoil in my clients, but because of the divine laws that govern Earth, there is a natural and unavoidable cost and penalty for doing so.

As this mind-bending download from God neared completion, I continued my prayer in tongues, surrendering, letting all that was faulty in me begin to crumble away. Then, a most peculiar thing began to exhibit in my body. As I prayed in the holy tongue, I noticed that certain areas of my body jerked in reaction, a response that seemed to be provoked by my prayer. *How peculiar. What could this be?* I wondered. Although cognitively I could not understand the words of my prayer language, my spirit could feel the divine presence and power of what I was saying.

The aggressive tugging manifested in specific areas of my body, areas in which I had held chronic pain for much of my life. For many years, I was plagued with severe neurological nerve pain and tension in my neck, as well as chronic abdominal and liver pain. The pain in these parts of my body intensified with my prayer in tongues, accompanied by the display of bizarre convulsions.

"God, what is happening?" I pondered aloud. A feeling of dread gripped me, as I hesitantly came to recognize there were things inside of me that were writhing under the power of God's glory held within my prayer language. Unholy things. Unrighteous things. Wicked presences. *Oh Lord, do I have entities on me like Gabriel does?* I thought anxiously, fear and paranoia seeping in from every direction. *No! It can't be!* I screamed in my mind, gravely unsettled at this possibility.

My mind spun out of control with questions and justifications. Are there really sinister forces in me, reacting to this prayer in my holy tongue? Is it the prayer language that stirs these things in me? How could this be? I am a caring, compassionate, good person. I live a spiritual and disciplined life. I get up at 5:30 am to meditate and pray. I have devoted my life to spirituality and serving others in the healing arts. I practice deep forgiveness and non-injury in my thoughts, words, and deeds. How could I have spirits or entities in me that quiver and resist the holy language of God?

A conversation I had with someone recently at church popped into my mind. Her words took on new meaning, as they echoed through my memory, "Yeshua of Nazareth has authority and dominion over everything in this world. He was the manifestation of God in the flesh. He paid the price with His crucifixion on the cross, and if we call upon His name, He has power and dominion over all darkness." In that moment of distress and panic, I turned my prayer towards Jesus.

Why not? If He has dominion over darkness, no better time to release His name over the stirring shadows I was perceiving within me. "Jesus!" I cried out. It was the first time I said His name sincerely in over 20 years.

As His name passed over my lips, I felt something inside of me jump in response, tugging at my physical body. I sat in stillness, trying to make sense of the unusualness of what I was experiencing.

"Jesus!" I shouted again. The mention of His name again resulted in an involuntary jerking of my abdomen and neck. *How peculiar*, I thought, *it appears these dark presences I've unearthed inside of me have a knee-jerk reaction to the name of Jesus.*

I couldn't help but recall the scene from *The Matrix* where Neo discovers a mechanical tracking device inside his abdomen, visibly crawling around in his stomach. Neo had been unaware of this parasitic machine hidden within his flesh until his rescuers informed him and provided the technology necessary to remove it. Now, in a similar situation, I felt something distinctly stirring within me, and it was the name of Jesus that seemed to act as the "technology" necessary to reveal these parasitic entities in a way that I could perceive them. My mind was crushing under the pressure of a truth I didn't feel ready to face. I wanted to hide and pretend like I didn't see what I had just seen. I was terrified of its implications, and the potential impact on my life. I pressed myself to be more objective, to be the spiritual scientist I had set out to be. I needed more data to make a proper hypothesis and conclusion about everything I had just experienced.

I found it difficult to digest what God was trying to show me about this matter in this first encounter but being in His presence stirred within me a deep desire to serve and obey Him. In the weeks that followed, God took my hand and dismantled my mental framework for reality as I knew it, making way for a greater truth to emerge.

The depth and magnitude of insight bestowed upon me in my first encounter with my Creator, astounded me. The supernatural knowing and unmatched intensity I experienced that day left me yearning for more of Him. After He encountered me, my previous spiritual experiences were unavoidably exposed as counterfeits that could never rival the true power and splendor of our Creator God. The Spirit of God that visited me that day as a translucent white dove I later discerned to be the Holy Spirit, as shown in Christian iconography.

The white dove has been portrayed in many ancient religious paintings as the Holy Spirit. In my research, I discovered paintings dating back to the 1300s, and the Holy Ghost is even pictured in catacombs—underground burial sites that date back to 100 AD (that's 1900 years ago). So, it turns out that this Spirit of God has been visiting humanity for a very long time.

7

Deliverance

The day after my encounter, I had a healing arts breathwork event planned with many confirmed attendees. As I stirred to wakefulness in the early morning light to do my meditation and prayer time, the presence of God that I had encountered the day before returned. In the silence, I heard a firm whisper of God's voice say, "Cancel your breathwork event, and instead go attend the three-day conference at Church of Glad Tidings called Show Us Your Glory."

It was difficult for me to listen and surrender to what God was asking me to do, since I had loyalty to my attendees and financial ties to my event. Yet, I had asked God to reveal Himself to me, and in return, I had offered my life. The experience I had the day before was so supernatural and powerful that I could not deny the unfolding of something extraordinary in my life. I reluctantly decided to cancel my event and surrendered myself to God's plan for my weekend.

In all the spiritual retreats I had attended in my life, I had never considered going to a conference at a Christian church. The wounding from Christian churches in my early childhood and teenage years kept me from including churches as part of my regular spiritual community. Despite my hesitancy, as I settled into my submission to go, a weight lifted off my shoulders. I sensed something of great significance was going to manifest that weekend and trusted the power of God was guiding me to go.

I had tasted God's true power, grace, and glory the day before, and I wanted more. Christian church or not, it didn't matter; I had felt and seen the Spirit of God in their church, and it was the speaking of tongues I received from a service there that brought down the holy presence of the Lord. The more time I spent at Church of Glad Tidings over the coming months, the more I realized that this church was different from any other church I had attended in the past. I perceived the Spirit of God moving in that church in ways I had never seen in a church setting before.

When I was gathering my things to leave for the conference, I quickly saw that I required a bag to contain my collection of items. I searched the back of the closet and fished out a shoulder bag, one I hadn't used in a long time. As I held it in my hands, I recalled that it was the bag that I used to bring with me to a class with a spiritual teacher whom my partner Gabriel had devoutly followed for over seven years.

After about a year of attending this spiritual discipleship with Gabriel and his Functional Symmetry mentor, I quit going because it was rather cult-like. Despite the spiritual nature and content, I sensed something sinister and dark about the group and setting. This bag had been repeatedly soaked in the energy of that circumstance and still carried a heavy feeling on it. I was in a hurry, so I decided to use it anyway.

I will never forget that day, when I first walked into the main sanctuary of the Church of Glad Tidings. I had that bag slung over my shoulder, securely held by its two, thick rope handles. The second my right foot crossed the threshold of the sanctuary and touched the floor inside, one of the rope handles of the bag suddenly split, the shredded rope falling in two pieces. Surprised, I paused, one foot in the door, and one foot out. *Huh, that's weird,* I thought, then, I lifted my left foot to pass through the doorway.

74

The moment my left foot touched the floor of the sanctuary, the remaining handle on my bag shredded and split, just as the other one had. My bag slammed to the floor because there were no longer any handles left for it to hang on my shoulder. I stood there stunned, staring at my downed bag, and thinking of its history. *Whoa,* I thought, *I'm definitely in the right place. If the power of God in this place can shred the haunted ropes of this bag, no telling what else God is up to in this place.*

I made my way to my seat and settled in. The Show Us Your Glory conference ran all day, and I spent much of the time with my head bowed in prayer. I basked in the wonderful and rich presence of God residing in that church, finding it immensely soothing to just be there and pray. Many intriguing things were spoken by the guest speakers throughout the day, but my attention was most drawn not to the words themselves, but to the electricity, excitement, and undeniable power of God in the words they were speaking.

At the end of the first day, they invited people to come up to the front for prayer. I contemplated the invitation, searching my heart for guidance from God on what He wanted me to do. Then I heard God say, "Go stand in line to get a prayer from the woman with red hair." At the time, I thought this woman was visiting the church as a guest speaker, but later discovered she is the wife of the pastor at Glad Tidings, and the granddaughter of A.A. Allen. (In case you don't know, A.A. was a famous evangelist known for the signs, wonders, and miracles God did through him.)

As I approached her, I became even more certain that God was insisting that I go to her for prayer. At the very moment she began to pray and laid her hands upon my head, my body unexpectedly collapsed to the ground. I was overtaken with surprise when my spirit then flew out of my body, and I suddenly found myself in an entirely different world.

All that I could make out was an all-pervading white, blinding light that penetrated through every part of me. My spirit took a step forward, and out from the piercing rays of light emerged an outstretched hand. I sought the face of the person offering their hand, and then, I knew. It was Jesus. I sheepishly took His hand, and He led me before an even more blazing light, the throne of God Almighty. I fell to my knees, and two angels appeared on both sides of me, anointing me with oil.

All of a sudden, I was back in my body, aware of the cold floor beneath me. The overhead lights of the church shone into my squinted eyes, and I heard a distant murmur of voices around me. My body was twitching in the areas of my neck and abdomen, like the day I first did my extended prayer in tongues. Something inside of me was fighting against the current of God that had just passed through my body and spirit.

I found my friend Kathy loyally kneeled beside me, announcing she had been guarding my body while I had been taken up in the spirit. I felt amazing, ripples of euphoric sensations still running through my body. I felt lighter, and strangely happy. *Wow*, I thought, *I searched for an experience like that when I was experimenting with drugs in my youth, but the real thing is a thousand times better!*

I got on my knees, my hands in prayer position, and fervently thanked God in a silent prayer: "Thank you, God, thank you, Jesus, thank you for bringing me into the heavenly realms. Thank you for blessing and anointing me on God's holy altar. Thank you for the angels who ministered to me."

My mind was reeling at what had just happened; I attempted to make sense of it all. In my vision, I had seen Jesus, but had also felt a larger, brighter, and more intense presence with Jesus in heaven. Could this be the answer to my question, who is God?

That evening on my drive home, I found myself to be exceptionally joyful. There was a buoyancy in my spirit, and I was inspired to sing—something I hadn't done in a long time. The songs bellowed out of me, with divinely inspired words and tunes proclaiming the goodness of God. I looked forward with anticipation to the final day of the conference and whatever else God had in store for me that weekend.

The next morning, I returned for the final day and sat attentively listening to the presenters. The energy of the weekend had been building up within me. I maintained a continuous prayer in my mind that matched the theme of the weekend: "God, show me Your glory!" Once I tasted God's majesty, I longed for more of it.

Through the temples of India, jungles of Peru, ancient ruins of Mexico, and a lifetime of meditation and spirituality, I had been searching for God my entire life. After my first encounter of supernatural revelation with the Lord, followed by the Godly current that swept my spirit up into heavenly realms, nothing could compare to the peace and power I had felt in those two encounters.

For the last 20 years of my life, I had been connecting and listening to the Spirit of God, but the knowledge of who God actually is, was an essential piece I was missing. Though my seeking was earnest and persistent, the world of deception I was imprisoned in kept me from an uninhibited experience of God. Now that the matrix of lies was beginning to dissolve, I had the pleasure of knowing God in a far greater excellence.

At the close of the Show Us Your Glory event, we were invited to stand for a final prayer. The presenter called it a deliverance prayer, explaining how there can be spirits or demons that enter us without us realizing they are there. I had certainly felt some "things" over the last week, and I had to know the truth about whether I had malevolent spirits in me or not. If they were there, I wanted to know, and I wanted to get them the heck out of me. Deep down, I already knew.

I boldly stood up and repeated the prayer of deliverance out loud. The presenter said that if after you say the prayer you notice a cough, twitch, body jerk, yawn, or feel pain, to come to the front for prayer. Sure enough, as soon as I said the prayer, I started to cough and feel that tugging in my neck and abdomen area. I took a step of faith and made a beeline to the front. As I arrived at the altar, I dropped to one knee and began to pray.

Right away, someone came beside me and began to pray over me. Before they even laid hands on me, my head was tossed back by some unseen force, and I was flung onto my back, hitting the church floor. Another person joined in praying over me, and as their prayers intensified, my body flailed around uncontrollably.

I felt completely out of control, my body being wildly tossed about by invisible power. I was in shock. My mind struggled to make sense of what was happening. Not realizing what I was gearing up for, I had launched headfirst into intense spiritual warfare, with no previous context to comprehend what was happening.

The room was a blur, and I was covered in sweat from the exertion of my body and limbs thrashing about in strange manifestations. It was highly disconcerting to feel so physically out of control. Amidst the confusion, I heard several voices praying over me. From time to time, I could make out things they were saying, as they repeatedly pleaded the blood of Jesus over me and commanded spirits out.

When the people praying over me sensed or saw a spirit, they called it out. Their words against the spirit caused my body to tremble, shake, convulse, and move in unnatural ways. The worst manifestation I experienced was the whipping of my spine, so intensely and hard that it felt like I was getting whiplash in my neck. Other than a soft hand here or there for comfort, no one was touching or moving me; it was the hidden agents of darkness within me, protesting against the power of God that were causing such a commotion. Out of nowhere, a blood-curdling shriek escaped my mouth. Was that me?

A supernatural manifestation of a wicked force just shrieked from inside of me. This is getting weirder and weirder, I lamented, wishing it would all just go away. Whatever the hideous things were, they had the ability to animate my body without my permission, which terrified me. I found myself enveloped in a shroud of darkness, desperately trying to break free from its grasp. It was as if I had been transported from the room, a dark cloud carrying me to a place where the sounds of the room grew distant, leaving me in isolation and fear.

My mind whirled with questions: How could these things have gotten into me without me knowing? How did they get there? Why are they revealing themselves now? Why have they never tried to control my body like this until now? Why is it that Jesus stirs them from their hiding places? Why does Jesus's blood make them squirm and thrash about?

I didn't have the answers to those questions, and I was in too much of a whirlwind to contemplate them further. Yet those very questions led me to a truth worth knowing, for without it I may have lived my entire life unknowingly held prisoner by secret shadows with dark agendas. God was making a jailbreak for my spirit that day as my body shook from the indisputable power of Jesus's name.

Into the faraway place I had been captured to, I heard the faint sound of someone calling my name. All at once, I was back in the room, lying on my side on the floor. I recognized the voice to be Tina's, a wonderful God-loving woman who organized the services at Grass Valley Glad Tidings Church. She said, "Bri. Open your eyes. Look at me."

I blinked my eyes several times, attempting to get my surroundings to come into focus. I saw Tina kneeling next to me on the floor, looking into my eyes. She said, "Say the name of your boyfriend who just left you."

She was familiar with my story, as I had confided in her one evening after a church service. That night, after our conversation, she had prayed for me, and had a deeper understanding of my situation compared to the others present. I struggled to find my voice. I felt so weak. "Gabriel," I finally managed to get out. The instant I said his name, a horrible vision of a demon with black wings flashed in my mind. It was an awful thing that looked like it had crawled straight out of hell. It was enormous and surrounded by a wicked group of smaller demons. God was granting me supernatural sight to see what possessed my boyfriend.

Along with the vision came supernatural insight about what I was seeing. The Holy Spirit revealed to me that the large demon was part of a group of twelve demons that my partner referred to as his Up-line. Up-line was a term that he learned from a "spiritual" teacher and mentor whom he had been under direct tutelage of for over seven years.

His teacher taught a system called Functional Symmetry and a spiritual doctrine that people are not able to connect to God directly, that they may only access the divine through the twelve teachers of their Up-line. The teachers of his Up-line were said to be in spirit form above his head. The practitioners of this philosophy consult their Up-line with muscle testing in order to access helpful information for themselves or their client, often containing supernatural insight into details that one could not know on their own. In my vision, God pulled back the veil on these seemingly benevolent and "helpful" beings, exposing their true faces as the malevolent demons they are.

Like myself, Gabriel and the practitioners of that system strived to live a spiritual life and do good things for others as healing arts practitioners, ignorant of the source of power. The spiritual aspirants of that system don't realize that the supernatural insight they are accessing is from a demonic source and comes with a hidden contract and grave repercussions.

I was astonished by what I was shown. I found it to be quite sad because I knew that the people following this teacher were earnestly and whole-heartedly seeking a connection with God. I believe that the teacher himself was also deeply seeking God, and according to what was revealed, they had all been greatly deceived.

My partner had been trained to consult and listen to "the voice of God" through consulting these twelve entities in his Up-line. He had become deeply merged with these evil influences in the spirit realm and believed with all his heart that he was serving and following God. *What blasphemy!* I thought, outraged at the level of deception good-meaning spiritual people get ensnared by. Who the heck did these evil entities think they were, and why are they misleading God's people?

Interestingly enough, the vision and the insight, all happened in a moment's time. It is undoubtedly amazing how God can download so much information and insight in a flash. I heard Tina say to me, "Bri, I am going to need to cut your soul tie to Gabriel."

No! I cried in my mind. I began to weep uncontrollably. I loved my partner so much, and I did not want to cut my connection to him. I wanted to *save* him. Then the vision of the twelve demons flickered in my mind's eye. I knew that I had to get free first, before I could help Gabriel. As much as I didn't want to, I agreed to the cutting of the soul tie between Gabriel and I.

She cut the tie through a prophetic act, and immediately, I felt lighter. The people who had been praying around me started up their deliverance prayers again. As soon as they began, my body again writhed around in response. What an intense battle it was, and clearly it was not over yet.

The pastor intervened, requesting I be taken into a private room to continue the deliverance. That totally made sense to me. If I was sitting in the crowd watching my wild exorcism take place, I would have probably felt pretty anxious. I was relieved to be removed from the front of the room and under the care of two God-loving ladies.

Tina and another woman from the church, Alicia, escorted me to a private area, where they continued to pray over me. Without knowledge of my previous spiritual involvement, they specifically called out the spirit of Kundalini. As they pressed into it with their prayers and spiritual warfare against it, my spine twisted and contorted in an unusual manner.

Spirit of Kundalini? My mind was blown. So many years of my life I practiced Kundalini meditations and yoga. I had been taught that energy cultivated through yoga and meditation that moves up the spine is divine spiritual energy that builds up over years of practice. I was told that this cultivated energy leads to higher states of consciousness and, ultimately, enlightenment.

During my meditation practices, I frequently encountered powerful surges of energy that I interpreted as a "Kundalini awakening." This manifestation of power often propelled me into heightened states of consciousness, accompanied by a rush of euphoric sensations throughout my body. In those moments, I felt a deep connection with what I believed to be the divine. Now suddenly, I was faced with an unsettling realization that perhaps my experiences weren't what I thought they were. I felt the presence of God envelop me once more, bringing more revelation in the form of a vision and deep knowing.

Being raised a Christian, I had the necessary context to comprehend the revelation being revealed to me. In this moment of insight, God brought to my mind the story of Adam and Eve in the Garden of Eden with emphasis on the pivotal moment of their original sin—the act of consuming the forbidden fruit from the Tree of Knowledge of good and evil. It was the serpent who came to tempt Eve, and thereafter, Adam and Eve acquired the knowledge of good and evil. God showed me that the fall of man was due to the temptation of the serpent, and the corruption it caused in man from that day forward. In my mind's eye, pictures of the way Kundalini is depicted flashed before me. God then revealed to me the connection between the serpent responsible for humanity's fall and its ongoing efforts to deceive God's people. This revelation showed how the serpent continues to tempt people into partaking from the Tree of Knowledge, much like the original temptation in the Garden of Eden, and how it leads to corruption.

Every depiction of Kundalini I had encountered portrayed it as a serpent, often illustrated as a snake ascending the spine of the practitioner or as a coiled snake resting at the spine's base. *Yikes,* I thought, *this whole time, so many years of practice, I thought I was connecting to God in a wholesome spiritual path, only to find out it was a demonic serpent spirit sent to deceive me.*

God later confirmed my vision in his Word in Revelation 12:9 (ESV):

"And the great dragon was thrown down, that ancient serpent, who is called the devil and Satan, the deceiver of the whole world—he was thrown down to the earth, and his angels were thrown down with him."

Satan himself is called a serpent, three times in the book of Revelation, not only in Revelation 12:9 but also in Revelation 12:1 and 20:2.

Looking back, it bewilders me how I missed something that is so obvious to me now. Such is the nature of deception. The notion of cultivating a serpent spirit in one's spine; how could I think that was God? I never believed the teachings of the Bible until God began to show me that it is the one thing in this world of illusion that I can count on most, the Word of God. Gradually, I came to understand how forces opposing God and His kingdom, like Lucifer and his fallen angels, craft counterfeit experiences that mimic God-given experiences. These are, in reality, traps designed to ensnare the unsuspecting in the lower realms of these deceitful beings. At a later time, I was led to Scriptures that indicate these truths. 2 Corinthians 11:14–15 (ESV) warns of this deception:

"And no wonder, for even Satan disguises himself as an angel of light. So, it is no surprise if his servants, also, disguise themselves as servants of righteousness. Their end will correspond to their deed."

None of my Sunday school lessons or years of involvement in New Age and occult practices had equipped me to confront the reality of a demonic serpent spirit that was contorting my body and causing hisses to escape from my mouth. I came back to a state of alertness after another surge of thrashing and spiritual battle between the women of God praying for me and these demonic entities. The struggle was intense, an unnerving battle in my own flesh. At times, I truly felt as if I were fighting for my life. In certain instances, I could feel sensations of something moving upwards and out through the top of my head and as if something was wrapped around my neck, making it difficult to breathe.

The women stopped their prayer battle and began to ask me questions about my life. After sharing some of my background, they led me through renouncing spiritual beliefs and practices I had from many years in the New Age and the occult. "All of New Age practices can open doorways to the demonic," Alicia explained. *News to me*, I thought. I had no clue the spiritual practices I was involved with led to demonic captivity.

I was crushed. It was difficult to fathom the magnitude of deception that had allowed evil spirits to get into me. My whole identity was wrapped around being a spiritual person in the New Age, someone who got up at sunrise to pray and meditate, who attended silent meditation retreats, who was a healing arts practitioner, who practiced and taught yoga. For so many years, I believed I was serving God and the greater good by participating in these things, and now my illusion crashed down like a tsunami without warning, crushing a lifetime of faulty belief systems.

As much as I wanted to deny or turn away from the painful and cumbersome truth of what was being exposed, I knew deep down that I had to face what was before me. I had asked for the truth. I had begged to know who was in charge of all the heavens and the Earth, and of humanity as a whole. I had inquired as to who had the most authority over this world. I even dared ask God to take spiritual authority over my life. And here God was, delivering mightily upon my request.

Whatever part of me was still hanging onto my past and the delusion I had come from, I let go of. I ceased my struggle against all of it in my mind. God was showing up in an extraordinary way, and whether I liked the answer or not, I needed to remain humble and grateful. From an objective perspective, the unfolding events were truly remarkable. Given God's heroic ability to cast out demons from our bodies, who wouldn't desire a God of such extraordinary power and authority?

There are many references to Jesus casting out demons. In Matthew 8:16 (NASB), it says:

"When evening came, they brought to Him many who were demon-possessed; and he cast out the spirits with a word, and healed all who were ill."

Then in Luke 4:41(NASB):

"Demons also were coming out of many, shouting, 'You are the Son of God!' But rebuking them, he would not allow them to speak, because they knew him to be Christ."

This Scripture reveals that the demons themselves recognized Jesus to be the Son of God.

The amazing part about Jesus coming as the Son of God is that by His sacrifice, we also have been given the power to cast out demons in His name. Mark 16:17 (NKJV) says:

"And these signs will follow those who believe: In my name, they will cast out demons; they will speak with new tongues."

When we believe in Christ, in His name we can cast out demons. That is the labor of love that these two women prayer warriors were faithfully enduring for me to gain my freedom.

There are some Christians out there who do not believe in demons, which begs the question...with all the accounts of Jesus casting out demons, where did all the demons go? And, if they were oppressing humanity then, what would stop them from afflicting humans today?

Following another round of struggles, one of the woman prayer warriors asked, "Do you have any tattoos?"

"Yes," I replied, wondering why they might ask this of me.

Then Tina said, "Certain tattoos and symbols can establish contracts with demonic entities without the person realizing it. Certain symbols mean specific things in the spirit world and can act as a doorway and free entry point for demons associated with the image to gain access to the tattooed person's body."

Geez, I thought, *what a crazy world we're living in. There is a whole world of demons lurking in the background, attempting to gain rights and access to our bodily vessels without us realizing we are under attack.*

I exposed a tattoo on my chest to the ladies. Alicia gasped, clearly shocked by its significance in the spiritual realm. My tattoo depicted the eye of Horus inside a triangle, covering my heart. Without hesitation, she sprang into action, placing her finger on the tattoo and rebuking any attached spirit, commanding it to depart. When she placed her finger upon my tattoo and unloaded her prayer, my body shook like I was being electrocuted, convulsing wildly as if I had come into contact with a live electrical wire. This unforgettable moment in my first deliverance was so peculiar and unsettling that it had a comical quality to it. It reminded me of the melting witch scene in the *Wizard of Oz* movie when she sizzled away into oblivion.

At that time, I didn't comprehend it fully, but it was the collision between the witchcraft within me and the authority of the God of this world that was jolting that demonic spirit around in my body.

For much of my life, I had a strong interest and attraction to Egypt, Egyptian mythology as well as Egyptian magic practices. I had envisioned the ancient Egyptians as sacred individuals who possessed secret knowledge about the world that was lost in the modern era. In my meditation sessions, mental images of Egyptian symbols would often arise.

The eye of Horus in a triangle was a symbol that had come to me many times in mediations throughout the years. During that period of my life, I believed that when I was meditating, I was communing directly with God, assuming the Spirit of God was the source from which I was receiving the eye of Horus symbol. The spirit I was communing with had instructed me to use the symbol in meditation and place it over my heart. At a point when I had been going through a relatively traumatic break up, that same spirit came to me in a meditation and suggested I get it tattooed over my heart to help it heal. It seemed like a great idea at the time, but I realized in that moment that I had been duped into placing a demonic symbol over the gateway to my heart. Our heart is intended to be the throne of God, and that malevolent spirit knew that if it could get legal access to my heart gate through the tattoo, that it could interfere with me having a real, authentic relationship with our Creator.

The spirit behind the eye of Horus was now exposed for its true nature, and it was shaking and quivering under the mighty power of Jesus's name. It became apparent to me in that moment, that whoever Horus was or represents, is only another counterfeit and layer of deception I had been living under. Despite the alluring stories of Horus being a healing and protective god, the spirit of Horus cowered at the mention of Jesus's name, its hidden evil intentions unearthed in the presence of the Son of God.

I subsequently learned that demonic spirits can enter us through points of weakness in our body, mind, or emotions. The combination of me being in the middle of a heartbreak when I received the Horus tattoo and the physical puncture wound from the tattoo needles, created the perfect entry condition for the demonic spirit to take residence in me. The tattoo established legal rights for the entity to enter and reside in me. Luckily, by the power in the blood of Jesus, those contracts can be broken.

When I had prayed for God to reveal Himself, I had prayed to know who the Creator of this world was, and who has the dominion and authority over this realm. I don't doubt that these other gods exist, nor do I doubt the powers they have, for I have personally experienced the impressive abilities of other gods and deities. However, what I found out, through this experience and many more to come, is that there is only one God and one name that has power, dominion, and authority greater than all others. It is written in Deuteronomy 4:35, 39 (NKJV):

"To you it was shown that you might know that the Lord Himself is God; there is none other besides Him... Therefore know this day, and consider it in your heart, that the Lord Himself is God in heaven above and on the earth beneath; there is no other."

I may have not believed this on my accord, but with all the deities that slithered out of me revealing themselves as the serpent spirits they are, God changed my mind.

In Isaiah 43:10–11(KJV), God reveals again that there is only Him:

"Ye are my witnesses, saith the LORD, and my servant whom I have chosen that ye may know and believe me and understand that I am he: before me there was no God formed, neither shall there be after me. I, even I, am the LORD; and beside me there is no savior."

I can personally attest that I spent years worshiping other gods and deities, and none of them could even come close to what can be done in the name of Yeshua of Nazareth. Not only that, miracles, signs, and wonders manifest to confirm the Word of God, as was happening during my deliverance. I don't know about you, but I'd rather serve the Master that has dominion over all heaven and Earth than a demonic spirit who attempts to be a god with only a fraction of the power and authority.

The worshiping of other gods opened me up to all sorts of dark spirits. Now, I had the promise of freedom on the horizon with Jesus in my life. In Galatians 5:1(NIV), it says:

"It is for freedom that Christ has set us free. Stand firm, then, and do not let yourselves be burdened again by a yoke of slavery."

I made the vow right then and there that I would never serve the enemy again—one I didn't even realize I had until that night.

I set myself firmly in the pursuit of God of the heavens and Earth, to discover all the truth that had been hidden from me most of my life. I was outraged by the betrayal I felt and the ways I had been deceived by the lower world. In Isaiah 61:1 (ESV), it says:

"The Spirit of the Lord GOD is upon me; because the LORD hath anointed me to preach good tidings unto the meek; he hath sent me to bind up the brokenhearted, to proclaim liberty to the captives, and the opening of the prison to them that are bound."

Jesus is a chain breaker; He frees us from the bondage of this world. That night tore the veil enough to reveal the matrix of lies I was living in—in turn, bringing my world tumbling down. Even though I was grieving the loss of my life as I knew it, I felt relieved after we closed the session that day. Little did I know that evening was just the beginning of a long battle for my freedom. I had only scratched the surface, and I was yet to discover the intricacy of the web which I had become entangled with.

8

Encounters with God

When I emerged from my deliverance session, I went to the altar to pray. My good friend Kathy came up, and we sat together quietly, discussing the details of my intense experience. A woman from the crowd approached us. "Hi. Sorry to interrupt. I just felt like I am supposed to come introduce myself. My name is Deanne," she said, offering her hand. Kathy and I shook hands with her. She was very kind, offering support and an insight that proved highly useful in the coming days.

She said, "Sometimes deliverance is a process and takes time. I have a feeling you might not be done yet." She gave me her phone number and offered to pray with me if anything came up. I thought it very considerate of her to go out of her way to show support. In all actuality, I was deeply disturbed by what I had just gone through. I was still in shock and hadn't yet had sufficient time to process such a mind-bending experience.

That night when I was driving home, I noticed a darkness creeping in all around me. I was abnormally fearful, as I made my way home on the dimly lit highway, squinting in the occasional rise and fall of oncoming headlights. I pulled into my driveway, letting out a long sigh of relief. What a crazy day it had been.

I opened my front door to a dark house and called out to the two kitties I was pet sitting at the time. Instead of them running up to me to get petted like they normally did, I heard them growling in the dark. *What on Earth?* I wondered. What I was unaware of at the time was that the swarm of demons that I had evicted earlier that night were attempting to find a way back in.

Then, in a flurry of fur, I saw them fighting. I shouted at them to cease, feeling increasingly unnerved, and began praying in tongues. I found their behavior unsettling. Once more, I attempted to call out to them, and their response came as growls in the dark.

"Forget it," I said. "I am maxed out on the creep-o-meter today." I went into my bedroom and shut the door, figuring I would check on them in the morning. Once I entered my room, they were silent and calm. *Weird,* I thought, *perhaps there are still spirits around me that they are sensing.*

I lay on the bed in my dark, lonely bedroom, trying to ignore the ache in my heart, praying unceasingly until I fell asleep. When I woke up in the morning, I felt dreadful. My body was burdened with heaviness, ached all over, and a dark cloud of doom and gloom loomed over me. My mind was unusually filled with dark thoughts. An agonizing anxiety sat heavily on my chest, causing my breath to feel laborious.

It was out of the ordinary for me to feel so awful or experience anxiety in that manner. I could only recall feeling that bad twice in my life: grieving Thomas's death when I was seventeen, and in the throes of the battle for my life against neurological Lyme disease. I was shaky, fearful, and my body felt unusually weak. Normally, I would go sit on my meditation cushion for a morning practice, but I felt so confused about my life and what might open a door and allow more of those horrendous spirits back into me.

Dark thoughts were a stark contrast to my normally upbeat attitude and peaceful nature. It was apparent to me I was greatly out of sorts, but my state was so overwhelming that I couldn't think clearly enough about what to do about it. I was burdened by paralyzing fear and a persistent feeling that I was going to die. At that moment, I didn't want to be alive. I felt inconsolably miserable.

When I walked into my kitchen that morning, I gawked at the freakish horror movie scene that had materialized; my counters were covered with insects. Everywhere I looked, I saw crawling things. *What is going on in here?* I wondered in disgust. I did my best to get rid of all the creepy-crawling things. We occasionally found ants here and there, but this was a full-on invasion. There were ants, pincher bugs, and other unidentifiable little bugs I wasn't used to seeing in my house. I hadn't yet made the connection that the infestation was a malevolent supernatural phenomenon, and I was now at the forefront of a spiritual war that would ensue for months to come.

I did my best to pull myself together and start my day, but I couldn't shake the depressed, anxiety-ridden state I was in. I was home all alone, and I didn't know who to turn to. I felt so isolated in the experience I had the night before, and I didn't know what or who I could trust. It wasn't as if I could just call anyone, tell them that I had demons exorcized out of me last night, that I was getting attacked by the possessed bug kingdom, and that I was now irrationally filled with troubling dark thoughts that were relentlessly assaulting my mind.

If I did, they would think I had clearly lost my mind and might even try to put me in a mental hospital. No, this had to be a spiritual attack. I need the right kind of help, I reasoned, not a psychiatrist who will try to medicate me out of my experience.

As I was contemplating what to do, the woman from the night before, Deanne, came to mind. She told me to call her if I needed help. At the rate I was going, I wasn't sure I would survive the day. I grabbed my phone and dialed her number.

By the grace of God, she answered. I divulged to her everything that I was experiencing, the unusual anxiety, the bizarre and unsettling dark thoughts, and even told her about the insect attack. I risked sounding like a complete whacko, but she didn't seem surprised at all. She explained some things that started to make a whole lot of sense. She said, "You could be experiencing backlash from the demonic spirits that you battled last night."

Backlash? I thought, as I listened attentively.

"The way to victory in spiritual warfare," she continued, "is to fight with faith and the Word of God." I recalled a voice that had been in my head all morning, trying to convince me that what happened the night before wasn't real and that I had imagined it all. "It's not real," the voice had said to me. "Jesus isn't the answer, it's just some other spiritual path that will lead you nowhere."

It became evident then that the voice had been attempting to make me so hopeless and depressed about myself and my life that I would lose faith in the power of God. The evil voice was trying to discourage me from using and trusting the one thing that could set me free, Jesus. Deanne offered to pray with me, and I eagerly accepted, desperately needing something to shift my circumstance.

When she began to pray, something incredible happened. The dark cloud around me began to dissipate. The fear, anxiety, and overall malaise left me instantly, and my reality slowly began to return to a normal state. "How do you feel?" she asked when she was done praying.

"Better!" I exclaimed. I was amazed how much better I felt and how drastically my perception had shifted. I thanked her immensely and returned to my day, hoping to get some work done.

After around two hours had passed by, a sudden shift in the atmosphere occurred and my world began to darken as if a storm were rolling in, my perception of reality distorting. What was happening at that moment seemed even worse than it had been earlier that day. The doom cloud sat heavy on my body. I couldn't move. I sat frozen in fear in my office chair, feeling like death was on my doorstep.

That moment seemed to stretch on forever, and I questioned if I was going mad. Nothing seemed to make sense; my thoughts were jumbled and confused. I knew I needed help. I was in over my head. Just over two hours ago, my new friend prayed for me and created an undeniable shift in my dire circumstance, causing all symptoms to disappear. Now, out of nowhere, they had returned.

I cried out from the depth of my spirit to God, begging for help and mercy. Out of nowhere, as though materializing from thin air, I sensed the presence of a mighty, towering angel behind me. This perception was not through ordinary senses but came in through extrasensory perception in the form of a vivid image that flashed in my mind's eye. The angel placed his hands on my shoulders, and as soon as he did, my reality instantaneously shifted back to normal again. The darkness fled the room; the cloud vanished. I was my normal self again; all traces of anxiety and fear having disappeared as quickly as they had come. *Wow, this is one of the most bizarre days of my life. My sanity is truly being tested*, I thought in bewilderment.

I enjoyed several peaceful hours after the encounter with the angel without any additional strange happenings. Towards the end of the day, I decided to try to eat some food. I hadn't eaten that day because I had been so on edge. When I entered the kitchen, I started to feel off again, sensing a shadowy presence around me. I tried to ignore it while preparing some fresh zucchini noodle pasta.

When I went to eat my food, just as I dipped my fork in, I saw maggots squirming on top of my pasta. This time, it wasn't a physical manifestation, it was a hallucination caused by psychological warfare. I could feel the dark presence casting this horrible image on me, though I couldn't see it. I then poked my food to investigate further and uncovered an actual, physical dead bug in the food. Needless to say, I lost my appetite. I didn't know what to do, I was way out of my league and not equipped for the level of spiritual warfare I was up against. I decided to head over to the Grass Valley Bible study group in hopes of enlisting some prayer support.

Towards the end of the Bible study and prayer group, people were taking turns saying prayers for the community. I was suddenly and unexpectedly moved by the Holy Spirit, prompting me to kneel and press intently into God, my body beginning to tremble with the intensity of His presence. During a brief moment of silence between the prayers being spoken out loud by others, the Spirit of God surged through me, and suddenly, a passionate prayer erupted from my lips.

The potent prayer I offered was for those in the Grass Valley community caught in a web of deceit, much like I had been, oblivious to being influenced by secret shadows with dark agendas. The words that billowed from my mouth were not my own, it was the voice of the Spirit of God speaking through me. At the end of the prayer, I heard myself make a vow that I would write a book about my experience to help those suffering at the hands of deception. *Did I just make a vow to God to write a book?* I questioned myself incredulously.

Well, a vow is a vow, even if I was under the influence when I said it. I take my vows very seriously, and especially when they are between myself and God. I vowed to God that if He revealed Himself to me, I would give my life to Him. I meant what I said, even if I didn't like the answers I received in return. I was wholeheartedly dedicated to giving my life to the Lord and obeying anything He asked me to do. When those words came through my mouth about writing a book, it was God's clever way of declaring what He wanted me to do through my own mouth.

At the end of the group, Tina came up to me and asked me how I was doing. I disclosed the details of what had been occurring. She shared biblical references for what I was going through, and I felt relieved with the insights that came through talking to her. She pointed me to Mathew 12:43–45 (NIV), which I looked up afterward. It recounts Jesus explaining to religious leaders:

"When an impure spirit comes out of a person, it goes through arid places seeking rest and does not find it. Then it says, 'I will return to the house I left.' When it arrives, it finds the house unoccupied, swept clean and put in order. Then it goes and takes with it seven other spirits more wicked than itself, and they go in and live there. And the final condition of that person is worse than the first. That is how it will be with this wicked generation."

The truth contained within that Scripture resonated with me. It appeared as though the spirits that had departed were now returning with greater force. I had never before experienced such intense spiritual attacks or felt so powerless. In our discussion, Tina consistently highlighted the importance of faith in Jesus as our protective shield. I must confess, at that time, my faith in Jesus was not strong. Regrettably, I had been immersed in an environment where Christianity and Jesus were often viewed with disdain and even ridicule. Many individuals with New Age perspectives tend to pity Christians, perceiving them as old fashion, religious zealots clinging to an outdated worldview. Such arrogant assumptions had so deeply influenced me that a part of me still held onto these misguided beliefs.

Tina offered to pray for me, and I readily accepted. Her prayer was one of protection, invoking the blood of Jesus over both me and my home. Late that evening, as I entered my house, I immediately sensed a noticeable improvement in the atmosphere. There were no bugs, no strange occurrences, just the familiar comfort of my own home. "Ahhh," I sighed, peace at last.

In the morning, I sat praying and meditating on the Lord, considering the declaration I had made about writing a book the previous night. I felt conflicted. What God wanted me to write about seemed like such a controversial topic, and I was apprehensive about facing ridicule, mockery, or being labeled as crazy.

A voice of doubt crept into my mind, and I began to question whether I should write this book or not. The voice said, "Nobody will want to hear your story. It's a waste of time, a story not worth telling."

I had many good excuses not to move forward. I might be judged, disowned, mocked by family or friends. Yet, I had told God that I would give my life to Him if He showed up. God delivered what I had asked of Him, and now it was my turn to do what I promised—give Him my life.

If God's first assignment for me was to write this book, I could not turn away from it. What kind of person would I be to cower away after God had shown up in such a big way for me? Before I committed myself to the task, I had to be sure that it was actually God calling me to write this book. I said, "God, if You really want me to write this book, I am going to need a big, undeniable sign from You."

As soon as the last word of that prayer fell from my lips, I was immediately startled by an emergency alert on my phone saying that an earthquake had been detected and to take cover. I sprung up from my prayer altar and ran outside of my house, the ground trembling beneath my feet, as my world tilted back and forth. I squatted down on the pavement in front of my house, trying to get my bearings.

Having removed myself from any potential danger, I suddenly burst into laughter. Was this God's response? The earthquake coincided with the exact moment I spoke the last word of my prayer. I had asked for an undeniable sign, and surely an earthquake would qualify as that. Even so, I was not yet convinced.

Once the earthquake had passed, I went back inside and decided to do a Google search on "God and earthquakes." I wasn't quite ready to rule it out as a mere coincidence, and yet I was not quick to believe it was truly God. My search led me to Isaiah 29:6 (ESV):

"You will be visited by the Lord of hosts with thunder and with earthquake and great noise, with whirlwind and tempest, and the flame of a devouring fire."

"Wow," I said out loud, sitting bewildered at my office desk. "So, the God that answered me is the God that was written about so many years ago in the Bible?" I pondered in disbelief. I know that probably seems obvious to some, but I had been living with such a radically different perspective that this was ground-breaking news in my world.

I got up from my chair and ran into my son's room to search for the Bible that a church had randomly given him recently. During my mother's recent visit with me post break up with my partner, we had attended the local church where the pastor had prophesied over me. That day, my son joined the youth group, and when I picked him up, he was sheepishly carrying a Bible in his hand. I remember thinking, *No one at our house is going to read that,* but thought it sweet they made sure he had one at home. When God revealed Himself as Yahweh, the God of the Bible, it was the first time in my life that I felt profoundly convicted to read His Word.

I searched fervently through his bookshelf, but much to my dismay, I couldn't find it. I sat on his bedroom floor feeling slightly discouraged. It really seemed as if God had a message for me, if only I could get my hands on that Bible. For so many years, I had scoffed at the thought of reading the Bible. Now, I regrettably realized that the presence of God could be found in those pages.

I let out a sigh and surrendered my defeat to God, whispering, "God, can You help me find it, please?" Instantaneously, an image of the Bible and its whereabouts popped into my mind, revealing its hidden location in the place it had fallen underneath my son's bookshelf. To confirm what I saw in my mind's eye, I moved some fallen books out of the way so I could reach underneath the shelf, and there it was!

I retreated to my prayer room, placed the Bible in front of me and stared at the cover while wondering what was next. I said aloud, "God, if there is something You want to tell me, I am willing to hear Your Word." Until that very moment, I was never humble enough to ask earnestly. I didn't know what was ahead of me on this path, but I was willing to find out. Although somewhat doubtful, I was pretty sure God had answered me in the earthquake, boldly declaring Himself as the Lord of Hosts of thunder and earthquake, whirlwind, and the flame of a devouring fire. I opened the Bible and was led to read Ezekiel 6:3–7 (NIV):

"Hear the word of the Sovereign LORD. This is what the Sovereign LORD says to the mountains and hills, to the ravines and valleys: I am about to bring a sword against you, and I will destroy your high places. Your altars will be demolished, and your incense altars will be smashed; and I will slay your people in front of your idols. I will lay the dead bodies of the Israelites in front of their idols, and I will scatter your bones around your altars. Wherever you live, the towns will be laid waste and the high places demolished, so that your altars will be laid waste and devastated, your idols smashed and ruined, your incense altars broken down, and what you have made wiped out."

I felt my stomach drop, astonished by what I had just read. Was that really God? I hadn't imagined God to be so full of wrath. I thought He was all loving, all forgiving, light, and goodness. My mind raced through memories of all the altars I had built in my life, all the idols I had worshiped, and all the gods I had prayed to. I had built Earth altars and made offerings to deities of the land; I had sat in many Indian Pujas offering fruit and ghee to Lord Shiva. At times, I had even worshiped the sun and the moon. My spiritual journey and exploration had led me through all types of activities that could be considered idolatry. Terror began to set in, and I couldn't help but wonder if God was going to "lay me dead in front of my idols."

It wasn't until further in my journey that I learned that reverential fear of God is mentioned over 300 times in the Bible. This fear differs from the way we typically relate to fear. Instead of a fear that causes retraction or repulsion, it is instead a deep reverence and respect for God. Reverential fear is the doorway into which we surrender to the awe of His holiness while honoring Him as the great God of majesty and power that He is.

In Proverbs 9:10 (NKJV), it says:

"The fear of the LORD is the beginning of wisdom, and the knowledge of the Holy One is understanding."

This type of reverential fear gives us access to knowledge and understanding only obtainable through God Himself.

Being led to that verse about idolatry aroused in me a fear of the Lord that I had never felt before. It opened the door for deeper humility and wisdom to take root in me. When I sat trembling at the thought of a wrathful God, the Spirit of God touched me, and in that intimate touch of the Lord, I became sorrowful for all the gods I had been worshiping, praying to, and building altars for. I felt so deceived, for in all sincerity, I had thought that all paths lead to God, and that the many gods and goddesses were different forms of God. I believed with all my heart that I had been worshiping God and living a spiritually focused life, yet God was revealing to me with His gentle touch, the depth of deceit I had been living in and how idolatry is blasphemy to the Lord.

I later verified in Exodus 20:3–6 (KJV), where God clearly states:

"You shall have no other gods before me. You shall not make for yourself an image in the form of anything in heaven above or on the earth beneath or in the waters below. You shall not bow down to them or worship them; for I, the Lord your God, am a jealous God, punishing the children for the sin of the parents to the third and fourth generation of those who hate me, but showing love to a thousand generations of those who love me and keep my commandments.

God also warns in Deuteronomy 8:19 (KJV):

"And it shall be, if thou do at all forget the Lord thy God, and walk after other gods, and serve them, and worship them, I testify against you this day that ye shall surely perish."

In that moment, I heard the Lord's voice in my mind say, "I am Yahweh, and the way to me is through the teachings of my Son, Yeshua of Nazareth." It was in that holy moment that I first started to grasp that God wants us to come to Him through the path that was made for us through the life, death, and resurrection of Jesus Christ. I understood that God was conveying to me that the only path He desires for me to seek Him is directly through Jesus Himself.

God also assured me that if I followed Jesus, I would not be killed for idolatry or any sin, for the path of Christ is a path of redemption. He has since confirmed for me in Romans 6:23 (KJV), which reads:

"For the wages of sin is death; but the gift of God is eternal life through Jesus Christ our Lord."

When I began to study the teachings of Jesus, I learned that the original laws and covenant that were in place between God and man before the coming of Christ differ from what was established after the coming of Jesus. The wage for sin is no longer death when we follow Christ.

That day of the earthquake, fresh seeds of awareness were sown into the cracks of my shattering world, and only in a humble and persistent seeking did they mature into a more profound truth. The encounter that day cast doubt on the ways I had lived and worshiped gods, thinking I was serving God, when in actuality I was caught in a well-disguised labyrinth unknowingly serving a sinister scheme. As 1 Corinthians 8:5–6 (ESV) says:

"For although there may be so-called gods in heaven or on earth—as indeed there are many 'gods' and many 'lords'—yet for us there is one God, the Father, from whom are all things and for whom we exist, and one Lord, Jesus Christ, through whom are all things and through whom we exist."

That evening, my mind was whirling. I felt unsure and uneasy about what was unfolding in my life. The answers I was getting weren't the answers I wanted. It felt like a burdensome truth and required me to massively change my perspective and understanding of God, the universe, and how things work. I attempted to rationalize what was happening, permitting myself to question the validity of the encounters I believed I was having with the Creator of our world.

Perhaps I am wrong, and just making all this up in my head, I thought. *Perhaps the harsh circumstance of my breakup had pushed me too far, and I had gone off the deep end.* I lay in bed that night, questioning all that had unfolded. What was so hard for me to accept was what it would mean if it were all true.

So much of my identity was wrapped around my spiritual path and beliefs, around being a "healer," as well as my allegiance to all of my rituals, practices, and deeply held assertions. My world was shaking, and the comfort of my established perceptions was disappearing. I was unsettled about whether I should actually follow through on writing the book I had vowed to God I would.

That evening in prayer, my hands folded in front of my heart, I asked God for greater understanding and peace. I drifted off, sinking into a deep, restful sleep. I woke up with a start at 3 am, surprisingly awake. I am not usually one to wake up in the middle of the night, and I found my unexpected alertness at that hour odd. "God, is that You?" I whispered.

Then, the booming voice of God resounded through my mind and declared, "BEHOLD, CHILD, you do not know what is coming! You must write your book." The moment those words were released, another earthquake hit my house, the lamp on the ceiling shaking back and forth. I didn't run this time. Instead, I laid in bed intently staring at the quaking ceiling while God gave me another revelation. This insight manifested as an intuitive understanding rather than the words that had just pounded through my head.

I understood the earthquake to be a very small demonstration of many more calamities to come. There was a sense of urgency behind the message, a distinct warning of times ahead. What I was left with was that the message God wanted to share through me would be important in times ahead, particularly to people trapped in the matrix of lies as I had been. I could sense that God was waiting for my response. "Okay. I will do it. If it is Your will, my Lord," I declared through the stillness of the early morning darkness. After saying that, a profound sense of peace enveloped me, knowing my choice had been made, my doubts now dissolving.

The next day, I woke up on fire with passion for God and a vengeance for the hidden enemy that had shadowed my world for my entire life. I tore through my house, ripping down pictures of deities, taking down statues, pulling books off my bookshelves, and ridding my house of anything that could be a gateway back to the world from which I was escaping. I filled six garbage bags full of items, making sure to include all tarot cards, runes, books on shamanism, anything to do with witchcraft or rituals, and all items with symbolism of the New Age or the occult.

Throughout that day, I sensed God's presence very close to me, and I continually sought to draw closer to Him. I entered a state of complete surrender to His will. I had asked Him to take spiritual authority over my life, and this is what it looked like. Letting go. Not needing to control. Trusting what He was showing to me day by day. It was intimate and vulnerable to be that close to God—to be that seen and witnessed by Him.

Throughout the day, the presence of God would suddenly intensify, bringing me to my knees. During these instances, my soul cried out, my mouth professing His power and glory in tongues, my body trembling under His touch. The message He said to me over and over again that day was the same, "Hold on to nothing, and I will give you everything."

I was shedding layers of my identity, things that were so deeply entrenched in me, that it felt like I was losing a part of myself. My whole mental framework was built on faulty belief systems, and the Lord was tearing them all down, one by one. My world resembled a barren landscape, its foundations collapsing, demolished by the relentless flood of truth from God. Resistance was futile; my only option was to surrender completely.

God seemed to be escorting me through the landscape of my inner being, directing me to evaluate collections of false beliefs that appeared as towering structures. There, He stood with me to witness, His very presence causing faulty belief structures to fall, crumble, and be exposed as the lies they were. It was painful to watch so many mental constructs I had been deeply invested in, be demolished in the presence of God; beliefs and convictions I had walked so boldly and ignorantly in were swept away in an instant by His witnessing.

I thought to myself, *By the time He is done here, I won't have anything left! Who will I be, and what will I have to stand on with nothing left?* The moment that question passed through my mind, I heard God say, "Me. I will be all you have. I will be all you have left to turn to. I will be all you need. With Me, you will have everything."

I reflected upon my long-standing devotion to my healing arts practice that I had served in for so many years. God's omnipotent appearance in my life shattered my identity as a healer. In a moment of divine love and firmness, God spoke, saying, "All healing comes from Me, and belongs to Me." It was then that I grasped the profound truth that genuine healing only comes from God, with the purpose of exalting His name and advancing His Kingdom. In my former practices, I was unintentionally trying to be God, and not allowing God to do what only He can do. My acts of healing until then were only band-aids and counterfeits of the one true Healer...God.

I knew I wanted to know God, be closer to Him, and live in union with Him, but there was so much still that stood in the way of that. I experienced great grief with the loss of the person I once was, but at the same time, I knew something much greater was on the horizon of the path I had just chosen. After hearing God say many times, "Hold on to nothing, and I will give you everything," I finally let go, surrendering to His divine plan.

In the places where I despairingly clung to the familiar, and in the areas where I resisted fully opening myself to Him, I eventually surrendered, relinquishing control. I stopped fighting the process, and when I did, God swept through me; through my house, through my castles of arrogant certainty until the disassembling of the matrix of lies was achieved. In the devastation of my world, everything felt bare. I stood there exposed and vulnerable, with nothing left to rely on except God. Looking back, I now see it was a mighty and great place to be, despite the desolation. Alone with God, nothing and no one else to turn to, be fooled by, or be distracted by. A clean slate. A new beginning. The burning pleasure of humility searing through every part of me that remained. It was holy, sacred, divine.

It was from this place of ruin that I knew my life could be rebuilt, restored, and made anew. A place where I could build a foundation on which I could stand, side by side with my beloved Creator. In His mercy, He tore down the house of delusion I had built around myself. My newly swept house was now transformed into an environment in which He could dwell within me.

God's design is for his Spirit to dwell inside us. 1 Corinthians 3:16–17(NIV) says:

"Do you not know that you are God's temple and that God's Spirit dwells in you? If anyone destroys God's temple, God will destroy him. For God's temple is holy, and you are that temple."

After the cleansing of my life, it felt so natural to then offer my body as a temple in which God's great and holy works could be done through.

I went seeking God's power and discovered power in all the wrong places, as is the case with many in the New Age and occult communities. The matrix of lies promises power and self-glory, built to distract spiritual seekers from knowing the supernatural power held only in our Creator God—the power of resurrection that raised people from the dead, that parted the Red Sea, that heals and restores, and that lives in those who have given their lives to God.

Many fall prey to the appeal of being god-like, like myself, desiring to be glorified and praised. The fallen ones devise paths of New Age philosophies that capitalize on seekers' desire for self-glory and self-exaltation. Much of modern society lives in self-obsession. It only takes a couple minutes of scrolling on any social media platform to see how intensely people are focused on themselves, on being seen, and receiving admiration from others.

When self-obsession and lust for worldly things are relinquished, we find God, in all of His greatness. The seeking of power and glory is the secret shadow that Lucifer and the fallen ones use to tempt people towards unholy desires. A great question I asked myself as I was transforming was, "Who is my Master? Am I serving 'self' and living in the world and values that Lucifer created? Or do I serve God, the Master of all?"

The New Age path I was on, is a path of great trickery that leads with a dark light, alluring people into the bright upper rooms of the lower realms in the Kingdom of Darkness. Being a healer in the New Age, I was blind to my unconscious seeking of self-glory, ignorant that I was trying to take God's place as Divine Healer. I unknowingly used demonic sources to do a job that was not meant to be done without God. Now I know that all praise and glory belong solely to the Master of this world, Jesus Christ. It is through Him that we can enter into God's Kingdom and be touched by His grace.

When God pulled back the wool and exposed all the deception I was living in, He promised to restore everything in His way, in His will, and in His time. He told me all the gifts and talents of mine that the enemy had distorted and corrupted, would be sanctified and used for good in the Kingdom of God. When the deceit of the dimensional doorway work that I got involved with was revealed, He said, "No longer will you tend doorways to lower realms, you will tend gateways to the Kingdom of God." I felt touched by

God's mercy; His compassion and capacity to bring all things back to the light is remarkable.

God told me that He longs to restore rightful power to all of His lost people, the power of light and life that is Jesus Christ. For those caught in occult practices using psychic powers, opening the third eye, cultivating Kundalini, and other similar practices that draw illegal power from the lower realm, you can find help and redemption through Yeshua, the Great Redeemer.

If you were lured into the serpent's snare as I was, you too can renounce those practices and ask the Holy Spirit to fill you with the light of Christ. The doorways inside us that lead to the lower realm can be closed with the blood of Jesus. God said to me when I still needed convincing, "You must not gather power from illegal sources, for you are breaking divine laws. "Illegal power that is drawn from the lower realm will slowly destroy and kill the one using it. It is never worth the cost of what is lost."

If you are a believer, I encourage you to share the insights found through my deliverance testimony with friends or loved ones who have been charmed into the New Age trap. It was nearly impossible for me to see the smoke and mirrors when I was so deeply entrenched. If my boyfriend hadn't left abruptly, claiming to be led by the voice of God, I may have never fallen to my knees to earnestly seek who God truly is.

The good news is we don't have to wait for difficult circumstances to invite God into our lives, either for the first time or to deepen an existing connection with Him. He is always there waiting, and He wants to be close to us, and desires for us to sincerely seek Him with all of our heart and soul.

9

Desperate for Freedom

After experiencing the backlash of darkness that came upon me the day after my first deliverance session, it was clear there was more work for me to do to obtain more freedom. With the Holy Spirit guiding me over the coming months, I began to grasp what spiritual warfare really was, and the strategy to win battles against demonic powers.

The next week, I returned to Church of Glad Tidings for an evening service. The service was presented by Mama Cheryl, Pastor Dave's wife. Her sermon was about readying oneself to share the message of Christ out in the world. At the end of her talk, there was an altar call for anyone who wanted to remove what was in their way of walking in and sharing God's Word. Being freshly on fire for the Lord, I made my way up to the front to receive prayer.

Once more, it was Mama Cheryl who prayed for me. When she laid hands on me, I again fell to my knees, overcome by the presence of God. The now familiar current of divine energy surged through my body as I began to involuntarily flop around like a fish out of water. Witnessing these convulsions, some others in the ministry came over to pray for me. As their prayers washed over me, the inner struggle between darkness and light resurfaced. My body again exhibited various physical manifestations, with my arms jerking and my spine contorting.

As I was reluctantly tossed into another round of deliverance that night, I felt tugging and pulling around my navel, as if something was wound up around it. The more I prayed to the Holy Spirit to purify me, the more I experienced a constriction around my belly button, accompanied by what felt like squirming inside of my lower abdomen. In Arhatic Yoga, a spiritual practice I had pursued diligently for seven years, a key component of the spiritual practice was Kundalini meditation. Following the meditation, we would "store" the energy in our navel by wrapping it first clockwise and then counterclockwise.

One of the women praying over me must have had a divine word of knowledge, because even though she did not know me or my past, she called out, "Kundalini spirit, I see you. I rebuke you in the name of Jesus. Get out!"

Oh right, I thought bitterly, *that dreaded Kundalini serpent spirit that I thought was the spiritual energy of God for so many years.* All those hours and hours of meditation I sat cultivating that energy, feeding the head of the serpent, and coiling it around my belly button. I burned with outrage at the deceit I had fallen prey to. I had faithfully thought I was meditating to be with God and live a spiritually wholesome life, only to realize it was the same wretched serpent that had caused the fall of humanity, disguised in New Age false doctrine.

Betrayal swarmed over me like an onslaught of enraged wasps, churning up vengeance aimed at destroying the works of Lucifer. At that moment, filled with outrage, I made a vow to uncover every corner of the dark labyrinth I had been led into by the lies of the serpent. Determination surged through me like adrenaline, compelling me to do everything in my power to dismantle, sabotage, and slay the framework that the lower dimension has laid to mislead God-seeking souls into a well-concealed trap.

Despite my hopeful aspirations, the struggle persisted within my flesh that evening. My body involuntarily flipped around as those in prayer waged a spiritual battle against the unseen entities within me. Their voices resounded with the name of Jesus, as they pled His blood over me from

114

head to toe. The physical manifestations made it evident the prayers had a significant impact on the malevolent spirits that had taken up residence in me, though they had not yet been fully expelled from my body. I lacked the right resources and understanding to rid myself of the wicked Kundalini serpent spirit that night. Yet, I recognized progress had been made, as I had felt other dark presences being disturbed and pushed out by the power of God in their prayers.

I hadn't anticipated that deliverance would break out that night, nor was I prepared for such a full-on and intense spiritual battle in yet another church service. These entities were really putting up a fight. Despite the challenge, I was determined to unwaveringly pursue my freedom. Now that the veil had been removed from my eyes, there was no turning back.

Following the deliverance session that night, one of the women who had prayed over me shared an interesting observation. She told me that while I was in the throes of the spiritual battle, my hands would often come together in a hand-on-hand prayer position. According to her, this specific gesture seemed to inadvertently grant authority to one of the entities I was contending with. Reflecting on the multitude of yoga postures, salutations to deities, and gestures symbolizing worship to other gods or the sun, I realized that she was likely correct. Hand mudras and positions are commonly known to supply spiritual power, yet from where does that spiritual power originate? I've now come to understand that the source is serpent power, originating from and linked to sources that are not of God. By assuming certain hand positions and mudras, demons can gain legal access and rights to a person's body. While one may acquire spiritual power through these hand positions or mudras, the question remains: at what price?

That night driving home, my confused eleven-year-old son and I discussed the events of that evening's service. I explained to him, "When I received prayer tonight, divine energy entered me, causing everything not of God within me to surface. That is the power of the Holy Spirit. That is the power of God, the same power which Jesus wielded when He healed the sick and cast out demons."

He didn't offer much in response, sitting quietly as he pondered what I had disclosed. If I had foreseen what would unfold that night, I might have reconsidered bringing my son along, Nevertheless, in hindsight, I was grateful he was able to witness a genuine battle between the light and dark in this world.

As my eyes gently opened the next morning, I began my day by praying in tongues. As I surrendered deeper into my morning prayer, the tangible presence of the Lord began to envelop me. Memories and images appeared my mind, the Holy Spirit prompting me to delve into a deeper level of deliverance.

A memory surfaced from my teenage years of attending renaissance fairs, accompanied by an image of a Celtic knot within my inner vision. Motivated by my newfound understanding of the power of symbolism, I declared out loud, "Any entities that entered me through the symbols at Celtic fairs, or any symbols I wore in jewelry, leave now in the name of Jesus!" It became clear to me through that moment of revelation that not only can tattooing a symbol grant malevolent spirits access; wearing the symbol in jewelry can also open a door.

With the Spirit of God as my guide, I revisited different memories being brought to my attention and began to unwind myself from hidden contracts and agreements forged unknowingly through what seemed like innocent enjoyment but carried weight and consequence in the spiritual realm. Through the authority vested in my covenant with Jesus, I annulled these contracts and sealed off any access of spirit influence.

The next memory that arose was of me as a young child, holding a bundle of worry dolls given to me by my grandmother. She had instructed me to tell my worries to the dolls, place them under my pillow, and that they would carry my worries away. At the time it seemed so innocent, but the Lord showed me that by engaging in this practice, I was inadvertently summoning a malevolent spirit to remove the worry from my mind, thereby forging an unknown contract that gave the worry doll spirit rights to my mind and body. I found it shocking how something seemingly benign could be so destructive. It is essential to use great discernment in any practice, and if you have worry dolls, get rid of them, burn them; they have connections to voodoo spirits that you certainly don't want to invite into your life.

Only God has the power to lift our burdens, and He does so freely, without any cost or hidden contract. Yeshua paid the ultimate price for our freedom in the sacrifice of His body on the cross. As God continued to teach me, He helped me to comprehend His meticulous design and how it governs our world. His laws and principles affect both the physical realm and the spiritual domain, which are intricately woven together. Whether we are aware of it or not, humans are bound by these divine laws and subject to their influence.

The forces that oppose God and seek to overthrow God's Kingdom, are well-versed in these laws and know how to corrupt them in a way that advances their wicked plans. It is through the technicalities of these laws that spirits are able to gain access and rights that are more often than not granted unintentionally. This can occur when one takes part in a ritual, receives a psychic reading, or consults tarot

117

cards, unknowingly giving permission and rights to a Luciferian source of power.

Before my encounters with God, I watched a movie called *Doctor Strange*. It is about a man who finds a teacher who helps him to miraculously heal an otherwise irreversible condition. In awe of his miraculous healing, he chooses to become a disciple and train under this teacher with extraordinary powers, only to discover later that his teacher draws her power and abilities from the dark dimension. God used my memory of this movie as an example to show the parallel to my own experience; the practices I was involved with from the New Age and occult indeed wield power, but that power is drawn from the lower realm of the fallen ones, a dark dimension.

Whether the lower realm power is used to do good things or not, the use of it comes at a cost. In the movie, Doctor Strange discovers for himself the formidable price of drawing power from the dark dimension, when he too falls into the same trap as his teacher. In a moment of desperation, he decides to use power from the dark dimension for a good cause. Despite Doctor Strange's good intentions, using the dark power source opened him up to great evil and torment, which continuously afflicts him through the doorway he opened.

Here on Earth, it is similar; misguided people desire power and end up using the improper source to gain it. Even though lower realm power can be employed to do outwardly good things, it is best to steer clear of it entirely. Engaging in practices such as rituals, magic, tarot, astrology, energy healing, and other occult activities, even when seemingly for good purposes, opens doors to demonic affliction. These practices are the fruits of the Tree of Knowledge (of good and evil), the very same tree that led to the fall of humanity. The power found within these practices originates from the dark dimension of the fallen ones; despite the allure of its temporary benefit, it is a dim light shrouded by the shadows it keeps concealed as one pursues the power it offers.

True power resides within the Tree of Life, the singular pure source of power that is obtained through Christ. It is only when we humbly allow God's Spirit to dwell within us, that we can access this power and perform righteous deeds. In Proverbs 11:30 (KJV), it is written:

"The fruit of the righteous is a Tree of Life; and he that winneth souls is wise." Through living a righteous life and adhering to the teachings and commandments of Yeshua, we walk the path that leads to the Tree of Life. Jesus said in John 5:24 (ESV):

"Whoever hears my word and believes Him who sent me has eternal life. He does not come into judgment but has passed from death to life!"

The promise of Eternal life by following Yeshua is given many times in Scripture. In 1 John 5:11 (NIV), we are told:

"And this is the testimony: God has given us eternal life, and this life is in his Son."

Having wandered in a veiled darkness, chasing after a deceptive light for too long, I turned my back towards the matrix of lies. I no longer meddle with things that are not of God, lest they open doors to things unholy. I firmly tread the path of Jesus, following the truths that He taught, for I know now it is the way to freedom and redemption. It is the path in which our Creator God has provided for us to obtain access to His untainted, undistorted, holy light and power.

I began my exploration with the intention to help my partner, Gabriel, who I suspected was oppressed by a dark entity pretending to be the voice of God, only to realize he was not the only one oppressed. From what I saw when God pulled back the veil, I perceived that the entire world is impacted by the shadow dimension of the fallen ones. Places of weakness within us are a point of vulnerability that shadows from the lower realm can target to afflict us. Be it physical weakness, emotional vulnerability, trauma, mental instability, or any other form of weakness, these are the openings through which we can be accessed and influenced by malevolent forces.

Malevolent spirits can gain access and control through the doorways we open into the dark realm by engaging in specific activities that are explicitly stated to avoid by God's Word in the Bible. In Leviticus 19:31 (NIV), God warns:

"Do not turn to mediums or seek out spiritists, for you will be defiled by them. I am the LORD your God."

The definition of defiled is to make foul, dirty, or unclean; polluted or tainted.

God's Word offers a warning of what happens when we dabble in New Age and occultism, not because He is controlling, but because He knows how the Kingdom of Darkness tries to corrupt His divine plan. Even if it seems as innocent as getting a tarot reading, by doing so, we are consulting the Tree of Knowledge and straying from the path of the Tree of Life.

Wisdom in the Word of God about this matter can be found in Deuteronomy 18:10–14 (ESV):

"Let no one be found among you who sacrifices their son or daughter in the fire, who practices divination or sorcery, interprets omens, engages in witchcraft, or casts spells, or who is a medium or spiritist or who consults the dead. Anyone who does these things is detestable to the LORD; because of these same detestable practices, the LORD your God will drive out those nations before you. You must be blameless before the LORD your God. The nations you will dispossess listen to those who practice sorcery or divination. But as for you, the LORD your God has not permitted you to do so."

I surmise that engaging in the aforementioned practices is detestable in the eyes of the Lord because it exposes our bodies to unholy spirits, whereas our bodies are designed to serve as vessels to the Holy Spirit. Be cautious not to fall prey to the allure of the forbidden fruit of the Tree of Knowledge. Walk steadfastly on the path that Jesus has illuminated for us, that guides us towards eternal life.

◊ ◊ ◊

Unknowingly, I opened countless doors to Lucifer's dark dimension, convinced of my own righteousness and good deeds, only later to comprehend the depth of my misconception. The schemes I was imprisoned by deprived me of experiencing the full radiance of God. Outraged by my discovery, I questioned God as to why He permitted me to remain enveloped in darkness for so long.

When God responded, He explained that my deep entanglement in the traps and mazes crafted by those who oppose Him allowed me to acquire the knowledge needed to expose and dismantle the works of His enemy. Upon receiving this revelation, I recognized the truth in it. Through years of meditating in the upper rooms of the lower realm, embarking on astral journeys within the great expanses of the lower realm, as well as tending gateways connecting different dimensions, I had developed a detailed mental map of the intricate labyrinth used to ensnare God's children. Now equipped with a profound understanding of the lower realm's maze, I can utilize this knowledge to bring salvation to the lost sheep of Jesus. In discovering God would use my experiences for the greater good, I was relieved, making peace with the journey I had taken to find God.

Despite God being by my side, imparting profound and powerful insights, I was still in the process of escaping darkness and had a lot to learn about how to more fully disentangle myself from what I had been involved in. The day following my second deliverance session, I encountered another wave of backlash from the demonic realm. Much to my dismay, the ominous black cloud of doom and its distortion of my perception returned to torment me. Through these trials, I learned that spiritual warfare truly resembles a battle; first you make a move, then the enemy responds with their move. Every time I gained freedom, the enemy would retaliate, seeking to hinder my progress.

Recalling my first doom cloud experience, I managed to navigate through its return, finding solace in knowing I could combat it with prayer and faith. My growing faith in God became one of my greatest weapons in my war against the Kingdom of Darkness.

The entities I faced attempted to convince me that they were stronger than I, insisting that they were capable of inflicting continual harm. They endeavored to trap me in a state of fear, doubt, and constant questioning of God's ability to deliver me. Yet, as I immersed myself in the Word of God and studied biblical verses about the authority given to followers of Christ to cast out demons, I began to take bigger strides on my path to freedom. The days that followed were a continuous battle between light and dark. The oppressive dark cloud and tormenting thoughts would surface to oppress me, yet I countered the attack with prayers and Scriptures. I read them aloud, asserting my authority in Jesus against their wickedness.

To empower myself in my quest of ultimate liberty, I engrossed myself in an intense study of self-deliverance. I ordered several books on deliverance, exploring various techniques and methodologies. I spent hours on YouTube searching through deliverance videos, uncovering numerous valuable resources (many of which are listed in the back of this book).

Even in my continuous learning and growing strength, I faced the challenge of ridding myself of a particular spirit that caused my spine and neck to twist involuntarily during prayer. Whenever I entered deep prayer or invoked the name of Jesus, the unseen shadow would abruptly jerk my neck to the right, deeply troubling me. Seeking guidance from God on how to address this issue, I received the message that undergoing a water baptism would be beneficial. Craving reprieve, I contacted my church and made the necessary arrangements.

10

Holy Waters

Having never attended a baptism before, I was uncertain what to expect, except that I would be immersed in water to symbolize the baptism of the Holy Spirit. In preparation, I fasted for three days leading up to the baptism, hoping that whatever lingering spirits remained would be swept away by the holy baptismal water. My hope was that through the cleansing, every door I unintentionally opened to Lucifer's deceitful world would be slammed shut, and I would emerge renewed in the light of Christ.

When I arrived, I noticed the baptismal prepared, with members from the church gathered around to witness my special moment. When it was time, I stepped slowly and intentionally into the water. Once I was inside the tub, I looked up at Tina's husband, Jim, who was the pastor leading me in the baptism. "Do you accept Jesus Christ as your Lord and Savior?" he asked.

I paused, then said, "Yes. I now accept Christ as my Lord and Savior," joy and anticipation beginning to bubble in my heart. It was an incredibly sacred moment, where my spirit humbly bowed in profound reverence, as I wholeheartedly surrendered my life to the Lord. There is a profound intimacy in allowing God to enter deep within us, to be fully seen and witnessed by His divine presence, and to experience the tenderness and love of His nurturing care.

"I now baptize you in the name of the Father, the Son and the Holy Ghost," Jim said as he lowered my head under the water. A rush of the Lord's presence surrounded me as I went under, the moment of sweet salvation seeming to linger on in the stillness beneath the water. When I emerged, my mouth began to fervently utter prayers in tongues, and Tina, along with her husband and other members of the church, gathered around to join in prayer. My baptism then took a surprising and unforeseen turn.

Once again, the unholy forces began to manifest physically, manipulating my body unnaturally, protesting against the Spirit of God in the atmosphere. What was supposed to be a quick dip in the baptismal waters unexpectedly turned into an hour-long exorcism. Suddenly my baptismal tub felt more like a birthing tub; me laboring intensely against the oppressive spirits that fought to maintain their place in my flesh.

Throughout the spiritual battle at my baptism, I periodically immersed myself under the water, which helped loosen the grip of all that had kept me in a secret bondage. The whole scene was quite dramatic; several people spoke intense prayers over me while my body continued to thrash about involuntarily in the water. As my arms and legs flailed around in the water, intermittent and unanticipated shrieks escaped from my lips, at times accompanied by weeping.

It wasn't me who was shrieking—it was whatever was inside me, protesting its eviction notice from the Kingdom of Heaven. As tears fell, I sensed God touching the tender parts of my soul that had been wounded, bringing healing to places where spirits had accessed me through traumas.

In the midst of this intense and chaotic experience, I vividly recall a moment in which spirits were manifesting physically through me, and a bystander placed a Bible on top my head. The moment the Bible made contact with my head, a shock ran through my body, causing another surge of involuntary flailing. It was as though the unholy spirits within me recoiled in direct opposition to its power and were in fierce conflict against the living Word of God. It was uncanny to experience the inexplicable power the Word of God has over the Kingdom of Darkness.

The whole scenario unfolded like a surreal scene from a far-fetched horror movie with demon possession, leaving me feeling like an observer from the outside looking in. I couldn't believe that this was my life. Questions swirled through my mind; What was happening, and how had it come to this? Just three weeks ago, I had been living a seemingly peaceful, spiritual life of meditation, yoga, and healing arts. I had asked to know God and now this. How had I been so fooled by what looked and felt like God, and only now discover how deceived I had been? Bewildered, I wondered how I was so easily duped into thinking I was serving God, while behind the veil, lurked an enemy I had no idea existed.

As I emerged from the baptismal tub that day, a sense of liberation washed over me, invisible burdens lifted from my shoulders. Dripping wet with a towel draped over my shoulders, I gazed out at the beautiful faces of those who had fought beside me in my spiritual battle that day. I felt altered, the unmistakable presence of God permeating through the atmosphere. Despite my weariness and trembling limbs, a deep sense of gratitude and peace welled up in me, as I recognized the significant progress I had just made on my trek towards freedom.

The following day, I woke up feeling thankful when the sense of lightness and brightness lingered, with no sign of the doom cloud or backlash that had plagued me prior to my baptism. *I am really making progress!* I thought excitedly. *The baptism truly made a difference. Thank you, God! Thank you for freeing me from the trenches of the lower world and guiding me into Your light.*

In the midst of savoring the sweet taste of progress and newfound freedom, a lingering awareness gnawed at my consciousness—there remained unholy presences that needed to be addressed. I had been fasting for six days at this point, and through all my extraordinary experiences, my faith had been strengthened and fortified; with fervent resolve, I was eager to claim my authority and purge residual darkness lingering within or around me.

I put some worship music on my Bluetooth speaker and grabbed my Bible along with John Ramirez's book, *Fire Prayers*. With reverence, I knelt before my altar, slowly reading out loud the prayers written by John Ramirez. After reading them aloud, I paused, allowing them to settle into me and the room. Some prayers I repeated, feeling their impact grow with each recitation. As I continued, I felt a growing sense of confidence and determination, accompanied by a noticeable physical response. A familiar and dreaded pain surged through my tailbone, right hip, liver, and right shoulder—a tangible reminder of the malevolent spirit's defiance against my prayers for its expulsion. With each spoken prayer, my neck continued to be forcefully pulled to the right by an unseen force. While I managed to maintain some control over the physical manifestations, the intensity of the pain increased, especially in areas of my body regularly burdened by chronic discomfort.

My body reacted to the prayers and declarations with bouts of coughing, attempting to expel whatever malevolent presence lingered within. Despite my efforts, the afflicting spirit stubbornly clung on, refusing to release its grip. I attempted to maintain my optimism, frustration setting in; I found it increasingly difficult to fend off the overwhelming sense of discouragement and defeat.

I resolved to retreat to bed, reminding myself it was only a matter of time before full freedom was obtained. I knew I had to persist in my efforts, I couldn't simply forget everything and return to the matrix of lies I had fought so hard to escape from. My only choice was to endure, push forward, and trust God's plan for me.

That night as I lay in bed, dark thoughts suddenly began to press into my mind, fear's false grip getting ahold of me. The physical pain I was experiencing in my back and stomach escalated, evoking a disturbing sensation as if something was pulling me apart from the inside out. *I know just what this is*, I thought to myself, *it is a spiritual attack*. I snatched my Bible and placed it on top of my stomach where the pain was emanating from, and surprisingly the pain subsided enough for me to drift into sleep.

As I awoke to the morning light, exhaustion weighed heavy upon me, and pain still plagued me. Refusing to succumb to despair, I brought my hands together in prayer, entrusting my weariness to the Lord, believing in His ability to heal me. To my delight, as I focused on Him, the pain and fatigue started to ease. My spine released after several satisfying pops, and the tiredness and discomfort gradually dissipated. Lying there in quiet astonishment, I marveled at how quickly my symptoms had subsided when I directed my focus towards the Lord, rather than dwelling on my discomfort.

I decided to listen to Katie Souza's audio recording called *Holy Spirit and Dunamis Power*. (Her work is amazing; you can find her online and she has great videos on YouTube). In this recording, she leads listeners in prayer, calling on the Dunamis power of God to seek out and examine the root causes of issues. I petitioned God to expose what the root of the pain I was experiencing was and assist me in overcoming the pestering spirit that was causing physical pain in my body. Through His boundless grace, God answered my prayer the very next evening in a divinely arranged connection.

11

Path to Freedom

On the Sunday night following my baptism, I found myself again at Church of Glad Tidings, attending a service where Jess Parker was the guest speaker once more. Knowing that Jess Parker is well-versed in the ministry of deliverance with more than three decades of experience, I was enthusiastic to learn more from him on how to cast out demons, the way that Jesus did when He walked this Earth.

During the evening sermon, Jess Parker focused on the topic of deliverance from fear. He described the differences between types of fear; fear that stems from reverence for the Lord and fear that is influenced by demonic forces. As I sat listening attentively, I found myself nodding in silent agreement when he emphasized the significance of cultivating a reverential fear of the Lord as a crucial aspect of spiritual growth.

I reflected on the moment when God spoke to me through an earthquake and led me to the shocking biblical verse, Isaiah 6:5, where God speaks of laying the dead bodies of the Israelites in front of their idols. Upon realizing I had unknowingly been practicing idolatry, reading that verse initially evoked a great sense of terror; yet, from that moment of fear, a necessary humility and profound reverence for the Lord emerged. The reverent fear I developed towards the Lord became the gateway to encountering God in a depth of glory that would have otherwise eluded me.

Jess Parker elaborated further in his sermon, highlighting that various types of fear often originate from demonic influences. Among the examples were fear of failure, fear of worthlessness, fear of sickness, fear of death, and fear of rejection. To conclude his sermon, he led the entire congregation in a group deliverance session aimed at freeing them from these oppressive fears.

Following Jess's prompts, we repeated a prayer of deliverance aloud. As he began to speak in tongues, invoking the power of the Holy Spirit over the room, the atmosphere became charged with spiritual energy. One by one, he called out the different spirits of fear by name. As his prayers saturated the room, things inside me began churning. As I stole a quick glance around the room, I noticed others were already exhibiting signs of deliverance. Coughing and sputtering could be heard as demons were being expelled. *Oh boy, here we go,* I thought nervously, *better out than in, I suppose.*

I seized the opportunity for more freedom, joining Jess Parker in speaking aloud the words of his deliverance prayer: "Fear of sickness, out in the name of Jesus! Spirit of infirmity, out! Fear of death, out! Up and out! Fear of loneliness, out!" *I'm finally getting the hang of this deliverance thing,* I thought hopefully.

With each sentence I spoke, my body shook in response, a miserable undulating motion rippling through my spine. Tina came to support me, placing a reassuring hand upon my back, as she unleashed prayers over me. Several other church members gathered around me in prayer, standing valiantly beside me as I endured yet another fervid battle in my flesh. *Heavens,* I thought confoundedly, *how many of these things could have possibly gotten inside of me? Aren't I done yet?*

The prayers from the mighty women of God surrounded me, tearing into the grasp of lingering spirits, who had been unwilling to relinquish their hold. The fight ensued much like the previous sessions, yet in this pivotal moment of deliverance, God graced me with vital keys to unlock greater freedom. Guided by the Holy Spirit, I was granted insight into generational curses embedded within the lineage of both my parents, intricate strands of bondage that had ensnared me for far too long.

Within my inner vision, appeared an image of one of my ancestors at war. God helped me to understand that through my great grandfather's actions as a soldier in the Nazi SS, a curse came upon my bloodline, which in turn gave access to a spirit of death and infirmity that had affected my familial line ever since. A spirit of death and infirmity can cause premature death and illness, and through revelation, I saw how the tragic consequences had played out, my grandmother's premature death, my father's grueling battle with a severe brain tumor and near-death motorcycle accident, my own prolonged battle with debilitating illnesses, and now my sister's battle with cancer.

From the shadows, a spirit of perversion also emerged, present on both sides of my family tree. This didn't come as a surprise, given the history of molestation that had occurred in both my mother and father's sides of the family. Then, the Holy Spirit exposed a soul fracture that occurred that treacherous night my friend died when I was seventeen, marking one of the most impactful discoveries of that evening.

I initially believed I had processed the intense experience fully, only to discover a lingering soul wound that allowed the spirit of death and infirmity to infiltrate through trauma. The Kingdom of Darkness works relentlessly to fragment souls through trauma and confine parts of them within prisons of pain, a habitable environment that demons can easily take residence in. Even though the dark realm uses emotional pain to trap souls, there is hope in the ability of the Lord to restore us and make us whole again. With His dominion over all heaven and earth, Yeshua holds the key to our liberation from the chains of darkness.

One of the women who were praying for me led me in a visualization to invite Yeshua into the traumatic moment of loss that happened so early in my life. With her guidance, I asked His presence to soothe, restore, and mend the wounds caused by that tragic event. When I invited Jesus into that memory, a flood of relief washed over me as His radiant light and boundless love enveloped the painful memory. Bringing the presence of God into that moment in my past helped me to close a festering wound, my soul now stitched up with His goodness.

The progress I made towards healing was made possible thanks to the guidance of a woman present during the prayers over me, who afterwards warmly introduced herself to me. "My name is Peggy," she said, with a kind smile. When I asked her about her background, she said, "I've been trained in a technique called Lie Busters. It's a method of deliverance that anyone can learn. It helps to identify or break off the lies of the enemy—lies that are used to stop us from claiming our true inheritance and fulfilling our destiny as sons and daughters of God. By joining with the Holy Spirit in this technique, it can help to get to the root of issues and lead to more freedom." (See the resources in the back of the book for more information.)

Under Peggy's guidance and expertise in the Lie Busters technique, I had managed to identify and dismantle sources of bondage that were holding me back. The exploration of underlying causes that evening provided me with the momentum I needed to move closer to the ultimate freedom I yearned for. Peggy graciously offered to conduct a follow-up session with me, and I gladly accepted.

With the significant progress I had made in uncovering and breaking generational curses related to destruction, warfare, masonry, and its connection to an afflicting spirit of infirmity, I was eager to continue to explore the transformative work. Determined to continue to forge my path towards redemption, I continued to fast; I had heard that fasting could be helpful in getting free from demonic strongholds, and I wanted to do whatever I could to hasten my process. As Jesus says in Matthew 17:21 (NKJV) in relation to a demon His disciples could not cast out, "However, this kind does not go out except by prayer and fasting."

The following morning, I lingered in bed in an in-between state, awakening in prayer then drifting back into sleep. My consciousness moved in and out of my dreams, and when I came to, I prayed to the Holy Spirit to reveal anything I needed to know from the dreams I received the night before. Suddenly, as I regained consciousness once more, a vivid image materialized in my mind's eye—an unmistakable silhouette of a dragon spirit in my inner vision. Uncertain of its significance, I delved deeper into my morning prayers, asking God for further insight.

As I prayed, the dragon re-appeared in my inner eye. Curious about its implication, I looked up the word "dragon" in one of my books titled, *The Divinity Code*. It is a resource used in decoding visions and dreams in a biblical context. After I located the word, I stared uneasily at the description; "the devil, principalities, or evil." Revelation 12:9 (ESV) refers to Satan as a dragon, "The great dragon was hurled down—that ancient serpent called the devil, or Satan, who leads the whole world astray."

Ephesians 6:12 (KJV) reveals the presence of these commanders of darkness:

"For we wrestle not against flesh and blood, but against principalities, against powers, against the rulers of the darkness of this world, against spiritual wickedness in high places."

Many fail to recognize how much of the wickedness of this world comes from the influence of these dark rulers who lead God's people astray.

I took a bold stance, asserting my authority in Christ, and demanding to know, "In the name of Yeshua, what rights do you have to be in my field of awareness?" In response, an image flashed in my inner vision: the Kabbalah. In the occultic spiritual lineage I had been involved with for the previous seven years, we had used the Kabbalah in the context of New Age mysticism. The Holy Spirit was now revealing to me that this practice I had engaged in contained teachings that opened a door to the dark realm.

Realizing the connection, I repented for the many years I used the Kabbalah ignorantly and immediately renounced the practice I had been involved with. I cancelled any contracts that were made without my knowledge, and with sincerity, I asked the Holy Spirit to seal off any doors opened by this practice. By revoking its rights, it made it easier to evict the dragon spirit. Upon completing this cycle of recognition, repentance, and renunciation, followed by commanding the spirit to leave, I physically felt its movement—a pressure that ascended up and out of my spine.

That weekend, I went to visit family out of town. While staying at my mother's house, the spiritual attacks returned with surprising intensity. Once again, the dark cloud resurfaced to cloak my heart and mind, causing a bizarre distortion of my perception. The grief of the loss of my partner became almost too much to bear, and I could not escape the weight of my sorrow. Accepting the finality of his absence and the end of our relationship seemed unattainable. I struggled to accept the reality that our relationship was actually over. I intimately knew the goodness of Gabriel's heart. I knew he was a true seeker of God like me. If only he could see beyond the same veil that God had lifted for me; if only his eyes could be opened to the deception he was living in.

The day after my initial deliverance, I poured my heart into an email to Gabriel, recounting the haunting vision I had witnessed—a hideous demon connected to him and his spiritual practices. Much to my dismay, he didn't respond. Our communication was strained and limited at the time, but he had agreed to meeting weekly on zoom to orchestrate our separation. If only I could get through to him. Each day, I turned a steady stream of fervent prayer towards God, asking for intervention for Gabriel. If God could supernaturally encounter me, there was hope for him, too.

I had yet to solidify my convictions about my newfound path with Yeshua. My life was in upheaval. I was isolated and shaky in my new belief in God and His unveiled identity. That weekend proved particularly challenging due to the presence of my sister and her partner, who harbored strong, oppressive views toward monotheism and Christianity. I didn't yet feel strong enough to confront their opposition at that point in my spiritual journey.

I could relate to my sister and her partner's perspective, as I, too, had spent many years of my life believing there are many paths to God and had embraced numerous representations of the divine. At times, I had even foolishly looked down on Christians, considering them unaware of a greater truth I believed I had discovered through years of meditation and the study of Eastern philosophies. I had, regrettably, dismissed Christianity altogether, harboring a disdain for organized religion not realizing that being a follower of Christ is the path to God Almighty and the heavenly realm. There is a big difference between religious dogma and the ability to truly follow Christ in our hearts and spirits.

I, like many others in New Age mysticism, had developed an allergy to religion and didn't realize that Jesus Himself opposed the rigidity of dogmatic religious beliefs. Had the Spirit of God not intervened and revealed Himself to me, I may have remained in ignorance of the profound truths that were unveiled to me.

An interesting observation I had as a person coming from the New Age and occultism is just how strongly people in that community oppose and ridicule the path of Christianity more than other spiritual paths. Other organized religions and even atheism is not as criticized by New Agers as Christianity often is. It is easily the most rejected, resisted, and mocked religious path in the world of spiritualism. Most New Agers believe in and respect Jesus as a person, but they fault Christians for being intolerant, narrow-minded, and religious, which is not untrue in some cases.

Yet, Jesus Himself, is not religion, He is not Christianity. Religious beliefs and askew religious interpretations of the Word of God is what kept me away from Jesus for so long. Dogmatic religious beliefs repel New Agers and occultists from discovering the unmatchable light of Christ. God is love. Jesus is the essence of what He taught, and being a true follower of Christ is not following religion, it is following the teachings of Jesus, and following His example of character. When the church, as a whole, quits being so religious and strives to become more spiritual, discovering Jesus from within the New Age and occult communities will be a far easier bridge to cross.

New Agers are Universalists, advocating for the belief that all paths ultimately lead to a higher power of divine source. They often criticize Christians for believing there is only one God and only one pathway to God. Having been immersed in that perspective for many years, I completely understand the appeal of said perspective. It offers convenience, inclusivity, and the freedom for individuals to forge their own spiritual journey. Part of me still wishes it were that easy and non-divisive.

It just wasn't the answer I received when I asked to know my Creator; it's not the message I received when God spoke to me in an earthquake and led me to biblical verses depicting His wrath against idolatry. It wasn't the revelation I experienced when I invoked the name of Jesus and witnessed malevolent spirits stirring in the shadows of ignorance, intertwined with the false doctrines I once believed in.

Having been immersed in a New Age worldview and mindset for decades, I was slow to admit that the God who revealed Himself to me as the Master of this world was indeed Jesus. Being entrenched in the belief systems of the New Age movement had profoundly impacted my perception of God and spiritual matters. Aware of the persecution that awaited me, I felt too feeble at that time to fully embody boldness in my allegiance to Yeshua.

I was genuinely surprised how quickly my shame regarding the truth of God dissolved as I gained more freedom from the spirits that had been afflicting me. As I grew in faith on my new walk with Christ, I came to realize it wasn't me who harbored an issue with Jesus; rather, it was the malevolent spirits within and around me that had such an aversion to Jesus and Christianity due to their proximity to the truth. However, these malevolent spirits don't merely pose a challenge for nonbelievers. I've seen evidence that there are also religious spirits and other types of hindering spirits within and around Christians that prevent them from fully experiencing the immense power and grandeur of God. In Matthew 7:13 (NIV), it states:

"Enter the narrow gate. For wide is the gate and broad is the path that leads to destruction, and many enter through it. But small is the gate and narrow the road that leads to life, and only a few find it."

I entered the narrow gate to the Kingdom of Heaven, trusting God's Word as true, trusting my spiritual Father in heaven had indeed revealed His truth to me.

I walk in faith that the answer I received is the answer from God that I cried out for, even if it means being judged, ridiculed, and mocked by people's opinions I once valued. It is a pain I will bear gladly that all may have the chance through my testimony to know the God above all gods, the ruler of all heaven and Earth. Zechariah 14:9 (KVJ) says:

"And the Lord shall be king over all the earth: in that day shall there be one Lord, and his name one."

I witnessed irrefutable evidence that there are spirits and entities that are not of God which enter through false doctrines and religions. Malevolent spirits attach to people and cause all kinds of mental, emotional, and physical problems, the source remaining hidden in the shadows until one boldly proclaims their authority through the Son of God, Jesus Christ. I noticed that when individuals who believe there are many paths to God react with anger, rage, and disgust towards Christians, I found that it often is not the person themselves, rather the indwelling malevolent spirits who react to the presence of God.

That which opposes God, dwelling in non-believers—the hidden enemy they unknowingly house—is what holds a deep-seated animosity towards followers of Christ. The indwelling spirits within non-believers despise the Holy Spirit residing in believers. This animosity stems from the recognition that Jesus holds authority and dominion over all heaven and Earth, posing a threat to them. Throughout the Bible, numerous examples depict indwelling evil spirits pleading to Jesus to have mercy on them, like in Luke 8:27–29 (NIV), when the demons beg Jesus not to torture them:

"When Jesus stepped ashore, he was met by a demon-possessed man from the town. For a long time, this man had not worn clothes or lived in a house but had lived in the tombs. When he saw Jesus, he cried out and fell at his feet, shouting at the top of his voice, 'What do you want with me, Jesus, Son of the Most High God? I beg you, don't torture me!' For Jesus had commanded the impure spirit to come out of the man."

In recognizing this potential dynamic, followers of Christ can more easily cultivate compassion, understanding that those who persecute them are not their true adversaries; rather, it is the dark shadow of the fallen ones within them that believers must confront. In Luke 23:24 (NIV) Jesus said:

"Father, forgive them; for they do not know what they do."

I have come to accept that there is only one God, the Creator of the Earth, who holds spiritual authority over this realm. Though I was uncertain about the response I might receive when I sought to know Him, God has undoubtedly revealed Himself to me. It would be foolish of me to reject His revelation.

In the midst of the reemergence of the dark cloud during my stay at my mother's house, I made the decision to reach out to Peggy to see if she could do the follow-up Lie Buster session she had offered me. We set up a time to meet the next morning before my journey homeward. I was uncertain as to what to expect, yet eager to receive support and break free from the grip of oppression.

It's intriguing to ponder how, in my past life of transcendental meditation and the pursuit of a seemingly tranquil state of mind, I convinced myself that I was genuinely happy and content. As my new spiritual journey unfolded, I realized that the mind-numbing "peace," that I experienced through hours of mediation is not the same peace that is found when in union with the Creator of this world. The presence of my Creator in my life broke the spell of the illusion of peace that the New Age path offered as counterfeit for the real thing. The "peace" I held in that season of my life kept me encapsulated in a cloud of confusion. I was confined to the upper chambers of the lower realm, unaware I had forfeited my opportunity to enter into an entirely different and higher realm of heaven.

During my session with Peggy that day, we began by joining together in a prayer, asking the Holy Spirit for guidance in uncovering the root of the affliction that had a hold on me. Gradually, step by step, the Spirit of God worked with us to unveil strongholds and gateways through which negative spirits maintained access to me. The session exposed unconscious agreements I had made, which remained active contracts in the spirit world, granting undesirable entities authority and permission to influence me. The precision with which the Holy Spirit pinpointed and highlighted each of these areas was truly remarkable. Memories surfaced that I may not have recalled on my own, nor thought to consider without God's guidance.

As the session progressed, symbolic images emerged within my inner vision, symbolizing different entities: I glimpsed various images of spiders, scorpions, and snakes. Jesus references these spirits in Luke 10:19 (NIV):

"Behold, I give unto you power to tread on serpents and scorpions, and over all the power of the enemy: and nothing will hurt you."

When this assortment of images was brought to my attention, Peggy sought guidance from the Holy Spirit to unveil the rights they held. It quickly became evident that these rights to affliction often originated from transgressions against God's laws and principles. Once their rights were exposed, Peggy guided me through visualizing the act of nailing my transgressions to the cross while at the same time renouncing unrighteous acts and offering repentance for my wrongdoings.

The particularly strong spirit that consistently appeared as a cobra, remained. This spirit seemed to be connected to the uncomfortable manifestations in my spine and neck. When we asked the Holy Spirit to reveal the root of this particular issue, an image of a book entered my awareness, one I had read in my early twenties called *The Serpent of Light*. In the book, the author presented the concept of Earth's Kundalini, describing it as a spiritual energy that flows through ancient archaeological sites as well as other power centers on the Earth. His story chronicled his journey to sacred ruins where he interacted with dimensional doorways and communicated with ancient spirits.

This book left a deep impression on my young mind and inspired my journey to Mexico, influencing me to enter into dimensional doorways and interact with the Kundalini spirit of the Earth. What I didn't realize during my involvement in what appeared to be a noble pursuit is that the ancient Kundalini spirit is a powerful serpent spirit and dark ruler, a principality in the shadow realm that encases and interferes with our world.

Innocently, I believed that the ancient spirits I interacted with were benevolent entities, whom I was assisting to bring light and balance to the light grid around the Earth. I followed their instructions obediently, ignorant that their mysterious light only illuminates the high places of the Luciferian realm. By participating in their hidden agenda, I unknowingly aided in advancing their unholy purposes.

My stomach churned in anguish upon discovering this truth; while seeking to serve God and the light in the world, I was ensnared by the very same darkness that I thought I was fighting against. I had been used as a pawn in a wicked game I didn't understand, a game that prevents much of humanity from realizing their true potential as children of God. In that moment, a bitter sense of betrayal washed over me as the truth set in. The Holy Spirit held back the veil and showed me that my engagement with those ancient spirits had bound me to powerful pre-Adamic spirits residing within the portals and gateways of the lower realm.

My heart sank and my spirit felt like it was being crushed under the immense weight of realizing my well-meant efforts did not have the impact I had intended them to. Yet, amidst my turmoil, I was grateful to solve the mystery of how I had become so oppressed by the powerful entities that I had been struggling to break free from for months now. Thanks to my session with Peggy that day, I uncovered numerous vulnerabilities that I had been oblivious to, that had left me susceptible to the influences of the Kingdom of Darkness.

Next, the Holy Spirit again addressed the impact sexual molestation had on my familial lineage, unraveling further revelation. Through deliberate exploration, we targeted the spirit of perversion lurking behind these tragedies. Immense peace came as I broke free from the grasp of that malevolent spirit and its hold on my family.

In the eye-opening presence of the Holy Spirit, I then understood the unfortunate ways that the spirit caused trauma and damage in my family, stealing innocence, breaking relationships, and creating deep wounds that perpetuated a tendency to repeat sexually immoral acts. 1 Corinthians 6:18 (ESV) states:

"Flee from sexual immorality. Every other sin a person commits is outside the body, but the sexually immoral person sins against his own body."

The Word of God seeks to protect us from unclean, afflicting spirits. Through my own journey towards redemption, I learned that when one participates in acts that oppose God's laws and principles (what the Bible calls sin), a door gets opened for unholy and unclean presences to dwell in the temple of that person's body. Transgression gives legal rights to demonic influences, not just in us, but also within the future generations of our descendants.

Throughout much of my life, I held a belief in reincarnation. However, towards the end of my session with Peggy, a vivid scene unfolded in my inner vision—a scene that I had witnessed countless times before in my mind's eye: a woman being burned alive on a cross. This mental image, experienced from a first-person perspective, resembled other "past life" encounters I had previously had. Based on my limited perception at the time, I concluded that these recurring images must be memories from a past life of mine.

The recurring "memories" that surfaced throughout my life consisted of specific scenes and characters, and I had identified with those characters as though they were myself. When I mentioned the familiar scene of a woman getting burned to Peggy, in response, she quickly declared, "We come out of agreement with that scene and the spirit that is projecting that memory onto Bri's mind."

What she said sent the wheels turning in my mind again. I had been deeply invested in my belief of reincarnation, particularly because I believed I had evidence to support it. It wasn't until just a month prior that I had dared to question my belief about reincarnation. In my search for truth and the answer to my question, *Who is God?* I came across a YouTube video series by a man who claimed to be the reincarnation of Jesus Himself. Following my recent encounters with God, I quickly realized that this man is not actually Jesus, but his access to compelling information about the spirit world and afterlife had captured my attention.

Through him, I was introduced to the concept of over-cloaking spirits for the first time, and I discovered how individuals can mistake the memories of over-cloaking spirits as their own. His insights into the afterlife, sin, and the teachings of "God is love" provided a deeper understanding than what I had encountered in similar teachings before. However, his claim of being the reincarnation of Jesus is a dangerous falsity that hinders his followers from genuinely knowing Yeshua.

Many spiritual teachers, religions, and practices provide valuable insights that encompass much of the truth, yet they are interwoven with subtle deceptions that obscure the full truth. When individuals engage with these partial truths and fail to recognize the shadows in the background, they become susceptible to detrimental misconceptions. Truth laced with deception is detrimental; people are drawn to and feel resonance with truth in new age practices and other religions, but don't spot the serpent that is twisting the truth. This leaves them vulnerable and unaware of the distortions and their negative impacts.

Suddenly, I was navigating unknown waters as I started to humbly reconsider my lifelong belief in reincarnation. In my quest for God to reveal Himself and unveil the truth about this world, I was completely open to exploring new perspectives that differed from my own. From that day forward, I adopted a new perspective and began to view "past life memories" as merely projections from spirit influence. Intriguingly, as I purified my life and removed lingering spirits, the memories and connections associated with them also began to diminish.

Although I had accumulated years of compelling evidence supporting the notion of past lives, I've encountered new evidence that counters that belief. I now hold the assertion that "past life" memories do not originate from past experiences of individuals, but rather are thoughts projected and impressions imposed upon unsuspecting people by spirits. When I began to regard these memories as the product of a spirit that needed to be evicted from my field of awareness, the memories I once believed were my own vanished, completely altering my worldview on reincarnation.

Throughout my twenties, I experienced recurring visions and "memories" of living in Egypt. Thinking back, I made a connection of how those visions had influenced me to study Egyptian magic and Egyptian Mystery School teachings, which contradict the divine laws and principles of God's design. When the eye of Horus in a triangle repeatedly appeared in my mind's eye during deep meditations, it compelled me to tattoo that wicked symbol on my chest, directly over my heart.

The legal rights I granted for this spirit to rule over my heart were what led to the grueling battle I faced during my deliverance process. My heart was intended to be the throne of God, not a gateway to affliction. During my deliverance, we battled that spirit associated with the Eye of Horus so I could make way for Jesus to reclaim His rightful place on the throne of my heart.

In the Lie Buster session that day, Peggy, and the Holy Spirit guided me in a thorough a meticulous examination of my past. One by one, I uncovered, renounced, and canceled hidden contracts created from engagement with witchcraft, magic, rituals, Earth ceremonies, sexual immorality, idolatry, and offerings made to other gods. The more I fought for freedom, the more I became conscious of concealed spirits lurking behind these revealed entry points, and they responded with backlash and a projection of unsettling images. At one point, I became disheartened by what felt like an uphill battle and broke down in tears.

Noticing my distress, Peggy asked the Holy Spirit to dispatch warring angels to stand beside me in my spiritual battle. Within moments, I found myself aware of several angels surrounding me from all sides. They engaged in combat with the dark shadows that had been bombarding me and removed them from their positioning around me; instantly, I felt peace. It was astonishing to see what a difference it made not to have those heinous spirits lurking around. Peggy prompted me to anoint myself with oil. With a deep sigh, I felt a wave of calmness envelop my weary soul.

I sat quietly for a while, enjoying the peace. From the depths of the stillness, a memory emerged. I saw an image of myself as a young girl participating in a pagan ritual from a book my sister and I had innocently discovered in our house. Alas, another doorway that had been opened. Overwhelm bore down on me. How was I ever going to find and close all the doorways I opened in my decades of spiritual exploration?

I recalled that during this ritual, a spirit had entered my sister, then causing her torment all throughout her youth. This malevolent presence drove her to make multiple suicide attempts and engage in extensive drug and alcohol abuse. The spirit's presence was eventually discovered by a set of psychic twin sisters who claimed to remove it. Unfortunately, I know now that using illegal sources of power to remove spirits generates hidden contracts in the spirit world. Although the spirit stopped tormenting my sister during that period of her life, I can't help but wonder at what cost?

Relief washed over me, accompanied by a profound sense of gratitude as the Holy Spirit brought this memory to the surface, providing me an opportunity to close the door I had unknowingly opened as a child. I repented and renounced my involvement with pagan rituals, evoking any rights and access that spirits may have had, sealing the door for good.

Throughout my life, I explored and studied various forms of sacred sexuality practices, such as Tantra and Taoist sexual energy cultivation. In these practices, I sought spiritual connection, desiring to bring sacredness to an area that is frequently distorted and perverted within American culture.

In God's mercy, He revealed to me the truth: the energy I had been cultivating through sacred sexuality practices actually originates from a serpent spirit that affixes itself to the spine of the practitioner. With time and humility, I gradually realized these serpent entities deceive practitioners by providing a false sense of enlightenment leading them to believe they are tapping into a spiritual energy from God, when in reality, the energy originates from a destructive source. While these practices may seem to offer spiritual benefits, they ultimately come with significant consequences. Unfortunately, I had to learn this the hard way, by enduring a difficult and exhausting battle within my own flesh.

To conclude the powerful session, Peggy lovingly guided my spirit toward Jesus. Instantly, His presence soothed and uplifted me, and I felt the tension in my muscles dissipate under the gentle touch of His grace. Throughout the session that day, I had felt as though I was lost in a dark tunnel with no sight of the light at the end. But now, a distinct burden had been lifted. I couldn't help but rejoice in the remarkable lightness I now felt. I deeply appreciated the opportunity I had been given to explore deliverance in such depth. Peggy's steadfast and unwavering guidance proved instrumental in unraveling the intricate layers of deception in the matrix of lies I had existed in.

12

Miraculous Healing

While the journey toward liberation was sometimes shocking and unsettling, I ultimately found tremendous light, peace, and wholeness on the other side. One of the biggest challenges I faced initially was developing the humility required to listen to the wisdom God had to impart and to pair it with the necessary willingness to make significant changes in my life. Fortunately, the perfect storm rolled into my life to stir up the winds of change and inspire fervent seeking of the truth.

Within my awakening process, my motto was: "Leave no stone unturned in your search for truth." Like me, many people are quick to dismiss ideas or impressions they disagree with or are skeptical about. Thankfully, when we are able to step outside our comfort zones and earnestly seek God the Creator of the world to reveal Himself to us, He does. Through deep and sincere prayer, we open the door for God to illuminate truth within a highly deceptive world, where nothing is as it seems. I can attest from personal experience that God comes to those who wholeheartedly and persistently seek Him.

Before my encounters, my worldview and spiritual practices were deeply woven into my identity. Finding God meant dying to self and breaking a false identity I had acquired in a world of delusion. It was not easy for me to be stirred out of a life I felt comfortable and adapted to, yet that difficulty was miniscule when juxtaposed with the gift of redemption I have received from Jesus Christ.

It wasn't easy for me to admit I had everything all wrong, to lay my misguided identity as an energy healer and yoga teacher on the guillotine and have the courage to disclose what God shared with me. I lost friendships, was heavily judged, persecuted, and even mocked by people whom I thought loved me. Even if some didn't understand what God revealed about my life, I could not deny what He revealed to me and go back to my old ways, pretending the veil had not been lifted.

When I escaped the matrix of lies, it opened the possibility of experiencing the Kingdom of God, a realm of extraordinary power and exquisite beauty. Had I not mustered the bravery to confront the hidden shadows of a lifetime in the New Age and occult, I may have never experienced the miracles that God freely gives to the righteous who seek Him.

Being someone who had many supernatural and remarkable experiences in New Age and Eastern religion spiritual paths, I can personally attest there's no comparison to the presence of God, The God who created the heavens and the Earth. The Spirit of God showed me that only one God has spiritual authority over this realm, and there is but one Creator God, who created all things in our world. Sadly, I came to the disheartening realization that the other gods I had been involved with are nothing more than governing entities and rulers of the lower realm. They deceive individuals into believing they possess the authority of the Creator God, when in reality they don't.

In the Bible, God is referred to by numerous names, but it is important to recognize He is only one God, the Creator of this world. His name is Yahweh, "the Lord," derived from the Hebrew word for "I AM," which means to "exist" or "be." His name is El Elyon, which means "God Most High" and is used throughout the Old Testament to reveal that God is above all other gods, and nothing in life is more sacred than He is. His name is Jehovah Rapha "the Lord that heals." His name is Elohim, meaning "Supreme" and "Mighty One." His name is El Roi, "the God who sees." His name is Adonai, "Lord" or "Master." His name is El Shaddai, "God Almighty." His name is Jehovah Raah, "the Lord my Shepherd." His name is Jehovah Jireh, meaning "the Lord will provide." His name is Abba, "Father." His name is Yeshua the Messiah, Jesus Christ, meaning "Salvation" and Christ, "the Anointed One." His Name is God, Creator, and He calls all people to walk in righteousness within our fallen world. He invites us to know Him deeply, that He may reveal hidden things to us. Jeremiah 33:3 (KJV) says:

"Call unto me, and I will answer thee, and show thee great and mighty things, which thou knowest not."

In my prayer room, hanging on a wall, I have a flag that God inspired me to create, which bears these names of God. In prayer, I call upon the many names of God, infusing them into my home. When I speak and call upon these names, I can perceive a spiritual shift in the atmosphere. When we call His name, He will come. (If you'd like this flag for your prayer room, it's available on my website.)

Deuteronomy 10:17 (NIV) says:

"The LORD your God is God of gods and Lord of lords, the great God, mighty and awesome."

In Isaiah 45:5 (NIV), God declares:

"I am the LORD, and there is no other; apart from me there is no God."

Nothing is more intimate, more fulfilling, more powerful than the presence of our Creator God. Throughout all my years of spiritual seeking, I could feel, touch, and interact with the Spirit of God, but I lacked the pathway and knowledge to profoundly know Him or experience Him in His great glory.

While there are glimpses of truth and virtue within the New Age and occult world, there remains a blanket of deception over those traditions which prevents the true knowledge of God from being known. The New Age movement captures some of the lightest and brightest souls, confining them to the many rooms and corridors of the lower realm, held in place by the never-ending maze of deception.

According to the beliefs in the New Age practices I used to engage in, chakras are spinning disks of energy in our bodies that correspond to bundles of nerves, major organs, and areas of our energetic body. My mentors emphasized the importance of maintaining one's energy centers, or chakras, in an "open" and "aligned" state. In these traditions, it is believed that these chakras play a significant role in influencing our emotional and physical well-being.

After an extensive study of the chakra system, I acquired the skill to manipulate energy, and create tangible changes in people's undesirable physical and emotional conditions. After being set free from the influence of the lower world ideologies, God revealed to me that my engagement with chakras and the utilization of techniques from the lower realm was symbolic of partaking fruit from the Tree of Knowledge of Good and Evil. By unintentionally eating of the forbidden fruit, I became bound by the Kingdom of Darkness.1 Corinthians 3:19 says:

"For the wisdom of this world is foolishness with God."

As difficult as it was to come to terms with, I discovered that the chakras serve as a mechanism employed by the shadow dimension to prime the individual's body for the entry of the Kundalini spirit, who, once established, acts as a counterfeit to block the person from receiving the True Light of God. Reluctantly, I came to realize that yoga, meditation, and certain breathing exercises are all intertwined with and harness energy from serpent power. Through extended periods of meditation, practice of yoga postures, and breath exercises, the Kundalini serpent coils at the base of the spine, increasing in power. While this serpent energy can be used as a source of power to generate signs and wonders, or even used to help "heal" people as I once did, the long-term effects on both the practitioner and recipient outweigh any temporary benefit gained.

I was utterly shocked to uncover that individuals engaged in practices tied to chakras and occult wisdom unintentionally convert their chakras into control mechanisms that are then exploited by the shadow realm. Over time, each chakra becomes an open gateway to the dark dimension, allowing spirits to infiltrate the unsuspecting vessels of spiritual seekers. In the spirit world, these control mechanisms are visible and targeted by malevolent spirits who seek to control and manipulate God's people. I now have reason to suspect these chakra gateways may play a significant role in the end times battle, as Lucifer and the realm of the fallen ones attempt to direct people ensnared by this energetic mechanism of control.

God is the ultimate power source, and He gives freely to those who seek Him and live a righteous life. Revelation 2:7 (NASB) says:

"He who has an ear, let him hear what the Spirit says to the churches. To him who overcomes, I will grant to eat of the Tree of Life which is in the Paradise of God."

It is imperative to discern if we are eating from the Tree of Life, which is Christ and everlasting life, or from the Tree of Knowledge which casts ominous light to attract the unsuspecting yet leads to an endless prison of darkness. In Genesis 2:16–17 (NKJV), when man was created, God said:

"Of every tree of the garden you may freely eat; but of the tree of the knowledge of good and evil you shall not eat, for in the day that you eat of it you shall surely die."

What perplexed me greatly in the spiritual systems I studied before encountering the Creator of this world, was the presence of substantial truth within those systems. The presence of truth mixed with deception created the illusion that all the teachings were valid. In the spiritual discipline I adhered to, known as Arhatic Yoga, we actively engaged in practices related to forgiveness, service, healing, and tithing. As devoted Arhatic practitioners, we sincerely believed we were serving a righteous and just cause. We were convinced that by studying chakras and harnessing Kundalini energy, that we could help to alleviate the suffering of others. We were taught that the more Kundalini energy we cultivated, the more impactful our potential as healers would be.

My colleagues and I were unaware that through our practice of Kundalini meditation, we were deeply merging our bodily vessels with the Kundalini spirit—a detrimental source of energy and power. We were caught in an intricately woven web of deception that lay beyond our field of awareness, interwoven with profound truths that made it difficult to discern the subtle, ominous light that was gradually and deceptively conditioning us to be controlled by an enemy we didn't know existed. Understanding these dynamics is crucial for believers who aim to assist those caught in Satan's cunning snares.

Through my use of the practices in that New Age occult system, I acquired psychic powers and abilities. I learned to see chakras, spirits, and even notice entities on people. The problem was that the power and sight that is gained through those means is subject to control by its power source, the

Kundalini spirit. That spirit permits psychic sight to the degree in which it will serve to advance its own dark agenda.

We undoubtedly contain God-given channels of light within us, and our own internal windows to heaven, but they are not as the New Age, occult, and Eastern religions depict them. The manner in which chakras are taught in various occultic traditions expose the practitioner to the nefarious light of the serpent spirit, which is a dangerous counterfeit. The desire for power and the allure of the supernatural drive many individuals toward exploring the New Age, occultism, and witchcraft. Additionally, the glamorous portrayal of occult practices in media and films influence people to desire supernatural power; seeking such power in that manner leads seekers into bondage.

While serpent power may yield results, it is essential to recognize that it is not of God. The utilization of serpent power, whether conscious or inadvertent, has the potential to cause illnesses, diseases, as well as mental and emotional disturbances. During the time I was unknowingly plugged into and using serpent power, I had a myriad of unexplainable sicknesses and pain.

God granted me insight into Lucifer's tactics, and how he uses pain as a tool to manipulate and lure the unsuspecting into systems that imprison them in the realm of the fallen ones. For example, the more I practiced yoga, the more reliant I became on it for maintaining a sense of well-being. Mistakenly, I viewed yoga as a remedy, unaware it was a gateway to affliction and one of the sources of my growing suffering. This revelation dawned on me as I began to experience liberation from malevolent presences within my body. Suddenly, much of the pain that had plagued my body disappeared upon being delivered from these undesirable indwelling spirits and ceasing the practices I was involved in. Consequently, I no longer felt the need for yoga; my muscles and mind were naturally relaxed, and I no longer felt compelled to rely on serpent power to alleviate the pain that yoga and its associated source had actually caused.

During the period of time in which I was practicing Kundalini meditation, my teachers warned me about the possibility of experiencing "Kundalini syndrome" as a side effect. According to their teachings, Kundalini syndrome stems from accumulated negative karma from past lives, which gets accelerated by rapid spiritual growth. What an incredibly misguided notion that was, that justified the negative symptoms and consequences I experienced when drawing power from the Kundalini spirit.

Being trapped in that matrix of lies had grave consequences for my body and health. Since I believed the worldview they taught on karma, I assumed that the pain and illness I was experiencing was because I deserved it from something harmful I had done in a past life. We were provided energy healing techniques to "heal" ourselves which would help the symptoms seemingly disappear but then later reappear or manifest as new symptoms.

Many yoga poses invoke Eastern deities, gods, and goddesses, permitting the shadow light of their presence to infill and control the person's bodily vessel. People may initially sense the power that enters them as peace, or relief from pain, but it is a counterfeit for the serenity only God can provide. The benefits the gods and deities in yoga offer are merely temporary and come with a hidden contract. It grieves our Creator that instead of turning to Him, we look for things of the world to solve problems meant for God alone. Other gods won't set us free; quite the contrary, they lead to bondage. The power to liberate us and bring complete healing to our bodies, minds, and souls resides solely with God, the Creator of heaven and Earth.

As I was set free, my body was miraculously healed by God Himself. For many years, I suffered through intense and excruciating periods of suffering from neurological Lyme disease. Even on my "good" days I was in constant pain, and my overall quality of life was greatly reduced.

Starting in my thirties, I had agonizing arthritis in my joints, and they would often swell to the point that I would find it difficult to perform basic daily tasks. I suffered from extreme neck pain that radiated down my spine, into my shoulders, and caused constant tailbone pain. My chronic neck pain and tension triggered severe migraines that could last for weeks, often requiring my boyfriend to inject pain medicine into me. I also had on-and-off severe sciatica since my early twenties, which made it difficult to drive long distances.

To maintain some level of functionality, I had to visit a chiropractor and massage therapist several times each month. I was plagued with constant fatigue and horrible digestion problems. There were instances when my abdomen would swell to the extent, I was unable to eat. I suffered from severe food allergies that limited me to an overly restrictive diet, just so I could eat anything at all. If I consumed corn, gluten, or dairy, my body would swell in response, causing significant inflammation. The relentless barrage of debilitating symptoms often left me feeling moody or depressed.

It is absurd how many doctors I visited over the years in an attempt to solve my complex medical conditions. I saw numerous neurologists, rheumatologists, naturopaths, and infectious disease doctors, among various others. Despite trying countless bottles of pharmaceutical medications and experimenting with numerous herbal and homeopathic remedies over several years, not one was able to cure my pain or illnesses. During prayer sessions, whether I was alone or had others pray over me, I often felt sensations of tugging, pulling, or pain in areas where my body typically experienced high levels of pain. As I progressed through the process of deliverance, the physical pain I had suffered from gradually diminished. Furthermore, during my encounters with the Lord, His presence within me helped me reach a deeper understanding of how certain pain or illnesses directly correlated to my behaviors that were out of alignment with God's laws and principles—my sin.

The more I devoted myself to God, through prayer, fasting, and seeking His presence, the more miraculous healing my body experienced. Sometimes, in deep raptures with the Lord, His presence would infuse me with powerful currents of energy, shaking areas of my body that were afflicted with constant pain. After a bit of shaking, the pain would simply fade away; God shakes what He is healing.

Within the first month, I was astonished to realize that my neck pain, back pain, and sciatic pain had all vanished! I was awestruck, elated, and filled with gratitude to witness God's goodness at work in me. Interestingly, my healing process was progressive, and in the weeks leading up to the resolution of my symptoms, I noticed unusual popping sounds and the release of muscle tension after periods of focused prayer.

A fog of heaviness that I hadn't realized was there, slowly lifted. In the mornings, I woke up full of energy, newfound love, and joy from the presence of the Lord. Within just two months of drawing close to the Lord, I noticed a major improvement in my digestion. Miraculously, my severe food allergies vanished, allowing me to indulge in wheat, corn, and other foods that had been off-limits for over six years. The constant ache and swelling in my joints disappeared, and I was able to sit long hours at my computer without the usual discomfort.

God is the ultimate physician! In this world, we often find ourselves misled into believing that we must seek worldly solutions for what God alone can provide. As disciples who study and follow the teachings of Christ, we are promised authority over all manner of illness. In Matthew 10:1 (KJV), it says:

"And when he had called unto him his twelve disciples, he gave them power against unclean spirits, to cast them out, and to heal all manner of sickness and all manner of disease."

Also, in Exodus 23:25 (NIV), it is written:

"Worship the LORD your God, and his blessing will be on your food and water. I will take away sickness from among you…"

God is Jehovah Rapha, the Lord that heals.

The healing I received from God was not merely physical. With each passing day, my world became brighter as I allowed Jesus to enter deeper into my heart. The more I surrendered to Him, the more the Spirit of God permeated the depth of my heart. I developed a new vulnerability and tenderness towards God as I learned to trust Him. The gentle care of His presence slowly healed a lifetime of heartache; heartache from failed relationships, heartache from betrayal, heartache from living in such a broken world, and heartache from grief and loss. Many times, the touch of God on my heart was so tender that it moved me to tears.

The human heart can endure many hurts in a lifetime, leading it to become hardened and calloused in its bracing against the pains of this world. My growing intimacy with God helped to gently loosen parts of my heart where I had been holding onto pain. As I allowed Him to enter my most vulnerable places, He began to heal and restore buried aches of my heart, ones I bore the burden of for far too long. In Ezekiel 36:26 (ESV), the Lord says:

"And I will give you a new heart, and a new spirit I will put within you. And I will remove the heart of stone from your flesh and give you a heart of flesh."

I cannot emphasize enough the importance of allowing our Creator God into our hearts; our hearts are the gateway to God. God is love, and the way to reach Him is through the heart. While God can certainly work mightily through our pursuit of knowledge and wisdom, relying solely on our intellect to find God may lead us astray, or tempt us to partake of the forbidden fruit of the Tree of Knowledge. In Jeremiah 29:11–14 (NIV), God provides insight as to how to encounter Him:

"'You will seek me and find me when you seek me with all your heart. I will be found by you,' declares the LORD, 'and will bring you back from captivity.'"

I believe that, deep down, we are all seeking a profound union of love with our Creator, whether we are aware of it or not. The issue is many of us don't know how or where to find that which we seek. People often look for this extraordinary love in relationships with spouses, with children, and even pets. Yet often we find ourselves brokenhearted, because such a level of profound and unconditional love cannot be found in worldly things; it can only be found in God.

Unlike humans in our lives, God will never betray us or let us down. He can fill the deepest voids in our hearts. Deuteronomy 31:8 (NIV) says:

"The LORD himself goes before you and will be with you; he will never leave you nor forsake you. Do not be afraid; do not be discouraged."

Isaiah 61:1 (ESV) describes how the Spirit of God works within willing vessels to bind up the brokenhearted, proclaim freedom for the captives, and release those who are imprisoned by darkness. I needed freedom, even if I didn't know it, and it is the Spirit of Truth who set me free.

In the two decades I dedicated to New Age, occult practices, and the healing arts, I was disillusioned by the belief that I was on a path to healing. Despite discovering numerous tools for healing, there remained a long list of revolving symptoms and complaints I could not break free from. I had seen some of the best energy healers, body workers, alternative healing practitioners, reiki therapists, astrologists, psychics, iridologists, acupuncturists, herbalists, and other healing arts practitioners. While these modalities sometimes produced seemingly miraculous results, marked by symptoms vanishing and supernatural insight into what was going on, I never experienced complete healing. When I overcame one problem, a new issue would soon arise.

The never-ending maze of false hope continually led me to believe I was making progress, only to realize I had made no real advancement at all. I spent all those years in the New Age, occult, and healing arts chasing the promise of healing, compelled to try each new healing modality I found, thinking it was finally the answer to all my problems.

In the end, all that searching proved fruitless, leading me to realize that there is only one answer to all our problems, and His name is Yeshua—the Healer, the Redeemer, the Repairer, the Restorer. What couldn't be accomplished in twenty years of natural medicine and the healing arts, was achieved in two months of sincerely seeking the Lord. The progress I experienced was nothing short of extraordinary and truly miraculous!

As I was going through my intense healing process with God, He directed me to discontinue taking all of the supplements and medications I was taking at the time. Following that guidance demanded a significant leap of faith for me; it required placing my complete trust in God to the extent that I was willing to suddenly cease taking all the pills and supplements that had been integral to my well-being for so long. Having adhered to a daily regimen of supplements and herbal remedies for over a decade, letting go of it all at once was a big challenge for me.

I relied on a variety of supplements to manage my health issues: turmeric formula for my swollen joints, melatonin so I could sleep, immune stimulants to avoid being chronically sick, herbs for stomach and organ pain, and more. Additionally, I intermittently took pharmaceutical medication to alleviate neurological and chronic pain symptoms. My cupboard was stocked full of countless bottles of prescriptions, all prescribed by my doctor in an attempt to "treat" my condition.

Moreover, I had been using birth control since my teenage years to regulate my cycles. I tried many times to stop taking it, but every attempt I made to discontinue it ended in excessive, irregular bleeding that was too difficult to endure. I experimented with various types of herbs and treatments in an attempt to regulate my hormones, but nothing helped.

Reluctantly, I stopped taking everything the day that God directed me to do so. As I was grappling with myself to trust God and let go, He reassuringly said to me once more, "Hold onto nothing and I will give you everything." Once I discontinued all herbs and medications, I had nothing left to rely on except God. Following my leap of faith, God immediately began the work of healing my body from the inside out.

Throughout my healing process, there were times when I would wake in the middle of the night, feeling the electric current of His presence surging through me. In response to His electrifying touch, my body shivered and shook in unexpected ways. In these visitations, the atmosphere became saturated with a deep peace, accompanied by a pleasant euphoria found only in His holy presence.

God truly is the best medicine. He knows exactly what we need. When I surrendered, He showed me that I can trust Him by healing all the ailments I was suffering from. Even when I stopped taking birth control after so many years, my hormones balanced, and my menstrual cycles normalized—something I hadn't been able to achieve all my life. I tried endless "remedies" in my search for a solution, but God was the only effective remedy.

Perhaps one of the most damaging beliefs I held in my years of New Age philosophy, was the belief of karma. Due to my strongly held assertion about past lives, it seemed plausible to accept that the deeds of "my past lives" were causing pain and suffering in this life, instead of realizing it was sin that had a negative effect on my body. Also, as I mentioned before, it was the perfect façade to conceal the repercussions of utilizing Kundalini serpent power from my "spiritual" meditations and the detrimental effects it had on my health and body.

This strategically placed veil kept me from realizing that my healing was promised by God 2,000 years ago when Jesus died on the cross and bore every disease and infirmity of humanity in His wounds, now and forevermore. The concept of karma was just the right fabrication to keep me from realizing miraculous healing becomes accessible when I look to God, the Great Physician. Believing in karma kept me from the authority I now have with Christ to lay hands on the sick and see them healed. Mark 16:17–18 (KJV) says:

165

"And these signs shall follow them that believe; In my name shall they cast out devils; they shall speak with new tongues; They shall take up serpents; and if they drink any deadly thing, it shall not hurt them; they shall lay hands on the sick, and they shall recover."

For those of you that were misled into the maze like I was, I want you to know that your freedom and well-being is promised by Yeshua. You too can escape the matrix of lies that may be keeping you from realizing that God is able to heal you. Healing becomes possible by the belief that the sacrificial act of Yeshua's death on the cross was for us to be able to obtain freedom from the curse of sin, which is death. If you are a follower of Christ, you can seek God's guidance on how to obtain health and wellness by having faith in what was established in the Earth realm through the death, burial, and resurrection of Jesus Christ of Nazareth. If we stand boldly in the faith that He has already carried every burden, we too can experience His resurrection in our bodies.

I've noticed that there are Christians who follow the religion of Christianity but haven't experienced profound intimacy with Christ in the Spirit. Some individuals who were raised in the church, possess a strong understanding of doctrine and are well-versed in God's Word, yet haven't fully surrendered their lives and spirits to God, preventing Him from entering and healing them. In my case, healing required full submission of my will to His will. Jesus Christ begins to dwell inside of us the moment we accept Him as our personal Lord and Savior. Romans 8:11 (NKJV) says:

"But if the Spirit of Him who raised Jesus from the dead dwells in you, He who raised Christ from the dead will also give life to your mortal bodies through His Spirit who dwells in you."

If we discover we have become spiritually deadened, God can revive us by breathing new life back into us through the power of His Spirit, just as He brought life to Christ when He raised Him from the dead after He was crucified.

When people dabble in Wicca, astrology, paganism, rituals and offerings to other gods and deities, consulting psychics, communicating with the dead, using Ouija boards, or participating in blood sacrifices, they open doorways to the demonic realm. Through these doorways, spirits can enter and bring about severe illness, disease, mental and emotional disturbances, and even death. Isaiah 8:19 (NASB) says:

"When they say to you, 'Consult the mediums and the spiritists who whisper and mutter,' should not a people consult their God?"

God is who we should turn to when we need help, and we are much better off to turn away from the deceptions of the world that lead us into darkness.

Witchcraft and divination aren't the only ways doors get opened to demonic forces. God showed me that malevolent spirits target our weakest areas to enter and afflict us. These vulnerabilities can stem from physical, emotional, or mental traumas. Fortunately, if you have experienced trauma, you can invite God to those memories and times in your life, and He can bring healing. He is the Great Restorer, and He can repair what was broken, heal what needs mending, and close the doors that were once opened.

From my own experience, I've also observed that certain emotions can open doorways. When individuals align in agreement with fear, grief, unrighteous anger, or unforgiveness, and stray from God's laws and principles, it acts as an open door for that which is not God to enter. Anger can be a doorway. Pride is a doorway. It is natural that these reactions arise from time to time, but if you accidentally open a door, be sure to close it through repentance, breaking agreement, and renouncing the action or behavior. Jesus's blood redeems us from all of our transgressions.

As I began to serve in the deliverance ministry, I encountered spirits of fear, anxiety, rage, and depression. In deliverance sessions, I was able to discern the type of spirit by observing how the afflicted person manifested as the spirit was being expelled from their body. In the case of a spirit of fear, the afflicted person would suddenly become inexplicably terrified. With a spirit of rage, the person displays sudden and intense anger and rage, sometimes with clenched fists or screaming.

The good news of the Gospel of Jesus Christ is that believers, through their relationship with Christ, have the authority to cast out all demons. Luke 9:1 (NKJV) says:

"Then He called His twelve disciples together and gave them power and authority over all demons, and to cure diseases."

Emphasis on *all demons*. Jesus is talking to his disciples here, and believers nowadays are the disciples of the twenty-first century. That means believers today carry the power and authority to cast out demons, but unfortunately, many don't exercise their God-given authority. Getting freed from afflicting spirits and receiving miraculous healing are some of the numerous gifts we automatically receive when we walk wholeheartedly with Yeshua. It's about time the church as a whole began to utilize their full inheritance from Christ.

Engaging in activities such as studying chakras, opening the third eye, practicing astral travel, or experimenting with psychedelic drugs grants demons full legal rights in the spiritual realm to afflict users. The way out of bondage is to repent to God for being led astray, cease, and renounce the activities that violate God's laws, and turn to Him for redemption.

Sometimes, particularly in dealing with complex issues, one may need to present their case to the courts of heaven. One of the afflicting spirits I dealt with was relentlessly stubborn in ceasing its torment upon me. I did everything I knew; I recognized sin and iniquity; I repented for transgressions against God's laws and renounced illegal activities. I pleaded the blood of Jesus; I unleashed intense spiritual warfare. I cleansed my family tree and lineage with the blood of Jesus.

Yet, despite my best efforts, this stubborn spirit still came back repeatedly to trouble me, often with intense physical pain. It wasn't until I started studying the use of the courts of heaven in spiritual warfare that I was able to make the progress that previously seemed unattainable. The spirit held no legal rights, so when I brought this matter to the courts of heaven, I was able to petition the heavenly governing body for a divorce and restraining order from the afflicting entity. (Please refer to resources in the back of this book for more info on how to use this technique in spiritual warfare.)

The enemy comes to kill, steal, and destroy, but God is the Great Restorer! Jesus explains this in John 10:10 (NIV):

"The thief comes only to steal and kill and destroy; I have come that they may have life and have it to the full."

I have noticed in cases of intense bondage that employing deeper deliverance tactics is crucial. Deeper deliverance helps to uncover rights that spirits may possess, which in my case was essential to gaining greater freedom. In the resource section of this book, you will find a link to a forty-page renunciation of the New Age and occult that aided me tremendously in my path to freedom. It helped me close hidden doors and break free from the grip of the Kundalini serpent energy that wound through the energy centers of my body.

In witchcraft, practitioners command the spirit world to do their bidding. This involves the use of magic, spells, and incantations that summon spirits in the spiritual realm that can then influence the physical realm. In white magic, spirits that may seem benevolent in nature are actually malevolent. Modern teachings, such as "The Secret," encourage people to willfully manipulate the unseen world to gain desires, and they may not realize that by using the technique they are engaging in witchcraft and breaking spiritual laws that expose them to undesirable spirits. New Age practices promote the idea of individuals becoming god-like, or being their own god, seeking power through spiritual practices that are the forbidden fruit of the Tree of Knowledge. Many who fall prey to this fail to recognize the consequences associated with this approach. They miss the connection entirely between the occult practice they engage in and their undesirable physical, emotional and/or mental problems.

When it comes to psychic abilities, having access to information doesn't equate to having authority. Just because someone has access to psychic information about you does not mean that it is from God. Even when someone operates in signs and wonders, it isn't always being generated from a holy and righteous light. In this day and age, maintaining incredible discernment is imperative, and the Holy Spirit serves as the ultimate guide. These are some of the primary avenues through which malevolent spirits can gain access to your physical vessel:

Direct Willful Sin

The Occult

Inheritance and Generational Ties

Unforgiveness

Trauma

Abuse

Ungodly Soul Ties

Addictions

Fears and Phobias

False Religions

Curses, Cursed Objects and Buildings

The process of recognition, repentance, renouncing, and resisting is the pathway to breaking the chains put in place by the Kingdom of Darkness. By following this simple sequence, unwanted ties connected to undesirable entities can be severed. If you find yourself struggling for freedom as I once was, utilize the resources provided in the back of this book and seek assistance from an established deliverance ministry. As we follow God and walk in His ways, we can affirm:

"Into your hands I now entrust my spirit. O Lord, the God of faithfulness, you have rescued and redeemed me," (Psalm 31:5–6, TPT).

"For blessed are they that do his commandments, that they may have right to the Tree of Life and may enter in through the gates into the city," (Revelation 22:1, KJV).

Part 3

The Glory and Power of God

13

God's Gifts

Even amidst the significant breakthroughs I was experiencing, a sense of grief lingered, as I attempted to process the loss of my life as I once knew it, the disappearance of my cherished partner, and the dismantling of my fractured belief systems. The truth I was uncovering proved to be inconvenient and uncomfortable, and shattered the artificial peace of my previous imagined version of God and the false reality I had been living in.

Until then, I hadn't realized my addiction to the approval of others and the unconscious drive to embody the New Age philosophy of aspiring to be God-like, constantly seeking praise and validation. Unknowingly, I had lived my life with a hidden agenda of self-glorification. The pain I faced in awakening was almost too much to bear as I came to terms with the reality of my misplaced priorities and motivations as I fully surrendered my life to God. As John 5:44 (KJV) says:

"How can you believe, when you receive glory from one another and do not seek the glory that comes from the only God?"

Having spent much of my life deeply invested in a New Age spiritual perspective, I held the belief that people could engage in a journey of spiritual evolution, expanding their power and consciousness to become increasingly more God-like. I believed in the concept that we are all one, and all is God. This led me to embrace the idea that one could cultivate their own divine nature by embracing the path of enlightenment, which involves meditation and achieving oneness with the world.

The pitfall with the above-mentioned road to enlightenment is that it often contains an element of self-glorification well-shrouded in justification. Psychics, gurus, healers, shamans, tarot card readers, New Age workshop facilitators, and spiritual teachers receive adoration from their followers who often idolize their gifts. While many of the solutions they offer provide access to the spirit world, knowledge, power, and tangible results, they come with undisclosed consequences as a result of contracts people don't even realize they have forged.

Surprisingly, this phenomenon also occurs within churches, where pride can infiltrate individuals who are operating in spiritual gifts. Deception can lead them and others to idolize their gifts. Satan exploits pride in order to prevent us from receiving greater gifts of God's glory. Humility is key. It was only when I humbled myself and relinquished my need to control and manipulate the truth, that I could even consider a radically different perspective that greatly challenged my beliefs. I came to understand that, unlike some spiritual traditions I once followed that claim to "take you to a higher level," true spiritual progress towards God requires great humility and a letting go of one's own self-focused ambitions.

God humbled me by exposing my ignorance and pride, revealing Himself as infinitely more magnificent than I had ever envisioned. Throughout my life, I pursued many gods and acquired power, insight, protection, and purpose from them. Yet, in the end, I realized that every deity I ever worshipped paled in comparison to the power and authority of Yahweh and His Son, Yeshua of Nazareth, for He is the Creator of this world. Chronicles 16:25 (NIV) declares:

"For great is the LORD and most worthy of praise; he is to be feared above all gods."

In 1 Chronicles 29:11 (NKJV), the truth of God the Most High is disclosed:

"Yours, O Lord, is the greatness and the power and the glory and the victory and the majesty, for all that is in the heavens and in the earth is yours. Yours is the kingdom, O Lord, and you are exalted as head above all."

In my pursuit of healing through spiritual practices, I employed elaborate New Age systems that initially seemed to eliminate illnesses, fears, addictions, emotional disturbances, and relational conflicts. However, I was simply chasing after illusions and grappling with shadows cast by smoke and mirrors. There was no real sustenance to the Band-Aid remedies offered in the healing arts world that I lived and worked in. I naively believed I could vanquish suffering in myself and others, yet never truly addressed the underlying issue, the reality that only God can bestow complete healing and freedom. The methods and approaches I used were merely superficial remedies, meant to deceive individuals into thinking they can heal without God.

Spending twenty years in New Age spirituality was like an endless game of whack-a-mole; I believed I was winning a battle and making progress, only to find that the same, or even worse, issues repeatedly resurfaced. Many of these New Age systems are a maze that keep people searching, enticing people with empowerment and results along the way, yet ultimately leading them further from the genuine truth, power, and fullness of God they long for.

Walking in the glory of God and coming back into alignment with our Creator is a simple path, without bells and whistles that glorify the "self." It is a simple act of dropping to one's knees in humility, asking God the Most High to reveal Himself, and repenting for worshipping other gods, idols, and ourselves. In Isaiah 42:8 (ESV), God establishes Himself in His rightful place:

"I am the Lord; that is my name; my glory I give to no other, nor my praise to carved idols."

As I came to know of the God of all creation, I was astonished to learn about God's gifts and miracles. I've always been drawn to and fascinated by the supernatural, but I had not yet seen manifestations of supernatural power in the church. On the contrary, churches I had visited seemed deadened in the spirit, suppressed by the weight of religious oppression.

As God stripped me of my unholy ways and practices, He promised He would replace them with virtuous, holy, and sanctified gifts of the Holy Spirit. At a time when I was grieving the loss of the healing arts work I practiced for many years, God responded with His recurring message in a firm yet loving voice, declaring, "Hold onto nothing, and I will give you everything. Your hands will be made to heal with the Holy Spirit, and you will be able to help many more people than when your hands were covered in a web of deception." As challenging as it was for me to let go of my entire career, I could sense the power in God's message and was inspired to pursue what He spoke of.

God's reassurance that my hands would again be used for healing, delighted me. Discovering that the gift of healing could be applied in my new journey with Yeshua brought profound peace, and I was relieved to learn I could continue to serve others in their pursuit of health and wellness. God shared with me that there are no limits to the extraordinary healing that can take place when led by the Holy Spirit.

As I studied God's Word, I learned there are nine gifts of the Holy Spirit that serve as a sign of the manifestation of the Spirit of God which dwells inside believers, as spoken of in 1 Corinthians 12:4–11:

"Now there are varieties of gifts, but the same Spirit; and there are varieties of service, but the same Lord; and there are varieties of activities, but it is the same God Who empowers them all in everyone. To each is given the manifestation of the Spirit for the common good. For to one is given through the Spirit the utterance of wisdom, and to another the utterance of knowledge according to the same Spirit, to another faith by the same Spirit, to another gifts of healing by the one Spirit, to another the working of miracles, to another prophecy, to another the ability to distinguish between spirits, to another various kinds of tongues, to another the interpretation of tongues. All these are empowered by one and the same Spirit, who apportions to each one individually as He wills."

From this passage, we can identify the following gifts:

Words of wisdom: Supernatural revelation or insight into God's will or plans.

Words of knowledge: Supernatural knowledge or insight, often about others, or situations that a person would not know without the Spirit of God.

Gift of faith: Supernatural ability to believe God without human doubt, unbelief, and reasonings.

Gift of healing by laying on of hands: Miraculous, supernatural healing of all types of ailments without human aid or medicine.

Working of miracles: Supernatural power and ability that can modify natural laws of physics to accomplish the will of God.

Gift of prophecy: God's voice speaking through people in order to edify, exhort, and comfort.

Discerning of spirits: Revelation or insight of spirits to detect their presence, intentions, and plans, in order to discern whether they are malevolent or benevolent.

Speaking in tongues: Supernatural language of the heavenly realms or other languages that are not known to the speaker.

Interpretation of tongues: The supernatural ability to interpret what is being spoken by a person speaking in tongues or other languages not known by the person who interprets by the Spirit of God.

In Matthew 5:16 (ESV), Jesus refers to these gifts as a means to demonstrate God's unparalleled power:

"In the same way, let your light shine before others, so that they may see your good works and give glory to your Father who is in heaven."

The first manifestation of God's glory I received when I fervently sought Him was the blessing of speaking in new tongues. It was that very gift from God that first set me on the path towards freedom, invoking my first supernatural encounter with God. Speaking in my prayer language has become a great asset to me on my spiritual journey with God. Whenever I pray in tongues, the majestic presence of the Lord permeates the atmosphere and otherwise inaccessible heavenly realms are opened. Each one of us has our own unique prayer language that assists us in communing with the Spirit of God. When speaking in tongues, we can declare things in our spirit that bypass the confines of mind and logic.

As I drew closer to God and allowed Him to take authority over my life, the gift of God's healing manifested in my body, reversing years of chronic illness. I believe that God's healing power is a gift that all believers can access, according to the Word of God. His presence itself is life and light. In John 8:12 (NIV), when Jesus spoke to the people, He said:

"I am the light of the world. Whoever follows me will never walk in darkness but will have the light of life."

God is the Great Healer, and He says so in Exodus 15:26 (NKLV):

"I am the Lord, who heals you."

Believers host the Holy Spirit inside of them, and the Lord can heal through them, as mentioned in Mark 16:17 (NKJV):

"... the Spirit of God Himself indwells and occupies the believer."

A few weeks after my first encounter, I began to attend a class at my church called Emerging Prophetic Voices. From the time I spent immersed in the New Age, I became well-versed in the spirit world. Throughout my career in the healing arts, I regularly received psychic impressions and intuitions about peoples' lives, challenges, and illnesses. I spent many years developing my spiritual capacity to sense and feel with my spirit. Years of meditation and healing work carved my vessel as an excellent conduit for the Holy Spirit.

After God revealed Himself to me, I renounced the ways I had been illegally accessing information from the spirit world and created a new alliance with the Holy Spirit. By surrendering to God and inviting the Spirit of God to speak through me, incredible new dimensions of spiritual insight opened for me. The prophetic class was the perfect environment for me to practice, learn, and grow in being a messenger for God.

During an exercise in class, I experienced the joy of hearing the voice of God speak through me to others for the first time. We were instructed to close our eyes and pair up with complete strangers. Upon opening our eyes, we looked at our partners and were given three minutes to share a prophetic message from the Holy Spirit. As we prepared ourselves, I sunk into a deep and fervent prayer in tongues, reaching my spirit towards the Spirit of God.

As I opened my eyes, in my inner vision, I saw exactly what the Holy Spirit wanted me to share with the man who was my partner for the exercise, accompanied by words of knowledge I was to speak. He was taken back by the intimate details about his life that the Holy Spirit revealed to me, information about his daughter, and knowledge of conflict they were going through. I delivered the specific advice God had given me to share with him about what to do in his relationship with his daughter as well as encouragement and confirmation about his decision ahead.

How awesome! I thought. God actually knows everything about everyone; since God knows all things, he can share information that only He knows through willing vessels. What a great way to build faith. All I have to do is listen to what He says and release it to the person. Great excitement stirred within me, as I considered all the marvelous ways God could use me to help minister to His people.

In my first encounter with God, He made it abundantly clear that He knows everything about me. I am completely exposed to Him; there is no hiding anything from His Spirit. He knows my actions, thoughts, and emotions—both past and future. He knows every person this transparently and knows precisely what people need to hear in order to be drawn to Him and His gracious mercy. When I listen to the Holy Spirit and allow Him to speak through me, He unfailingly discerns the precise message that the person I am prophesying to needs to hear. It is profoundly humbling and fulfilling to become a vessel of inspiration and encourage others through the guidance of God.

Upon sharing what the Holy Spirit led me to share, I observed the man's face and expression change; he looked brighter, more joyful, and more at ease upon hearing the message. He looked at me in awe, exclaiming, "You're special. You have a special gift!" I could tell he still felt surprised at what had happened. I knew I wasn't any more special than anyone else in that room, including him. I believe we can all tune ourselves to hear the voice of God. When believers are baptized in the Holy Spirit, they all have the capacity to empty their vessel, surrender themselves to the Lord and allow Him to use them as an instrument of His will.

In that same class session, we also explored the realm of dreams, and how the Holy Spirit can use them as a channel of communication with us. I've been fascinated by dream interpretation from a young age, and the prospect of embarking on a new exploration of the dream world with the Spirit of God as my guide thrilled me. That night, before I went to bed, I said a prayer and invited God into my dream space, asking His help in creating a new dreamscape that contained the sanctity and wisdom of His essence.

My new dream journey with God began that night when I had a prophetic dream. In the dream, my hand was stuck in a sticky black widow spider web, then a black widow got bound to my hand and bit into my flesh three times. In the dream, I told my mother that I needed to go to the hospital. At the end of the dream, I woke up with a start, feeling disturbed by the dream, not yet understanding the nuance of interpreting dreams in the language of the Holy Spirit. Desiring further insight, I decided to confide in my friend

Deanne, knowing her to be a prophetic individual deeply attuned to the Spirit of God.

The next day, I carpooled with Deanne to a church event, and we sat together in the back of our friend's car. This was the perfect opportunity to ask her about my dream. After recounting the dream, she helped me interpret it explaining to me, "The web represents deception; the hospital in the dream world can symbolize the church." *How interesting*, I thought.

Now that I understood the symbolism, the dream began to make more sense. For the last seven years, I had been using that very same hand that was stuck in the spider's web to administer energy healing on clients, genuinely believing I was helping them. However, in reality, I had been caught in a web of deception. The poisoned bite of the black widow signified the contamination of my healing hand from the practices I participated in. The message of the dream was now clear: I was to seek the remedy for the venom of the deceptive practices in the church, symbolized by my need to go to the hospital in the dream.

That dream marked the beginning of a series of many more, as the Holy Spirit opened a doorway into the world of the prophetic. I began to communicate with the Kingdom of God, regularly getting visions, seeing angelic presences, and discerning afflicting spirits of individuals in need of deliverance. In Job 33:14–15 (NLT), it says:

"For God speaks again and again, though people do not recognize it. He speaks in dreams, in visions of the night, when deep sleep falls on people as they lie in their beds."

At the beginning of the following prophetic class, we bowed our heads in a potent and heartfelt prayer. I pressed my spirit close to God, asking for a vision or message for the class for that day. As the sacredness of the presence of the Holy Spirit enveloped me, I was granted a vision.

In the spiritual realm, I saw golden scrolls descending from the heavens above, showering upon us. Within this vison, people from the class reached their hands up to grab the scrolls, and as they did, they began to glow brighter with golden light. While witnessing this, I comprehended God was conveying that we are stronger united, especially when we agree together on the Word of God. Then, I saw a golden force field surrounding us, intensifying in strength and brilliance.

In the next part of the vision, we walked together to a pool of water, and each person immersed themselves in it. As a person emerged from the water, a white dove took flight from them, symbolizing the presence of the Holy Spirit. This message seemed to affirm messages we were to receive from heaven as a prophetic group and confirm that we were being baptized in the Holy Spirit. In John 3:5 (NIV), Jesus says:

"Very truly I tell you, no one can enter the Kingdom of God unless they are born of water and the Spirit."

When believers are baptized in the Holy Spirit, they enter into the Kingdom of God and into divine communication with the Kingdom of Heaven.

In the second part of my vision, angels came and placed luminous golden gloves over each of my hands. I took this as an affirmation of what the Holy Spirit promised me when stripping away the deceptive practices of my past; that now my hands were being made to heal with the Holy Spirit. God had said multiple times, "Hold on to nothing, and I will give you everything," and as I let more of my old life and identity go, not only did He heal me in body and spirit, but He used me to heal others, as well.

As I drew closer and closer to the Lord, seeking Him constantly, the oppressive spirits and presences that had afflicted me fled. God, who made all the heavens and Earth, has unrivaled power, a power that we can hold when Christ dwells within us. The more we go after God, the more intimate we become with Him, the more His magnificence manifests in our lives. In such a short time of fervently seeking God, I experienced miraculous healing, holy encounters, revelatory visions, and dreams from the realm of heaven. Yet this was only the beginning of what God would do in and through me over the course of the next year.

When I picked up the Bible, after avoiding it for most of my life, I was completely surprised by what I found. It was as if it was an entirely different book. When I had read it from a religious perspective, it appeared to be a rigid book of rules and bizarre stories. Yet, when I learned to pray and read the Bible in the Spirit, God's words came to life and shed a new light of understanding. As I asked the Lord to lead me in his Word, God's blessing of revelation came upon me, granting supernatural insight into what He was showing me.

God validated the experiences I had been having through His Word. His Word is eternal and forever settled in heaven; time and space have no effect on the Word of God, and the Spirit of God enlivens His Word, which is why it is called the Living Word. Psalms 119:89–91 (NKJV) affirms:

"Forever, O LORD, Your word is settled in heaven. Your faithfulness endures to all generations; You established the earth, and it abides. They continue this day according to Your ordinances, for all are Your servants."

As I was learning how to sincerely follow Christ, I was confronted with my own resistance to reading the Bible. Though I was excited to read it the day God showed me where my son's Bible had fallen under the bookshelf, as the weeks went on, I rebelled against reading it. God kept pressing me to study, however, and I quickly began to understand the quickening power of reading the Bible. The words of God are the pillars upon which this entire world is upheld. In the beginning, there was the Word, and it is the Word that this world is built upon. John 1:1 (NIV) says:

"In the beginning was the Word, and the Word was with God, and the Word was God."

The Spirit of Jesus brings the words of the Bible to life in our hearts when we read it; it is a living book.

The truth of God, the knowledge of God, and the Word of God were what I was missing in my years of spiritual seeking. God's Word is the power and the foundation on which believers can stand to become carriers of His glory. Without the Word, followers of Christ are not plugged into the power source of the Almighty God. Many of us hunger for power, and many people, like me, get fooled into drawing power from false doctrines, false gods, and the lower realm that is beneath the Kingdom of Heaven.

◊ ◊ ◊

Discerning spirits is an additional gift of the Holy Spirit. As the Spirit of God began to dwell within me, I learned how to discern malevolent spirits from benevolent ones. I would simply ask the Holy Spirit to pull back the veil and expose the true face of the spirit.

God's presence reveals the true nature of spirits to me. It is only possible to correctly discern with God our Creator as the inner witness and judge inside of us, and this cannot be done without Christ. I have seen "angels" in the spirit world, that when I asked God for discernment, they were unveiled as demons posing as an angel of light. 2 Corinthians 11:14 (NKJV) says:

"And no wonder! For Satan himself transforms himself into an angel of light."

Even with all the profound ways in which God's grace had already touched my life, I was merely just beginning to get to know God. God had more in store for me, as I was destined to sing His praises, and He had plans to dispel any lingering doubts about His truth. Over the next few months, I had the delight of experiencing even greater levels of God's magnificence as He continued to restore me, my family, and my life.

If you are suffering from affliction, Christ can restore you. With Him as your personal Lord and Savior, He can teach you discernment of spirits, be the light of your life and take dominion over darkness. With the power of God within us, we can break free from the unseen realm that oppresses us, if we have faith in Him.

No matter how broken we are, no matter how bad our traumas have been, no matter how far we have slipped into darkness, there is nothing that the great Lord cannot overcome. There is no feat too big. God is miraculous and His powers reach far beyond the laws that govern our world and can stretch as far as our faith can take us. Never underestimate what's possible with God.

God's power and strength brought me to my knees, penetrated to the depth of my soul, and miraculously healed my most deeply embedded wounds. And it is only with God that such things are possible. If you are tired and weary, God offers restoration in His Spirit.

As we invite Jesus into our lives, His Spirit begins to reside within us. The resurrection power of Jesus Christ lives in us, and has the potential to strengthen, refresh, and restore us, if we know how to use it properly. It is Satan's ongoing plan and effort to trick us into believing that we don't have access to that restorative, resurrection power. It is the resurrection power activated by faith that can bring healing and restoration to long-standing issues.

God waits for us to cry out, to long for His embrace, to desire Him above all things. If we yield to His plan for our lives, He will do a much better job than we could ever have done on our own. In Proverbs 25:2 (NIV), God invites us to search for Him:

"It is the glory of God to conceal things, but the glory of kings is to search things out."

In building a personal relationship with Yeshua, we can learn, grow, and walk in the gifts of the Holy Spirit by seeking Him above all other things; we can build an alliance with the Kingdom of God and access an entire heavenly realm of supernatural grace. Whether you're emerging from a spiritually dark world outside of the teachings of Christ or you are seeking to experience the miraculous realm of the Holy Spirit from within the church, the time has come for all of us get to know a God without the limits we place on Him. It is time to break free from the shackles of lies that hinder us from experiencing the full majesty of our Maker.

14

Visions of Heaven

I reveled in the thrill of my new venture of discovering God and His ways, yet the unresolved sense of disconnection from Gabriel persisted. The peace I had not yet found became apparent in the quiet moments of each passing day. Something about the separation between my partner and me still didn't sit well with me. I prayed constantly to God, asking Him to encounter Gabriel in the glorious way that He had for me.

If I was to walk with confidence on my new path, I knew that I needed to seek God's assistance in reaching a greater level of redemption. One day, in my exasperation, I threw my arms in the air and exclaimed, "Lord, show me more of Your glory! Reveal Thyself in all of Thy splendor! Let Thy thundering voice shake my world, and Thy lightning strike my flesh, may all the world know Thy glory through me. Use me! You have swept my house, now I lay my life at Your feet. You have shown me who You are. Lord, my soul cries out for You, my soul longs for You. Nothing else will do. Now that I have tasted the honey of Thy nectar, I know You are the only thing that can satiate and fulfill me, God. I don't want to live a moment without You. Stand by me, oh Lord the Most High, be with me every moment in my heart and in my mind. Be the voice that guides me. Awaken the gifts of the Holy Spirit in me so I can expand Your kingdom. Use my life as a testament to Your power, resplendence, and grace!"

I prayed this prayer over and over, in every moment I could muster throughout my day, every so often dropping to my knees to declare it in a deeper sincerity. The more I lowered myself to exalt the Lord, the more humility I allowed to penetrate the proudest parts of me, the more I eradicated hidden desires of self-glory, the more I could feel God's sensational presence and unmatchable power. Within a few days of engaging in my fervent and radical prayers, God began to release sweet tastes of His richness.

While in this process, I opted to pursue a follow up Lie Busters session with my friend Peggy. We arranged a time and met online in her Zoom room. The session began that day with the anointing of ourselves with oil and calling on the presence of the Holy Spirit to guide us. We continued the work we had begun in our initial session, entering into even deeper levels of deliverance. The Holy Spirit guided me through labyrinths of deceit, identifying doors that still needed closing from my involvement with the occult.

During the session, different spirit influences again appeared as shadowy visions of spiders and scorpions in my inner vision. Together, with Peggy and the Holy Spirit, once more we uncovered practices or situations in my life that had given the entities a right to access me. When I found the root cause of their presence, I went through the recognize-repent-renounce process, ensuring their access was revoked.

As unpleasant as it was for those creepy entities to be exposed, I was relieved to kick them out and slam close every door they had entered through. A significant element of the session was the need for renunciation of my involvement with opening energetic portals between the physical and spiritual worlds.

God revealed to me that there are realms of the spirit world forbidden to us, and that accessing them with illegal power exposes people to all kinds of demonic attacks. What is so perilous is that undesirable spirit influences enter silently and unnoticed, yet are always working in the background, affecting individuals in negative ways. They are excellent at concealing their presence until the authority of Jesus is invoked, at which point they can be cast out in Jesus's name.

On my spiritual journey, it was essential for me to understand God's laws that govern both the physical and spiritual worlds, and the law of dominion that was established by the crucifixion of Yeshua. Through Jesus's death and resurrection, believers are given power and access to the Kingdom of Heaven and the unfathomable glory of God Almighty that is unmatched. This is an access that was unavailable prior to the sacrifice of Yeshua, Son of God.

A veil between heaven and Earth was lifted in this Holy sacrificial act, and a passage to heaven granted. Hebrews 10:19–23 (KJV) confirms:

"Having therefore, brethren, boldness to enter into the holiest by the blood of Jesus, by a new and living way, which he hath consecrated for us, through the veil, that is to say, his flesh; And having an high priest over the house of God; Let us draw near with a true heart in full assurance of faith, having our hearts sprinkled from an evil conscience, and our bodies washed with pure water. Let us hold fast the profession of our faith without wavering; (for he is faithful that promised)."

The sacrifice of Jesus forged a pathway to our Creator, and God is calling all of His people to the path He has created for us to find Him.

In this ultimate atonement, Yeshua Himself became our Lord and Savior. Philippians 2:9–11 (ESV) says:

"Therefore, God has highly exalted him and bestowed on him the name that is above every name, so that at the name of Jesus every knee should bow, in heaven and on

Earth and under the earth, and every tongue confess that Jesus Christ is Lord, to the glory of God the Father."

The path to God was laid before us on a red carpet with the sacrificial blood of Yeshua. Through humility and gratitude, we can receive the gifts He bestows upon us by studying and living according to His teachings, emphasis on *living* according to His teachings. It is one thing to study and learn about Jesus's teachings, and another to act them out in your life. In the Old Testament of the Bible, we hear word of the coming of Christ, and in John 1:14 (ESV), God speaks of His Son, saying:

"And the Word became flesh and dwelt among us, and we have seen his glory, glory as of the only Son from the Father, full of grace and truth."

Hebrews 1:3 (ESV) speaks of Jesus's purity, power, and place with God:

"He is the radiance of the glory of God and the exact imprint of his nature, and he upholds the universe by the word of his power. After making purification for sins, he sat down at the right hand of the Majesty on high."

Peggy completed the session with me that day by leading me into the splendor of God. When I opened myself up to humbly receive Him, I was met with a series of visions. In the first vision, the sky was ominous and dark, and I saw myself standing with an army of angels, lions, and griffins behind me. I was carrying a large book with empty white pages in my left hand and a large glowing golden key in my right. Later, when I sought the meaning of what I had seen, I discovered that griffins are protectors from evil and witchcraft, and known in Christian symbolism to represent courage, leadership, and strength. As God improved my spiritual sight, I often saw griffins with angels and came to recognize them as heavenly creatures.

The day after this vision, the Spirit led me to Matthew 24:29 (ESV) while I was praying:

"Immediately after the distress of those days the sun will be darkened, and the moon will not give its light; the stars will fall from the sky, and the heavenly bodies will be shaken."

This Scripture discusses what Christians refer to as the End Times, which preface the return of Jesus.

Upon reading this verse, my mind raced to the night I was awoken at 3 a.m. when the Lord said to me, "Behold!" as the earthquake shook the ceiling above my bed. I pondered the message I had received: *You don't realize what is coming, the earthquake is a small example of what is yet to come.* God our Creator is a just and righteous Lord, and I believe in times ahead He plans to put an end to wickedness happening on Earth.

It is prophesied in the Bible, that the signs of the approaching End Times of Jesus's return are famines, wars, and earthquakes. In Mark 13:7–8 (NKJV), it is said:

"And you will hear of wars and rumors of wars. See that you are not troubled; for all these things must come to pass, but the end is not yet. For nation will rise against nation, and kingdom against kingdom. And there will be famines, pestilences, and earthquakes in various places. All these are the beginning of sorrows."

While considering the messages I received and the accompanying vision, I couldn't help but notice all the parallels between the current affairs of the world and what had been prophesied in biblical times. God was speaking to me, His Spirit coming to life through His Word, despite it being written thousands of years ago.

Being someone who speaks a second language, I know how easily things can get lost in translation. When I think about the Word of God being in the many translations of the books that make up the Bible, I have to admit I have been reasonably skeptical. It's not that I don't trust God, it is that I don't always trust man's interpretation of God.

Yet, when I am in union with the Holy Spirit and praying while reading, I find that God's presence brings His Word to life in the stories of our ancestors who had many direct encounters with our Creator. The Spirit of God Almighty flowed through the prophets and servants, who were instructed by God to record His Word for the generations to follow. When I was humble enough to hear, God directed me to study His Word in revelation and allow it to restore my mind with timeless truths.

I felt hesitant to share the second part of the vision I had in the session with Peggy, feeling unsettled about the bizarre imagery. Peggy insisted I share what I had seen, and I am glad she did, as her feedback was highly insightful. Now that I have more experience interpreting Holy Spirit led dreams and visions, I've noticed that visions or dreams may initially seem peculiar, but when I seek to interpret them, I often discover poignant and precise messages concealed within them.

In this particular vision, I saw an image of myself sweating blood followed by a flash of an image of the crucifixion of Yeshua. Upon telling Peggy what I saw, she asked, "Have you ever heard the Bible story of Jesus in the Garden of Gethsemane?" Having spent much of my life avoiding reading the Bible, I lacked context for the story she was referring to.

"No, I have not," I replied to her.

She explained patiently, "The night before Jesus's execution, He prayed in the garden of Gethsemane and, in some interpretations, is said to have sweat blood. He was in anguish, for He knew in painstaking detail the events that were to follow."

It was challenging for me to fathom what Jesus endured, but it seemed plausible that if someone knew they were destined to suffer a gruesome death, the mere thought of it could lead to sweating blood. Subsequently, I researched it, and there is a medical condition called hematidrosis, which causes one's sweat to contain blood. Some known causes are extreme distress, fear, and stress. When I was reading this information, in revelation, I realized that the vision I had was foreshadowing my own trials and tribulation that lay ahead as a result of sharing my testimony.

This concept appeared to align with my ongoing experience, as I had already endured a significant amount of anguish due to the profound transformation of my life; a transformation that caused upheaval to my previous way of life, the complete loss of my identity, the mournful conclusion of my career in the healing arts, and the shattering of the mental framework I had relied on for most my life. It had been a monumental struggle. I could sense a coming wave of persecution, mockery, and criticism that would be directed at me for faithfully sharing what God had called me to share. Despite being forewarned, it was still hurtful when certain friends and family members distanced themselves from me after hearing my testimony. Over time, I came to realize that it wasn't them rejecting me; it was their own past traumas from religious settings that caused them to turn away from Christ. Furthermore, I observed how principalities and rulers of darkness in or around unbelievers influence them to repel the light of Christ residing within followers of Yeshua.

In a revelatory insight, I saw how the tough periods of my life were a preparation for the rough road ahead. God can turn around even the greatest challenges we have faced and use them for good. I reluctantly saw that the years of extreme suffering with neurological Lyme disease I experienced were miniscule compared to the trials of faith that lay ahead of me. God was disclosing to me where the path I was choosing led, testing my commitment to stand for truth, even if it meant persecution.

I deeply considered what God was presenting. Would I face persecution or symbolically sweat blood for God's cause? I couldn't imagine turning back at this point and pretending I didn't see or understand the truths God had offered me. The thought of being so stressed or scared that I sweat blood was troubling, but not as disconcerting as returning as a prisoner to the matrix of lies I had just escaped. I drew a shaky breath, realizing I was standing at the crossroads of my destiny. Should I go back to the matrix of lies or face a treacherous narrow road that leads to my Creator God?

Okay God, I resolved, I will do it. Whatever it takes, I want to serve the Kingdom of Light, not the Kingdom of Darkness. A sense of relief washed over me, the taste of righteousness on my lips. I will burn for you, God. I will light myself up with Your Holy fire, that others might know Your goodness through me.

After all, in exchange for God revealing Himself to me, I offered my life, promising to surrender in a way I never had before, giving Him everything I had to give. What kind of person would I be to make such a bold declaration then run away because I didn't like the incommodious truth I received? No. I could not turn away from the first assignment God gave me. Ignorance is not bliss, it is darkness, and though what God presented was challenging,

I would rather be persecuted for the truth than continue to live a lie. 1 Peter 4:12–14 (ESV) says:

"Beloved, do not be surprised at the fiery trial when it comes upon you to test you, as though something strange were happening to you. But rejoice insofar as you share Christ's sufferings, that you may also rejoice and be glad when his glory is revealed. If you are insulted for the name of Christ, you are blessed, because the Spirit of glory and of God rests upon you."

Now that I was sure there was no way I was turning back, I settled into my new path as a follower of Christ more peaceably. Joy swept over me. Encouraged, I declared, "Yes! I will share the suffering of Yeshua of Nazareth, the great Messiah, whose name freed me from a bondage I didn't know I had. Yes! I will bear the burden, the agony, the pain, the humiliation, and the sacrifice. I will brave the narrow passage that leads to God Most High, whose authority reigns on Earth. No longer will I serve that which is against God, nor serve the hidden enemy that manipulates God's design!"

I could have it no other way. I would rather die righteously fighting to free a world caught in a web of deception than let my spirit die a little bit more every day by being a coward and avoiding a painful truth. There is a big difference between the suffering we endure at the hands of the enemy and the suffering we undertake to serve God. For far too long, I unconsciously lived for self-glorification in my life, bending to the approval of others. Now, I prioritize living a life not dictated by the opinions of others; God defines me. Self-exaltation and superiority only bring pain, suffering, and isolation in a world built within the walls of deception. John 15:19 (ESV) says:

"If you were of the world, the world would love you as its own; but because you are not of the world, but I chose you out of the world, therefore the world hates you."

American culture is the poster board of self-glorification; social media is crowded with posts that say, "Look at me, look at my self-glory! Be like me! Get rich by following me! Be more beautiful by doing what I do! Look at my photos of how spiritual I am! I am a god! I am a goddess!" Many get trapped playing this game, seeking fame and credit, but the time has come for God's people to come to their knees before Him and take their humble and righteous place beneath God.

When suffering is at the hands of the enemy, we can get overwhelmed with hopelessness and lost in darkness. When we firmly walk in alignment with our Creator, the radiance of God fills us, illuminating the path, even during our greatest trials of faith. Our Creator God, Yahweh, is the most powerful force in the world. When we come under the protection of God, we can rest knowing He is mightier than all darkness and any other god, goddess, saint, or deity to whom we could pray.

The vision I had symbolic of the persecution ahead was not the only insight I received that day. Once I decided to follow Jesus, I was drawn up in the Spirit and suddenly standing at the gates of heaven. Ancient, enormous golden gates. The doors opened, a blinding white light spilling from the entrance. A golden scroll came flying to me in a blast of wind. Startled, my hands flew up in front of me, and I grabbed it. I glimpsed the writing on the scroll, noticing it was in a language I could not interpret. I peered curiously at the foreign language, then understood that it wasn't yet time to comprehend its message, so I tucked it into the gown I was wearing. Psalm 24:7–8 (NIV) describes heaven's gates:

"Lift up your heads, O gates! And be lifted up, O ancient doors, that the King of glory may come in."

From the entrance emerged two massive, magnificent angels. They came to stand at each side of me, then with great eloquence, slowly walked me inside the gates. They led me gently to kneel before a pool from which they drew out water, pouring it delicately over my body. As the water flowed over my body, the angels pulled snakes out of my spine, emerging from areas they had been wedged in between vertebrae. I couldn't help but draw a parallel to a moment in *The Matrix* when Neo's spine was disconnected from the matrix, finally freed from his bondage as a slave to the machines. Now, within the heavenly gates, it felt as though I, too, was being unplugged from the deceit and influences of the matrix of lies.

Once my purification at the heavenly pool was complete, a gleaming silver garment appeared in the sky above me. It was slowly lowered and then draped like a cloak over my body. The garment was made of chain mail (many tiny, linked rings of metal), and it covered my entire body, including a hood for my head. Later, I discovered the garment is called a chain mail hauberk, which is a tunic of chain mail worn as defensive armor.

After my chain mail armor was in place, the angels escorted me back to the gate entrance. While walking, I stole glimpses of what lay inside the gates. White billowing clouds, landscapes on a horizon that glimmered in an all-permeating glow; scenes that seemed to blur the more I tried to focus on what they were. Some things, I gather, were not meant for me to see on that first visit.

When my spirit returned to my body, I began to piece together the elements of my vision and their significance. The dark horizon, with an army of angels and griffins behind me. The armor from heaven. A prophetic word I had received in church that day with my mother, when the pastor said, "There is a time coming that I am going to use you to go where angels fear to tread." All those messages led to one conclusion: I was being prepared for battle.

Intriguing. A battle. Why else would I have been given an army of angels and armor? I didn't like the idea of going into any battle. However, I had offered my life to the Lord. I surrendered completely. If this was the path God had in store for me, I was committed to trusting Him. I was reassured by the army of angels and griffins I had seen gathered behind me. If nothing else, I knew I would not have to fight the battle alone.

While writing this recount, I was led in revelation to Ephesians 6:10–17 (NIV):

"Finally, be strong in the Lord and in his mighty power. Put on the full armor of God, so that you can take your stand against the devil's schemes. For our struggle is not against flesh and blood, but against the rulers, against the authorities, against the powers of this dark world and against the spiritual forces of evil in the heavenly realms. Therefore, put on the full armor of God, so that when the day of evil comes, you may be able to stand your ground, and after you have done everything, to stand. Stand firm then, with the belt of truth buckled around your waist, with the breastplate of righteousness in place, and with your feet fitted with the readiness that comes from the gospel of peace. In addition to all this, take up the shield of faith, with which you can extinguish all the flaming arrows of the evil one. Take the helmet of salvation and the sword of the Spirit, which is the word of God."

I have experienced firsthand that the battle we face is not against flesh and blood, but against spiritual forces of evil in other realms and here on Earth. I have the ability to perceive that darkness thanks to God opening my eyes for me to see. I now saw how much of my past had prepared me to fight in the battle ahead.

The visions and insight I received in that session with Peggy sparked a flood of more visions, words of wisdom, revelation, and miracles from the Kingdom of Heaven. The messages I receive now differ immensely from messages I received prior to my encounters with the Holy Spirit. The numerous deceptive messages I was exposed to from untrustworthy sources in the spirit world led me far away from the truth I was searching for. The insights I receive from the realm of heaven carry a tangible weight, authority, and power that emit the radiance of God.

In this world, many people seek information from astrology, from divination, from tea leaves in a cup, or some even by consulting dead ancestors. It is a great desire of humanity to know what the future may hold, and herein lies the attraction toward the use of these types of methods to look for answers. Psychic readings, palm readings, and other forms of divination seek information in a manner that is unlawful to God. Deuteronomy 18:10-11 (KJV) states:

"There shall not be found among you any ... that useth divination, or an observer of times, or an enchanter, or a witch, or a charmer, or a consulter with familiar spirits, or a wizard, or a necromancer."

I was guilty of many of those things. I used tarot cards, runes, and pendulums as a means for guidance for many years, not perceiving that by doing so, I was inviting the Kingdom of Darkness to dwell in me. When one consults pendulums for guidance, it's important to note that familiar spirits, essentially demons, are often the source providing information to the inquirer. Familiar spirits offer the seeker the information they desire to hear, providing enough details to build trust in them, yet these spirits never truly have the best interest of the inquirer in mind. Through the exchange of information, the "helping" spirits unfold a hidden agenda unknown to the seeker.

However, there is someone that always has our best interest in mind: God. He wants us to turn to Him for the guidance we seek. The Kingdom of Heaven is an ally in this world of darkness, and the only source we can truly trust. Leviticus 19:26 (NIV) explicitly says:

"Do not practice divination or seek omens."

Obtaining access to information with forms of fortune-telling, a hidden contract is forged in the spiritual realm, leaves a door ajar to the dark dimension.

Even established followers of Christ can be tempted or deceived into divination or seeking omens. We live in a world where asking someone's astrological sign is as common as asking their name. Tarot cards can be found in common stores, and the use of magic that is perpetually romanticized in media, creates a hunger in mankind for what is forbidden. When tempted or deceived into acquiring information by unlawful means, remember that the Lord is the only one who has your best interest in mind, and He can provide the guidance you need.

The Kingdom of Heaven seeks the allegiance of the people of God in such a time as this when wickedness and deception abound. Matthew 5:14–16 (NIV) says:

"You are the light of the world…let your light shine before others, that they may see your good deeds and glorify your Father in heaven."

May we each strive to be light unto the world, standing firm in righteousness and become holy in the eyes of the

Lord. Let us extend our hands to those being deceived, leading them with compassion towards safety, ensuring they do not remain in unknown bondage.

15

Persistent Prayers

I steadfastly continued to say passionate prayers for my estranged partner, refusing to give up on him or allow the enemy to triumph over his life. The unease I felt knowing some demon was masquerading as the voice of God to Gabriel, served as the driving force to my constant intercessory efforts. If there was hope for Gabriel, I knew I could find it in God.

When Gabriel first left me, I questioned God, begging to know if it was actually Him that was leading Gabriel away from me or not. "Are you taking him away from me?" I demanded to know. "Why is it that Gabriel and I can't be together? Is he really not the one for me, nor I for him?"

After shedding countless tears and persistent pleas for an answer, God graced me with mercy. He gave me insight into His design for humanity, in that man and wife are meant to join together in a sacred marriage with the Lord. Since Gabriel and I had not yet sanctified our relationship with a marriage and covenant to God, we were living out of alignment with God's laws and principles, and outside the protection of God's covering.

When I asked God about whether Gabriel was the right man for me, He said that if we were to get married, the Holy Spirit would sanctify and guide our union. Without the vow of marriage to each other, our relationship could easily be torn apart. Though we were unaware, we had transgressed into sin by living in sexual immorality. God's desire for His people is that sexual intimacy is experienced within the bounds of a loving marriage covenant.

1 Thessalonians 4:3–8 (ESV) states:

"For this is the will of God, your sanctification: that you abstain from sexual immorality; that each one of you know how to control his own body in holiness and honor, not in the passion of lust like the Gentiles who do not know God; that no one transgress and wrong his brother in this matter, because the Lord is an avenger in all these things, as we told you beforehand and solemnly warned you. For God has not called us for impurity, but in holiness."

Then I heard God's voice in my head ask, "Will you abstain from sexual activity until you're married?" Astounded, I didn't know what to say. I had been living in the commonality of the world as it is today. I had not met one person in the entire thirty-seven years of my life who waited to have sexual relations with their partner until marriage. I attempted to imagine what it would be like to marry a new person that I had never been intimate with; sad to say. it was a foreign concept to me at the time.

I didn't reply to God's question right away, inadvertently avoiding it, hoping it would go away. Over the next few days, I felt Him pressing for an answer. When I didn't get let off the hook, I asked, *Would that include kissing?*

He answered me and said, "Yes, it would." Though this may or may not be the standard for everyone, it was what He was asking of me. After grappling with the decision for several days, I surrendered, submitted to God's will, and said yes.

I made numerous heartbreaking attempts to reconcile my relationship with Gabriel. On several occasions, he said, "I think you are an extraordinary woman, and you will make an excellent partner for someone else, just not for me." Ouch. Each time he uttered those words, it was a painful blow to my heart. I was convinced that he was the man for me, and the thought of starting over with a new partner was daunting. When I questioned him as to why he thought I wasn't the right one for him, he always reverted back to saying, "I don't know why exactly, but God told me to leave, and I want to follow God."

During my first deliverance session, I was stunned to discover the legion of demons afflicting Gabriel. It wasn't just one demon as I had initially believed, but rather a group of twelve of them. The sheer injustice of it all weighed heavily on my heart. How is it that demons could hijack my boyfriend, control his mind, and lead him astray? Yet, in the face of the disturbing revelation, I felt powerless and unsure of what I could do.

With little hope of a shared future with Gabriel, my new commitment to God in abstaining from sexual activity may have meant meeting a new person, then spending years together platonically until we either marry or move on. Despite it feeling like an overwhelmingly big task, I made the commitment, and was surprised how at peace I felt about my decision.

I wanted to do things the right way for once, and I had offered my life to God, and for me, that meant my body as well. If God wanted me to abstain, I would follow His guidance wholeheartedly and loyally. 1 Corinthians 6:19–20 (NIV) says:

"Do you not know that your bodies are temples of the Holy Spirit, who is in you, whom you have received from God? You are not your own; you were bought at a price. Therefore, honor God with your bodies."

A deep sense of holiness and honor came with my decision, as I recognized the sacredness of my body as a temple of the Holy Spirit.

◊ ◊ ◊

After not seeing any progress in my attempts to save my relationship with Gabriel, I reluctantly agreed to weekly meetings to arrange our separation. We owned a home together, had joint bank accounts, joint phone accounts, and other shared utility costs. Our lives were deeply intertwined, not just physically and financially, but also emotionally. As hard as it was to face this trial, I kept my word to God, daring to love Gabriel through it all.

The day before our separation meetings, I fasted and prayed fervently. The Lord had guided me to refrain from eating food any time that I was going to see Gabriel, so as to be in the spirit with him and not in the flesh. If I were to be in the flesh, I could easily be offended and upset at his decision to end the relationship. Not only that, but I was also still attracted to him as my partner, and God had warned me not to engage in any form of physical intimacy with him should feelings arise.

In our meetings, Gabriel would sometimes allow for the exchange of spiritual and philosophical questions. In those opportune moments, I pressed fiercely into God, asking God to speak through me, so I might get through to him. At times, I heard God's voice guide me to say key things, challenging Gabriel on the choices he was making for his life.

Looking back, I realize now that I was sowing seeds in his awareness, asking poignant questions about God, such as how he was sure that the voice he was hearing was actually the voice of God. I challenged him the way he challenged me when he first left, pointing out that he seemed so certain, and lacked the humility to know if what he believed was actually the truth.

210

On one occasion, I said to Gabriel, "You told me one of the reasons you left is because I was so certain about everything; you told me that I needed to let go, to learn to be humble. Well, I listened. I surrendered all my assumptions. I relinquished my firmly held assertions. I crumbled the castle of certainty in my mind, and when I did, I found out that the world is nothing like I thought it was. Even God is different than I imagined Him to be. I discovered that I had only been worshipping a convenient version of God, one that merely echoed my desires rather than confronting me with what I truly needed to hear. I came to realize that the sources I consulted for divine guidance weren't actually God. You compelled me to ask the right questions, questions I had been too afraid to ask about God and this world. You told me to break, to let go. You sent me ahead of you, and now I have found the incredible presence of God that is more real than anything else in my entire life. I have been broken in humility, and my pride has been crushed. As I listen to you speak, I can hear the same arrogance and pride I was walking in before I dared to humble myself the way you challenged me to. Now it is your turn. If you can talk the talk, it's time you walk the walk."

Surprisingly, what I said landed. He was quiet for several minutes before admitting there was at least some truth to what I was saying. He agreed to consider what I had said more deeply before our next meeting. That's one of the things I have always loved about Gabriel—he is always willing to reflect on himself and consider feedback I offer about his choices and behaviors. Finally, I had made a crack in his seemingly impenetrable certainty.

I heard from mutual friends that he had already become intimately involved with other women only weeks after he left, not even allowing space for us to complete our separation. Finding this out provoked a deep ache in my heart and a festering feeling of betrayal. It would have been so easy for me to become bitter, resentful, and cast him aside instead of fighting for him. Yet, God directed me to stand beside him and love him, no matter what happens.

So, I fought back feelings of rage and resisted the urge to push him out of my life. If I were to turn my heart from him, the enemy would win. I realized then, the wisdom in God's advice to love him. Love is the greatest weapon we have against darkness, for love conquers all things. I have since studied 1 Corinthians 13:4–7 (ESV) deeply, and in it, God reveals the true nature of love:

"Love is patient and kind; love does not envy or boast; it is not arrogant or rude. It does not insist on its own way; it is not irritable or resentful; it does not rejoice at wrongdoing but rejoices with the truth. Love bears all things, believes all things, hopes all things, endures all things."

It all became clear in that moment; God wanted me to love because God *is* love. By choosing love, we are choosing to express God within us. Love is the one thing we have that our enemy does not, making it a valuable asset in the battle against darkness. I also came across John 4:7–8 (ESV):

"Beloved, let us love one another, for love is from God, and whoever loves has been born of God and knows God. Anyone who does not love does not know God, because God is love."

I was convicted. I decided to fight even harder and with even more love. I began to pray unceasingly for Gabriel. I've never prayed for anything or anyone else in my entire life like I prayed for him during those months. In my ardent prayer sessions, I imagined myself in the courts of heaven incessantly petitioning the Lord and courts to intervene on his behalf. I envisioned myself standing boldly in the courts, a written appeal in hand, requesting the powers that be to save him from the dark entities that had captured his life.

The more I did this, the more the courts of heaven became familiar to my spirit, almost as if I could sense and get glimpses of it in the spiritual realm. Day after day, I visited what I believed to be the place of justice in the heavenly realms. When I arrived, I would declare Gabriel's name, shouting aloud his first, middle, last name, and birthdate.

Once his name had been spoken, I followed it with a detailed account of the injustice of the demons that were oppressing him, and how they were pretending to be God's voice. Next, I would list every single one of Gabriel's amazing qualities, being sure to emphasize why he is a good candidate for an intervention from God. My plea for his case sounded something like this: "Gabriel has a good heart, he is kind, he is obedient. He is loyal, and he has been wrongfully deceived into thinking he is serving God, and instead is being led by a demon's voice. He has a hunger and love for the Lord, even if he is confused about who God is. God, if you encounter him, surely, he will serve You and be a great asset to the Kingdom of Heaven!"

Countless times I protested the blasphemy of the evil spirits being allowed to shadow his perceptions and lead him toward destruction. I demanded justice on his behalf, pleading God to show him the truth. Some days I would stand in the courts, shouting his name into the realm of heaven over and over again, desperately hoping someone would notice and do something.

As the courts of heaven took on a familiar form after repeated visits, I started to discern faint impressions of other presences in that realm. When I encountered an angelic presence during a visit, I determinedly ran to them to present Gabriel's case, describing what was happening to him and how I needed help from the courts of heaven. I was stubborn and unyielding in my mission to help him, and willing to do whatever I could to assist in his freedom, even if it meant resorting to strange, desperate, and unconventional means.

At this point, it was no longer a matter of me saving my relationship with Gabriel; it was a matter of divine injustice being done to a great man who was held captive by malevolent spirits impersonating God. I attempted to tell Gabriel's parents and one of his friends what I believed to be happening, and lamentably they dismissed my supposedly wild story about Gabriel being commandeered by evil spirits.

The unsettling realization that I was the only one in the world who had seen the truth haunted me, and I knew if I didn't fight for him, no one would. I could not bear the thought of Gabriel living his entire life in an unrecognized bondage, so I persisted in my fight for him. I committed myself to loving him the way God loves him. Painstakingly, I endured, obedient to the instruction God had given to me, being relentlessly loving in the face of painful rejection.

Gabriel had a history of bipolar disorder and was hospitalized as a teenager for an episode he had. In the years following, he was heavily medicated. It wasn't until a few years ago that he was able to discontinue the medication. He functioned reasonably well without the meds, but I had known him to have frequent mood swings, sometimes drastically switching between highs and lows. Although this dynamic was challenging at times, he consistently maintained his kindness, even when he was struggling, and our family had learned to adapt to his mood instability.

Another significant source of strife, especially in our relationship, had been Gabriel's heart. Throughout most of our relationship, he struggled to keep his heart fully open to me. Often, he would enter into "numb" or dissociated states, displaying a noticeable absence of human emotion. As a deeply emotional and sensitive person myself, it proved difficult for me to endure the constant cyclical opening and closing of his heart towards me, and too often I took it personally.

When I began to learn about various malevolent spirits, such as spirits of fear, spirits of anxiety, and other spirits that can affect people, I became wondrously hopeful for Gabriel. Considering his myriad of manifestations at times, I realized that many of his mood swings could easily be due to demonic influence. When I observed his mood swings in the past, I noted distinct shifts in his composure and even shifts in his facial structure, at times appearing as if he had become a different person. Now that I had personally experienced how demonic influences can manifest physically, it made total sense that this may also be the case with Gabriel.

On one occasion, I told God that if He were to encounter Gabriel and save him, that it would obliterate any remaining doubts I harbored, that He is Lord. If this were to occur, it would be an unquestionable display of His power and authority, and certainly eradicate lingering questions in my mind. After fifty or more hours of radical prayers, pleas, and visitations to the courts, I received a vision.

In it, the Lord showed me Gabriel, completely restored by the power of God. I understood that if Gabriel were to accept Jesus, there was a promise of healing and deliverance over his life. I saw that the Holy Spirit would enter Gabriel and completely heal and restore both his mind and heart, just the way He had entered me and healed my most challenging issues.

Through my personal journey with deliverance, I learned God makes the promise of deliverance and healing to all who turn to Him. Jesus is the great Healer and Restorer. He has the power to heal all the places in us that have been broken. In Jeremiah 30:17 (ESV), the Lord tells us that the power of healing lies within Him.

"For I will restore health to you, and your wounds I will heal."

Undeniably, Gabriel needed to experience what I went through, and have his own individual process of being freed. He was caught in the web of deception, and the bite of the enemy was upon him, leading him down a path of destruction. Friends of mine had approached me, concerned about Gabriel, one even communicated a concern that he might be on drugs.

Could he actually be taking drugs? I wondered. He had always been so straight and careful because of how fragile his mind was. *How could he believe he was listening to the voice of God and then dabble in drugs and meaningless relations with women?* I thought, trying to sort through facts and make sense of it all. The two of us had waited eight months in our relationship before engaging in any physical intimacy, and now he was out being reckless?

One time, while praying for him, the Holy Spirit forewarned that the path he had chosen could lead to insanity or even death, because of an assignment of the enemy on his life. It sent a shiver down my spine. *Yikes, I* thought. But what was I to do about it? How was I going to help him encounter the Spirit of Truth, like I had?

The way I found God was face down on the floor, desperately crying to know the truth, even if it meant the end of my life as I knew it. Gabriel was not yet at that point. His pride and certainty kept him bound in deception. Gabriel needed humility, but it wasn't something I could just hand over to him, it had to come from within him. Knowing that all things are possible with God, I prayed for God to use me for Gabriel's salvation, promising to submit to His lead.

If only I could get Gabriel to church. The Spirit of God moved through my church in ways I had never seen anywhere else. Recently, when Gabriel had come by to get some of his things, we sat together on the sofa and shared a long, intimate conversation. I shared with him the potent experiences I had been having, and how the Holy Spirit encountered me. I recounted how God had revealed Himself in an earthquake as the God of the Bible and instructed me to follow the teachings of His Son, Yeshua. I even shared some details about my baptism and the manifestation of demons I had experienced.

Gabriel listened attentively and politely as I poured my heart out. When I was finished, he said, "I am so glad you told me all that."

"Really?" I asked.

"Yes," he replied, "it helps me know that I made the right decision with you. I could never go with you down the path you have chosen. I will never be a born-again Christian." The slim hope I had been clinging to for us to get back together quickly slipped out of reach the moment he said those words. I knew I needed a man of Christ to go where the Lord was calling me.

As disheartening as it felt for Gabriel to say what he said, I understood where he was coming from. I prefer to describe myself as a devout follower of Christ rather than a Christian,

217

considering some claim the word Christian stems from the Greek "Christiano," a derogatory term coined by 1st century Romans to taunt the original followers of Yeshua. Many people today have an aversion to the word Christian or Christianity, because of how intensely religion has distorted Yeshua's teachings at times.

However, I wasn't going to give up on helping Gabriel find freedom. I was determined. With a whole lot of grace from God, I was able to convince Gabriel to attend a church service. When he said yes, it was an absolute miracle, especially considering how close-minded and resistant he had been when finding out that I was now following Christ.

We made a plan for Gabriel to come over on the upcoming Friday evening to finalize matters in our separation, and afterwards to drive to the big church in Yuba City for Freedom Night. Knowing this could be my best opportunity to help Gabriel, I fasted and prayed the two days leading up to our scheduled time together.

On the day we met up, as I sat through the meeting intended to separate our lives, I held my tongue and gritted my teeth, still feeling like Gabriel was making the wrong decision. I knew Gabriel needed Jesus more than ever, and some part of me still hoped that with Christ, there might be a future for us. I steadied my focus on God and my heart, careful not to disrupt any part of a divine plan that could be unfolding.

On the drive down to Yuba City, our conversation somehow drifted into the causal relations he was exploring with other women. I expressed the deep hurt I felt that he wasn't giving time or space for our relationship to come to a close before involving himself with other people. I pointed out how out of character it was for him, him having waited months before we even shared our first kiss. When I inquired to God about this matter with Gabriel, He revealed that Gabriel was under the influence of a spirit of lust.

To make the situation even worse, Gabriel then disclosed he had been intimate with a friend of mine—someone I had been close to. I was horrified. This was a woman that I reached out to when Gabriel left, being vulnerable, opening up to her, only to find out three weeks after I told her, she then sought out Gabriel to declare her secret and deceitful passions towards him before we even finished separating.

The overwhelming feeling of betrayal crept in, taunting me. I feared losing control, my boiling emotional reaction threatening my commitment to be loving. I wanted to turn around and drop him off, pushing him out of my life forever. I was so angry and hurt. But that's not what love would do, nor what I thought God would do. I drew in some deep breaths, reaching for God's wisdom and grace. As soon as my spirit unified with God, I recognized the situation for what it was—a low blow from the enemy.

The enemy knew exactly how to tempt me towards anger, even hatred. When I recognized it was just a tactic of the principalities to disrupt what had been set in motion, I was able to overcome the overwhelming temptation towards anger and resentfulness. I could not let bitterness poison my heart, not at a moment like this, when Gabriel finally agreed to come to the church. I would not allow my enemy to win by using division.

It wasn't even a matter of me and Gabriel anymore; this was about something much bigger. I was at war, and I would not step down from my battle ground, no matter what happened. Every move had to be precise and guided by God's lead.

Fortunately, we arrived at church—our arrival breaking up the tense moment. Relief washed over me as we entered the church. Instantly, I was comforted by the distinct, noticeable presence of God. The evening began with worship music, heart-felt melodies saturated the atmosphere in increasing holiness. I seized the opportunity to lay my burden on the altar and rid myself of the dark emotions stirred by discovering the betrayal of Gabriel and my supposed friend.

I surrendered myself into God's arms, desperately pleading with Him in my mind. God, I brought Gabriel here under your roof, now it's your move. This is your moment to do what only you can do, God. He is in your house Lord, show him your magnificence! I am counting on You. I have done everything I can. I have done everything You asked me to do. I have fought and prayed, even frequented the courts of heaven. His life is now in your hands, I am letting go. Do what You do best. He's here on Your doorstep Lord, bring him home.

For the entirety of the service that night, I prayed silently in intense intercession for Gabriel. For that reason, I don't recall much of what was said. What I do know, is that Freedom Night is about just that: freedom. Gabriel needed freedom, and all the rest was up to God.

At the close of the service, they did an altar call. I urged Gabriel to come and get prayer with me. By the look on his face, I sensed the shame around what he had done had started to sink in. He was noticeably afflicted, his facial expression tense and shoulders slouched.

He refused prayer. I didn't want to accept no for an answer. I had convinced myself that if only someone were to lay hands on him, the power of God would pass through and stir him to redemption. I tried another angle, "Will you go up there with me to pray about our relationship?" I asked.

Again, he refused, so I turned my back, took in a shaky breath, and began a slow walk to the front. I held back tears, my soul crying out to God for Gabriel's salvation. *Do something! Please God, don't let this opportunity slip away,* I pleaded to God. Just before I got to the front, Gabriel called out to me, so I walked back to where he was sitting.

He said to me, "Okay. I will pray for the ending of our relationship." That statement struck my heart like a dagger, only then realizing some part of me still hoped that he would be saved, and our family restored. I didn't want to agree to what Gabriel had offered, a prayer for us to break up, but I did want to get him out of his chair and into the hands of the pastors. Being desperate for his freedom, I agreed to his terms for the prayer, even if in my heart I didn't want to say a prayer to end our relationship.

God, take spiritual authority over this situation, I said silently in my mind. *Use this opportunity, Lord, to do not my will, not Gabriel's will, but Your will.*

We went up to the altar, and the wife of the worship leader approached us. When she asked us what we would like prayer for, Gabriel said, "I want to pray to end our relationship."

Then I quickly added, "He wants to pray for that, but I want to pray for him."

She looked at him, and the Holy Spirit started to speak through her. I don't recall the exact words, but I do remember that she called out the affliction in Gabriel's heart, saying that God wants to heal his heart. As she prayed, she mentioned personal details about Gabriel that only God would know.

When we discussed the events of the evening some weeks thereafter, Gabriel said that he thought I had spoken to the worship leader and told her things about his life. He was surprised to find out that I had not disclosed any information, confirming that what she said was indeed prophetic words from God. As she finished praying, she ended by telling Gabriel that Jesus is the only way to the Father, and to God Almighty. Upon hearing this, Gabriel immediately challenged her on her declaration, refusing to accept that Jesus is the only way to God.

The worship pastor's wife didn't back down and shared some of her background being raised in India. "I worshiped many gods and deities growing up, but none of them are like Jesus," she said to Gabriel. I could see her words were falling on deaf ears. After some time, we returned to our seats.

A heavy discouragement surrounded me as we sat down. I noticed my concealed expectation for a visible miracle to have happened to Gabriel when he received prayer that day. I wanted a confirmation, similar to when the Holy Spirit knocked me to the floor and transported me to heaven. I could no longer fight back the sinking feeling of defeat when I didn't immediately witness an observable manifestation of God. Alas, my hope for a grand display of miraculous, supernatural power had been greatly disappointed.

Hopelessness burdened me as we headed to the car. On the ride home, Gabriel and I got sucked into a heated argument, a rare occurrence for us. In the years we have known each other, when in conflict, we have made a point of maintaining honor for one another, being mindful to preserve our respect and kindness. I found it unsettling that our words had become sharp, exposing a deterioration of respect for each other.

222

I felt let down by God, and I was beginning to lose my cool. I had done everything God told me to do, but I wasn't seeing the results I wanted. I had fought to get Gabriel to come to church; I had fasted and prayed; I had stood unwaveringly in love, even when so much of me wanted to cry out in anger. Now, we were leaving the church, seemingly empty-handed, with Gabriel still under the influence of dark forces. I could feel my heart turning away from God. I could no longer fight back the descending cloud of hopelessness.

Our conversation became increasingly tense, reaching a devastating peak in conflict where we both decided we didn't want the other in our lives anymore. That was the first time we ever said anything of that nature, as we had always desired to remain friends so that my son would be able to maintain his relationship with Gabriel.

The wicked claw of bitterness clasped over my heart, as I clenched my jaw to choke back tears. The situation was spinning out of control. I had given up hope and faith; I had stopped being the love of God. I was failing. I attempted to regain control of the situation by returning to a state of peace, love, and strength in the Lord, but I was slipping dangerously into anger and rage.

In a last-ditch effort of determination and wisdom, I put on some worship music and turned myself back towards God. *I can't let the enemy win,* I thought to myself. *I can't let the enemy win!* I screamed into the silence of my mind; *God is the victor! Righteousness reigns. I will be the love of God. Jesus is the great Deliverer. He will make a way, even when it seems like there is no way.*

By the time we pulled into the driveway, the atmosphere in the car had shifted noticeably. I again felt the presence of the Lord. I pleaded with God to give me the right words to get through to Gabriel. I needed God's grace to overcome the division that had been stirred by the enemy.

God responded to my plea, providing me with the boldness and wisdom I needed. With my newfound confidence, I calmly and firmly said to Gabriel, "You are the biggest fraud I know." I didn't say it with contempt; I said it with love, which made the statement all the more potent and curious.

"What do you mean?" he exclaimed. Those were the words that God had influenced me to say. I waited to respond. I wanted to see what the Lord would say through me. I completely surrendered to His will, knowing that God knew the way to get through to Gabriel.

I steadied myself in the silence of my pause, then continued, leaning on God for the right words, "You pretend to be humble; you pretend to care about others, but every decision I've seen you make, has been a decision that only considers yourself. You have not once considered me or my son since you left or shown any amount of compassion to the difficulty we faced when you left us behind. Everything you are doing and saying right now demonstrates that you are living in a world of self-glorification and pride. You pretend to follow the voice of God, but I tell you that it is a voice of self. God is love. Nothing about what you have done is love. You blindly worship an idol of self and the god of your mind, not realizing you have yet to encounter the true Lord."

There, I said it. I got it out. Thanks to the Holy Spirit infusing my words with great power and presence, I could feel the impact of what was said landing like a pile of bricks hitting concrete. When what I said hit Gabriel, he began weeping. He knew, and I knew that there was great truth to what I had said. With his façade shattering, he now had the humility to hear the message I had been trying to get through to him. God's words through me shook his world, creating a crack in the matrix of lies he was living in.

Being aware of what was beginning to unfold, I began to pray over Gabriel in tongues, pleading to God to encounter him in this rare moment of vulnerability. Only in humility can the truth of God penetrate the greatest of delusions. As my prayers saturated the atmosphere, God's presence filled the car, a radiant glow appearing around Gabriel.

God was definitely up to something. When God's presence arrived on the scene, I went with it. I began to rebuke all unclean, unholy spirits, calling them out of Gabriel. Then God spoke through me and declared, "The Kingdom of Heaven has come upon you." All of a sudden, deliverance broke out! Gabriel began to physically manifest different demons, his head shaking back and forth, crying out as if in pain.

Having just endured intense deliverance myself, then spending countless hours studying deliverance books and videos, I knew exactly what I needed to do. I was finally ready to face the demons that had hijacked Gabriel and were leading him down a path of destruction. At last, the moment I had been waiting for!

"In the name of Jesus, I command all unclean unholy spirits up and out of Gabriel. I plead the blood of Jesus over him from head to toe," I said with authority. As I ordered the entities to leave, his body writhed in response, twisting, and whipping about. The battle was on! I was determined to take them out one by one, the drive for vengeance of demons fresh on my hands.

In the midst of action, an overwhelming sense of gratitude for God's presence overtook me. I immediately felt foolish for allowing myself to become disappointed on the car ride and losing faith in His plan and timing. I apologized to God for my lack of faith, giving praise to Him for using me to evict the demons out of Gabriel.

After engaging in fierce spiritual warfare in the car in my driveway for some time, I asked Gabriel if he wanted to come inside to be more comfortable. I knew from personal experience how intense it was to discover dark presences inside my bodily vessel. Once inside our home, I continued to command the spirits out of him, in the name of Jesus. His physical manifestations persisted, his body being tossed about like a rag doll, much like the wild scene of my own deliverance.

The demons openly displayed their objections to leaving Gabriel's body, sometimes growling, yelling, and making Gabriel's body thrash around. The whole scene was surreal, as if time was sped up and slowed down at different moments. I surrendered myself to God, allowing the Holy Spirit to teach me how to cast out demons, just like Jesus did.

Seeing Gabriel's struggle, I remembered how we can unknowingly give demons rights to inhabit our body, giving them permission to remain. Considering this, I said, "Gabriel, you need to repent to God for your sins and renounce the activities in your life that are outside of God's laws and principles. Without repentance and renouncing, the doors remain open to these demonic influences."

He received what I said with openness, a fresh humility detectable in his demeanor. There's nothing quite like having one's body thrown around by demonic forces to get motivated in submitting to God's will for your life. With the Holy Spirit directing me, I helped lead Gabriel in a repentance process. He repented for sexual immorality, pride, selfishness, lust, and a slew of other unholy things. It was beautiful to witness his soul being cleansed, his tears of remorse loosening the hold of bondage. Following this process of repentance, we managed to make more progress in persuading some of the demonic spirits to depart from his body.

Being so engrossed in Gabriel's deliverance, we were surprised to realize it was 1 a.m. Upon discovering the hour, we decided to call it quits for the night. A lot had transpired!

We hadn't finished settling our entangled affairs during our meeting earlier that evening, so he agreed to return the next day to complete what needed to be done. Before he left, I warned him, "Since you have not yet accepted Christ as your Lord and Savior, there is a chance that the dark presences could come back stronger. Jesus has dominion over all heaven and Earth, and it is His name and authority that shake demons out of our flesh. Once they are gone, it is important to fill the void with the light, love, and presence of the Holy Spirit." I told him to call me if he fell under spiritual attack, assuring him that I would pray with him at any hour.

When he left, I fell to my knees praising God. Though Gabriel was not yet free, we had made a crack in the matrix of lies he was bound by. God had shown up, given me the right words to say, and fought hand in hand with me in a spiritual battle against the demons that had been oppressing Gabriel. God became a lot bigger to me that night. As I lay down to rest that early morning, an outpouring of love and appreciation towards the Lord surged from my heart.

16

The Glory of God

The next day, I heard a knock at the door. When I answered the door, there stood Gabriel on my doorstep, a bouquet of flowers in hand, an unspoken apology. I opened the door gently and our eyes met, our souls touching in a silent and humble embrace. We walked to the dining room table, with the intention of sitting and discussing our affairs.

We stared at each other in silence for some time, the air thick with many unspoken words. After a while, he said, "I would like to request some time to consider before proceeding with our separation."

"Okay," I said. This was certainly a big shift, and I didn't want to make any decisions without God's guidance, so I said, "Would you like to pray with me?"

"Yes," he agreed timidly.

As I began to pray, the room filled with an all-consuming presence of the Lord, my skin suddenly covered in goosebumps. I was deeply comforted by His presence, my heart leaping for joy knowing that God's embrace was there that day to enfold us. Sensing an electrical charge course through my body, I gently laid my hand on Gabriel's shoulder. As I placed my hand there and continued to pray, I felt a surge of power transfer into Gabriel. It reminded me of Luke 8:46 (NIV), when Jesus said:

"Someone touched me; I know that power has gone out from me."

I knew that the power of God had just passed into Gabriel.

The Holy Spirit took control of the situation, speaking through me to Gabriel, and said, "Close your eyes and picture two roads before you, one that leads to a path with God, and the other path being the path that you chose the day you left. Now, turn your attention towards the road that you chose when you left." As I said those words, I had the insight that the presence of God that had transferred into Gabriel would provide him supernatural sight and revelation about the crossroads he was facing.

Then I said, "Holy Spirit, reveal to Gabriel where this path leads. Pull back the veil and show him what is behind his motivation and choices." After a moment, Gabriel's face grimaced and his body began trembling. I continued, following God's lead, "Now, Holy Spirit, take him further down that path and show him where it leads."

After a moment, Gabriel began shouting, "No! No! No!" while flailing his hands wildly in the air.

At a different time, when I asked him what he had seen, he likened what he saw to the Eye of Sauron from the *Lord of the Rings* movie, an all-consuming darkness and hellish place. He said that in that moment, he witnessed that all the choices he had been making from pride, selfishness, and arrogance led to a dark doorway. At the very center of all the darkness was a giant demon of "self," the very pinnacle of hell. He was also shown that if he were to continue on that path that it would lead to either insanity, death, or both.

He began sobbing, his head shaking back and forth, still muttering, "No, no, no..." I could sense that Gabriel was seeing the truth for the first time since he left.

Then the Holy Spirit gave me a cue, and I said, "Okay, now focus on the path that leads to God, a path with me and a path with Christ."

His eyes were still closed. He wiped his face and sat up. His demeanor instantly changed. A slight smile lifted the corners of his mouth. I saw a light wash over his face, illuminating a look of awe and completely transforming his composure. Then I said, "Holy Spirit, take him further, show him where this other path will lead him."

He drew his hands together over his heart, tears streaming from his eyes…this time in joy. Light filled the room, and there was a noticeable shift in the atmosphere as he focused on where the path of Christ would lead him. Curious, I asked him what he saw. He said, "I see us together, married, and a child… I see myself serving others, living a life helping others instead of only serving myself. I see myself in happiness, joy, and fulfillment."

I was in awe of the way God was touching Gabriel's spirit. The supernatural insight that he was receiving was exactly what God had been revealing to me. What Gabriel didn't know at that moment, was that a week ago, God had granted me the same vision, of Gabriel and I married with a child. I was surprised to see a child, as I had long passed the moment I would have considered birthing another child, and Gabriel had always been opposed to having one.

When Gabriel was shown the same vision, I took it as a confirmation that God was guiding us to be together. Although I wasn't fully onboard with having another child at that time, I would gladly do it, knowing it was God's will. We sat in silence for some time, Gabriel processing the visions that God had given him, and me fervently praising the Lord for the good works He was beginning in Gabriel. Then I heard God say, "I am not done yet, there is more."

When I opened my eyes to look at Gabriel, I saw a sorrowful look on his face, and sensed the remorse he was feeling for what he had done. When he left, he thought he was done with the relationship for good, never imagining a future with me as his wife. Now, faced with the reality of God's plan for his life, I could see that he was laden with shame and guilt.

I invited him to the living room floor, with the intention of enlisting God's help in healing his shame and sadness. I knelt beside him, prayed in tongues, and asked the Holy Spirit to help me. Again, I led Gabriel in a repentance process, explaining how the blood of Jesus washes away our sin and transgressions. As he was kneeling face down on the ground, a magnificent angel suddenly appeared standing beside Gabriel's head.

I had at times seen or sensed various angelic presences, but this angel was different, of high rank, his appearance saturating the atmosphere with a distinct aura of holiness. I looked towards him respectfully, in my mind asking, *Why are you here?*

The angel responded back saying, "I am here to give Gabriel the gift of speaking in tongues."

Oh, how wonderful! I thought. I placed my hand gently on Gabriel's shoulder, and said, "Uhhh, Gabriel. There is this big and powerful angel here for you. He said he's here to give you the gift of speaking in tongues."

Gabriel was still face down on the floor, deep in his emotion-filled repentance. He turned his head to the side and mumbled, "Okay…" in a shaky voice.

The angel instructed me to place my hand on the back of Gabriel's neck, and that he would release the gift of tongues through my hand. I passed on the message to Gabriel, saying, "Ok, Gabriel, the angel said for me to place my hand on the back of your neck, and when I do, try to start speaking in tongues with me." What happened next shocked me!

As soon as my hand struck the back of his neck, his mouth erupted with a loud, Germanic tongue. To my surprise, he was speaking in a thick, heavy accent. I had known Gabriel for years, and never had I heard any such sounds leave his lips. It was extraordinary! I had seen others receive their prayer language, and they started speaking their tongues shyly and softly; Gabriel was shouting in his newfound tongues with an incredible boldness and stature, the heavenly tongues echoing through our house.

There was such a power and presence in his prayer language, that as his tongues saturated the atmosphere, a great glory filled the room. Suddenly, a strong persistent tongue also burst forth from my mouth, in unison with his. Instantly, I was inexplicably compelled to start marching around the room, glorifying God, praising Him in rapid fire tongues.

Thanks to the intensity of the presence of God in the room, there were several moments in which I had a supernatural ability to understand the tongues that both Gabriel and I were speaking. That evening was the first time that I could actually interpret and understand what was being said. What was being spoken in tongues were expressions of passionate adoration to the Lord, proclaiming His greatness, power, and splendor. Our declarations of the goodness of God resounded throughout our home as we praised and worshiped His mighty omnipresence. I pressed in, prayed harder, praised louder, asking God to show us the fullness of His glory—for Him to reveal Himself to us.

I found myself strangely and wildly leaping for joy, stomping my feet, completely enraptured by the presence of

God. I became intoxicated by God's presence and felt the urge to laugh and cry in the same moment. I teetered about in my divine, drunken stupor while my mouth rattled on in new and strange tongues. Although the ability to understand the tongues came and went, I understood the overall message that streamed uncontrollably from my mouth to be a proclamation of the goodness of God.

I glanced over at Gabriel, and he too was yelling and singing in tongues while tromping around the room. Apparently, the presence of God in our living room was having the same effect on him! When our eyes met, we laughed hysterically. What a strange scene it was, us frolicking around, intoxicated, and elated by the touch of God. It was a full-on Holy Spirit takeover, and at certain moments, I even heard faint music and horns sounding from the celestial realm.

Suddenly, an intense shock struck my body and Gabriel's body at the same time, throwing us both to the floor. I barely had any time to think about what was happening, I felt so out of control. Then, it felt as if someone was on top of me, a heavy blanket of glory weighing on my body. As I was pressed into the ground by the invisible glory, I was propelled into intense repentance, with past sin being highlighted by the overwhelming presence of God. Many things I had done, I had long forgotten, and suddenly, the memories and secrets of my past poor decisions emerged all at once.

Being faced with such an onslaught of my past negative actions, I began shaking and weeping, asking for forgiveness, vowing to be a better person. I could hear Gabriel's sobs and cries as he lay on the floor beside me, also begging God for mercy and forgiveness. Nothing inside of us could escape the all-permeating presence and all-seeing eyes of God. Being fully seen by God is unlike any other experience because God knows everything about us and can see into every hidden chamber of our souls. In the company of such holiness, everything that is unholy is unavoidably unveiled, all darkness exposed in the all-penetrating light of God.

When I was lying face down on the floor, it felt as if the Spirit of God was scanning through every part of me, searching my heart and mind. As God's touch reached places of my body burdened with chronic illness and pain, I could feel an uprooting of remnants that had been the source of suffering for so many years. This great cleansing and sanctification from God, tilled the soil of my soul's garden, making room for new seeds of righteousness to be sown.

Gabriel and I continued to get rocked by the omnipotent power of the Lord. After a period of intense repentance, our cries abruptly and simultaneously shifted to sudden and uncontrollable laughter. In that same moment, we both sprung abruptly to our feet, my body now feeling light as a feather. We joyfully paraded around the room, once more speaking in tongues, overwhelmed by a delightful ecstasy that can only be experienced in the presence of the Lord.

It was a peculiar sight, both of us being engulfed in God's glory. The manner in which the overwhelming presence of God orchestrated a shared, supernatural encounter between Gabriel and I, was utterly fascinating. I had no previous point of reference for the unfolding events and had never before found myself in the midst of such an unusual display of spiritual power. I marveled at the flawless synchronization of the moments when Gabriel and I rose and fell together under God's influence—an exquisite display of God's eminence.

During the subsequent two hours, a continuous outpouring of the Spirit enveloped us as we cycled through moments of repentance and remorse, followed by elation, joy, and ecstatic celebration of the Lord. At times, we were both yelling and singing in uncontrollable tongues, then without warning, simultaneous jolts would then strike us both to the ground at the same time. It was an experience of both exquisite beauty and fearful awe to be so affected by God's mighty presence.

After we had risen and fallen several times, we rose again, this time not merely speaking in tongues, but singing a song in our distinct prayer languages. Incredibly, our singing harmonized into the same melody. It was at that moment I recognized we were singing the same song, each in our own unique tongues! The song carried a profound aura of sacredness. As our voices joined in harmony, I saw in the spirit realm the enormous, ancient, etheric gates of heaven begin to open to us.

I recognized the song we were singing under the influence of the Lord's presence as a celestial melody sung in the heavens themselves. It seemed familiar, as if from a distant dream. I felt the presence of angelic beings surrounding us and noticed heavenly creatures beyond the gates. It was a grand celebration, and everyone was singing and dancing. It was truly a miraculous moment, made even more remarkable by the fact Gabriel had only received his prayer language just minutes before; now we found ourselves singing a heavenly hymn in unison, completely overtaken, and surrendered to the Holy Spirit.

While some unseen magnificent force held the gateway to the glory realm open, I received a vision and succession of revelations. In my vision, I saw both Gabriel and I engaged in ministry, traveling, and standing before vast crowds of people. I beheld entire crowds of people getting jolted by the same electrifying surge of God's power that had descended upon us that very evening. When the power of God came down, the entire multitude, which consisted of hundreds or perhaps thousands of people, would fall to their knees. This part of my vision was shown repeatedly, where I saw similarly large crowds of people in different locations falling under the power of God. Each time the power brought people to the ground, I heard the voice of God say, "Every knee will bow!"

When I heard this, Philippians 2:10–11 (KJV) came to mind:

"...so that at the name of Jesus every knee should bow, in heaven and on earth and under the earth, and every tongue acknowledge that Jesus Christ is Lord, to the glory of God the Father."

Another bolt of power pulled us down from that glorious moment onto our knees. When the power of God hit Gabriel, some of the demons that had been oppressing him began to manifest. In that moment of deep union with God, I received supernatural sight and awareness of the demons on and around his body. A surge of energy rushed into my hands, causing my fingertips to tingle with an electric sensation. When I looked down at my fingers, I understood what to do. Job 36:32 (ESV) states:

"He covers his hands with the lightning and commands it to strike the mark."

I pressed my index and middle fingers onto the areas of Gabriel's body that the Holy Spirit had unveiled hidden demonic entities. When my fingers touched his body, the demons residing in him squealed! Gabriel's head thrashed back and forth helplessly, the dark spirits within him writhing under the glory of God. I was astonished; God had turned my fingers into a demon taser!

When this "God power electricity" passed into Gabriel, his entire body shook, expelling the hidden demonic presences. A few of them manifested in bizarre and grotesque form, the whole scene surreal and fantastical. Amidst all the craze unfolding, I pondered how my life seemed to have suddenly transformed into a scene from a sci-fi thriller. After many of the unwanted presences were chased away by the "demon taser," a malevolent spirit stubbornly remained.

I prayed to God, asking what to do about it. In the realm of the spirit, I saw a sword being lowered down to me from heaven. My mouth began to rapidly speak in tongues, then out of nowhere a supernatural voice of divine authority spoke through me, cackling then saying, "You filthy leviathan. You are finished!" Without conscious thought, my hand reached out and seized the ethereal sword that had appeared from heaven, and the voice speaking through me declared, "Leviathan, I take the sword of the heavenly realm and strike you with the wrath of God!"

As I sank this "Spirit sword" into Gabriel, the demon fully manifested in Gabriel's flesh, thrashing his arms and head around, squealing at top volume. I continued to stab it with the invisible Spirit sword, but still it refused to leave Gabriel's body, putting up a frenzied fight. In my mind's eye, I then saw a fiery arrow descending from heaven. Instinctively, I reached up to grab it and held it just above Gabriel's body.

"Leave or die, by the wrath and glory of Yahweh!" I cried out. When it didn't leave, I plunged the etheric fiery arrow into Gabriel and instantly stopped manifesting the demon. It was over; the wretched thing was finally gone. Subsequently, when I asked Gabriel about his experience, Gabriel said that when the heavenly arrow pierced through him, he felt as though the surrounding darkness shattered into fragments and exited through the top of his head.

238

After a moment of stillness, I felt an overwhelming presence of the Holy Spirit once more. God spoke through me to Gabriel, declaring, "The white dove descends! The Lord Himself stands before you." A flash of light burst forth, and I bowed my head to the floor. I could then distinctively feel and perceive, in my inner vision, the feet of Jesus, standing beside Gabriel's head.

I later found out from Gabriel, that even before I made the declaration of Jesus's arrival, Gabriel had already felt Jesus's hand on his shoulder. When Gabriel was a teenager, he had a severe psychotic break that landed him in a mental institution for a period of time. I could sense that Yeshua had come to minster to the mind fracture that had happened during Gabriel's youth.

Prophetic words continued to flow out my mouth as the Lord spoke through me, "You are going to receive your anointing, God is going to heal your mind. He is stitching jewels, rubies, and diamonds into your brain. They are not for right now. The Lord says, 'Seek Me and bow in humility, and your treasure will unlock. The more you seek Me, the more treasure you will receive. It is not a treasure for you, it is a treasure for my people. Only in sincere humility can this gift be accessed.'"

In the spirit realm, gems represent spiritual giftings to me. I interpreted the jewels that Jesus brought as an impartation of a gift that would be more fully revealed as Gabriel grows in humility and his walk with Christ. Then it was said through my voice, "The white dove ascends!" At the utterance of that declaration, both of our bodies jolted and shuddered, and once again I heard heavenly music and horns sounding from a higher realm. In the spirit, I saw the back of Jesus with a white dove on His shoulder, walking into an opening of light—a portal to heaven.

The air was thick with His omnipresence, and we lay stunned on the floor in silence. The sacredness of that moment resounded through the stillness, the echo of glory still reverberating in our spirits. Our bodies lay motionless for a long time, full of awe and wonder as waves of bliss washed over us in the aftermath of what had just transpired.

All of a sudden, Gabriel stood up and gazed into my eyes. He slowly lowered one knee to the ground, taking my hand delicately in his. "I don't have a ring," he said, "but this moment is too precious to delay any longer." His eyes seemed to glisten with tears that had not yet fallen, and his body was still trembling from events that had just transpired.

"Will you marry me and spend the rest of your life with me as my wife?" I hesitated, letting the anticipation linger and allowing time to ensure it was within God's will.

After I was certain, I looked Gabriel in the eyes and said, "Yes. I want to spend my life with you and the Lord." We sat there taking in the fullness of the moment, gazing deeply and lovingly into each other's tear-filled eyes. We were both still shaky from all the thrills God had bestowed upon us that evening.

From deep within that sacred moment, I felt God guide me to ask Gabriel to join me in communion. "Would you like to take communion with me and seal our new vow with each other in a sacred covenant with the Lord?

"Yes," he agreed joyfully. We gathered together some cups, juice, and bread, and sat next to each other before my prayer altar. We took our communion together that night for the first time, making a promise to enter into marriage not only with each other, but more importantly, to enter a marriage together with God. John 11:40 (KJV) says:

"Did I not tell you that if you believed you would see the glory of God?"

I believed. God's convincing appearance in my life established within me, great faith. Through my persistent prayers, I petitioned God to touch Gabriel with His supernatural power. At times, I had envisioned God's electric power passing through me into Gabriel, much like the day when I first fell under God's power and decided to take the hand of Jesus.

God had not only brought Gabriel to salvation but had also restored my family. God is truly amazing! There are no limits to what is possible with God. Philippians 4:19 (NKJV) states:

"But Jesus looked at them and said to them, 'With men this is impossible, but with God all things are possible.'"

God, and faith in God, is what makes the seemingly impossible, possible. Ephesians 2:8–9 (ESV) says:

"For by grace you have been saved through faith. And this is not your own doing; it is the gift of God, not a result of works, so that no one may boast."

A profound sense of admiration and gratitude swelled within my heart. After that majestic night, my humility and reverence towards the Lord increased substantially, as did my steadfast allegiance to serve God. Though the trials were bitter, the reward of my restored family and a life with God made the strife worth the struggle. Hebrews 11:6 (NIV) says:

"And without faith it is impossible to please him, for whoever would draw near to God must believe that he exists and that he rewards those who seek him."

Thankfully, my humility and faith to seek Him and His rewards made the seemingly impossible, possible.

God Himself came to my rescue, bringing irrefutable evidence that he is Lord of the heavens and all the Earth. He left no room in my mind for doubt, shattering the very framework and interpretation of the reality I had clung to. The profound experiences I had stretched my understanding far beyond the bounds of what I thought to be possible, birthing an entirely new direction for my life.

Psalm 97:4 (NIV) says:

"His lightning lights up the world; the earth sees and trembles."

The Lord had unquestionably revealed Himself in the most potent manifestation of power I had ever witnessed or been a part of. In our encounter, we both trembled in fear and awe of His presence. His bolts of lightning struck our bodies to the floor, annihilating hidden temptations towards self-glory, placing God in His rightful place above us.

There is no greater fulfillment than basking in the profound peace and all-permeating presence of holiness found only in the Lord. So sacred is He who created this world, and He loves us all so deeply. He wants nothing more than the children of God to turn to Him, to trust Him, and love Him. Even if you are a seasoned believer and already said yes to Him, there are even deeper and more profound levels of loving God, surrendering to His will, and faithfully choosing His path each and every day.

◊ ◊ ◊

God will test our hearts and faith. Jeremiah 17:10 (ESV) says:

"I, the Lord, search the heart and test the mind, to give every man according to his ways, according to the fruit of his deeds."

In the encounter with God that Gabriel and I shared, the Lord meticulously examined my heart and mind, purging away all that was impure and unholy.

Gabriel was my first test of faith; facing that trial while staying faithful to my commitment to God to be love, strengthened, and fortified my spirit. James 1:3 (ESV) states:

"...for you know that the testing of your faith produces steadfastness."

In our greatest challenges, we are refined, and how we face them is a testament to our faith. Job 23:10 (ESV) says:

"But he knows the way that I take; when he has tried me, I shall come out as gold."

Like rough stones in rivers, we are polished in the tough trials of our lives, God's holy waters refining us along the way. If I hadn't experienced the agony of Gabriel leaving, I may have never experienced the glory of God.

Not long after Gabriel accepted Jesus, the Lord came to test his heart and faith. It was a week before our wedding day. I awoke one morning to discover dark presences seriously afflicting Gabriel. Remembering the many-months-long battle I myself had endured, I imagined Gabriel still had quite a battle ahead.

I was not surprised at all that the enemy was showing up to oppress Gabriel. The force of darkness we were escaping from would do anything to prevent us from sealing our union with a marriage to each other and the Holy Spirit. Having acquired the knowledge of my rights and authority in Christ, I was prepared to stand and fight for the freedom that is rightfully ours. Jesus paid the price for redemption on the Cross of Calvary, and I would stand firm until we defeated every one of those demons.

As he kneeled in prayer beside our bed, I could see the shadow of a dark entity covering him. I peered at him in the early morning light, noticing his face was grimaced with fear and unease. I bowed my head in prayer, and the Holy Spirit revealed to me what was causing his affliction.

God spoke through me in a prophetic voice, naming each hovering spirit that surrounded Gabriel. "Spirit of rebellion. Spirit of pride. Spirit of fear…" I placed my hand on him, casting out each demon by name. As I commanded them out, Gabriel's physical body exhibited their resistance to leaving.

I knew God had touched Gabriel when he burst into tongues, followed by an outpouring of repentance. "I repent for all the ways I have been prideful; for how I have caused hurt to others with my pride. I renounce my prideful ways. I repent for rebelling against You. I submit to Your will," Gabriel prayed aloud, his body trembling. I love watching the way God moves in His people; how He brings light to darkness. I love how He mends, restores, and washes away transgressions, providing wisdom on how to live a righteous life.

Festering, unconfessed sin can be a stronghold for the enemy. The presence of God so naturally moved Gabriel to be able to see the ways he was living out of alignment with His laws and principles. In doing so, God eradicated rights that demons had to Gabriel through pride, rebellion, and fear. When we come into agreement with things that are not of God, such as pride, it is an open door for spirits to torment us.

As I was observing, one of the entities manifested like a gremlin, wildly shaking Gabriel's head and shrieking. *Ugh, I hate these things*, I lamented. *Why can't I just have a normal, peaceful morning with my soon to be husband?* A different entity manifested like a snake, and when I commanded, "Unwind!" Gabriel's body gyrated in semi-circles. Despite the progress we were making in pushing the tormentors away, I saw there was still an evil presence hovering over his back.

I prayed, asking God for help, then received a vision from the Holy Spirit of an AED, the medical instrument used to shock someone when their heart stops. *How interesting*, I thought to myself. God then directed me to place my two hands on Gabriel's scapulas. Obediently, I climbed up on a chair behind him and hovered my hands over his upper back and shoulders, waiting for God to instruct me on what exactly I was supposed to do.

As I continued to practice in the ministry of deliverance, I learned that this location on the shoulder blades is a common area for evil spirits to attach. The heart is the gateway to God, and demons attempt to interfere with our connection to God by obstructing the entrance to our hearts. When I worked in the healing arts for many years, I would say three out four people had chronic pain between their shoulder blades; now I know where their mysterious pain was likely originating from.

As I stood on the chair behind Gabriel, I noticed a potent surge of God's power hit me, and I planted my fisted hands with a thud on Gabriel's back. Gabriel's whole body bounced back in shock, and the spirit that had been manifesting through him immediately flew out. "Wow!" I exclaimed, genuinely surprised.

I delighted in the magnificence and absurdity of the way God moved to help us that morning. I raised my praise to God, feeling sincerely grateful for the assistance in chasing away Gabriel's oppressor. I marveled at the creativity and wondrous display of His authority. I already believe God is so powerful, so wonderful, and yet I recognize there's so much for me to learn and mature in to fully understand God without limits. Our human minds and the illusions of this world put many limits on what God can do.

Once the room and Gabriel had been cleansed of the dark influences, we both sensed the presence of God fill and illuminate the space. It was as if a heavenly sun had cast its radiant light upon us, evoking more praise, and song in our prayer languages. After some time, Gabriel and I fell into a deep silence. I became aware of a holy presence in the room and saw in the realm of the spirit that once more an angel stood at Gabriel's side.

As my attention went to the angel, he told me he had a message for Gabriel from God. I told Gabriel and then waited patiently to see what the angel would say. The angel then released God's message to Gabriel through me, saying, "Will you serve Me? Or will you serve yourself? Will you drink from the well of My holy waters? Or will you drink of the poisons of this world? Will you surrender and submit your life to Me or be held captive by My enemy?"

There was a moment of stillness, as the message sank in. Gabriel responded, "Yes, yes, Lord, I submit to You. Yes, I give my life to You."

The angel replied, "But will you submit not with your words, but with your spirit?" When the angel said this, I sensed an even deeper surrender in Gabriel's spirit; his body posture relaxed, and he lowered himself closer to the ground.

Through Holy Spirit-led awareness, I sensed the places in which Gabriel had been holding and clinging onto his old ways begin to loosen. In that moment, I witnessed Gabriel surrender to God in a manner he had not yet done.

Then the angel said, "Will you surrender your mind? The Lord wants to use you as a messenger of truth, but you must let go of everything you think you already know." Upon hearing that, I sensed a struggle in Gabriel against his mind.

After some time, Gabriel said, "Yes, I will surrender, even my mind."

When I looked up, the angel unexpectedly held a sword in his hand, and he said, "This sword is a representation of the Word, the truth of God." The angel then gently touched Gabriel's head with the sword.

After a moment of waiting, there came an influx of divine energy. Now the angel was holding a key in his hand and said, "I give to you this key as a representation of salvation through surrender; and finally, I place upon your chest the breastplate of righteousness, that you may live henceforth unto the goodness of God." The angel then departed. We sat quietly, awe-struck by the angel's visitation and the significance of what had just happened.

I was ongoingly astonished at how greatly God continued to move in our lives. A should-have-been ordinary morning turned into me standing on a chair over my fiancé to shock a demon out, followed by a divine visitation from an angel with a message from God. Such an all-pervading humility and reverence bloomed in my heart. Witnessing His greatness fortified my trust in God.

In preparation for our upcoming marriage to each other and God, Gabriel and I endeavored to write our own vows. It felt important to us to be very specific and intentional with our promises. While writing the vows, it took several attempts due to strong interference from the enemy trying to prevent us from completing them. After much effort and prayer, we wrote:

"(Gabriel, Bri), on this day, I commit myself to you as your (wife, husband), not only in the flesh but also in the spirit. May our union be made holy and sanctified by the Holy Spirit today as we weave our souls together. May all stand witness that today our marriage is not only to each other as husband and wife, but as a couple, we now enter into a sacred union and marriage with God. I offer my life and my union with you as my (wife, husband), to the works of the Kingdom of God. Amen."

I am thrilled to report that on July 16, 2023, Gabriel and I were married by Pastor Dave and Cheryl Bryan at Church of Glad Tidings in Grass Valley, to the glory of God! It was attended by our parents and close friends of the church. May this story of the healing and restoration of our family be a great testament to God's ultimate power, magnificence, and wonder. Through God, all things are possible.

17

God the Healer

For many years, I suffered immensely from unbearable pain, chronic illness, and various debilitating ailments. Through my encounters, I was suddenly and inexplicably made well. Years of prayer were finally answered by my desire to genuinely know God. I was excited to eat foods I hadn't been able to eat in years due to inconsolable food sensitivities. I was able to walk without pain, even run, finally free from agonizing and persistent joint pain. I relished my newfound wellness for two seamless months, until one day, the enemy came to steal and destroy my progress.

Right before our wedding, my fiancé and I attended a family reunion for my father's side of the family. I enjoyed the opportunity to see my family and spend time with them, but over the weekend, I became progressively ill. By the time I got home on Sunday, my joints were aching badly, my stomach swelled up with inflammation, and I came down with a horrible migraine.

What is this? What is going on? I questioned, stunned those symptoms that had been gone for months reappeared so abruptly and intensely. It didn't make sense.

A flood of thoughts rushed into my mind. The symptoms I was experiencing had been resolved and now suddenly, they all resurface at once for no logical reason? *Didn't God heal me?* I wondered. *How could this be? How could the healing be taken away?* I felt the all too familiar fear, panic, and hopelessness of experiencing physical affliction, not knowing if or when it might end.

A voice of doubt crept in, saying, "Maybe God isn't who you thought He is; maybe this path isn't the right path.

Maybe God didn't heal you at all, and this new path isn't any better than all the other ones you have tried that didn't work out in the end."

For the first time since God had instructed me to cease taking all my medications, I thought about taking my prescribed pain medication to escape the almost unbearable symptoms. I was lying in bed in my dark bedroom, so sick that I couldn't even eat dinner with my family. *No!* I screamed feebly in my mind. *This can't be happening! I can't go back to living this way! This can't be right. How is this happening?*

Over the next two days, I grappled with this demon of doubt in my mind, struggling to find my way back to the truth. For a brief moment, I entertained doubts about whether everything that had transpired over the past months had genuinely occurred or if I had merely imagined my way into feeling better; I even doubted whether my perceived healing had existed at all.

I found myself in a state of confusion, and knew I needed to break free from my emotional reaction to the return of symptoms. I struggled to regain my capacity to think clearly. I decided to redirect my attention towards making simple and objective observations. I sorted carefully through the facts in my mind. *For the last two months, I was completely healed,* I thought to myself. All symptoms had mysteriously vanished with the appearance of God in my life. I had proof! I had eaten foods I couldn't previously eat and experienced no ill effects whatsoever. My neck pain really had been absent; I canceled all the standing chiropractic and massage appointments I had on the books, no longer needing relief.

Two months prior, during my family's visit, we went for a walk together, and I had moved with a new lightness in my step. There were times in our family walk when I even ran and jumped around. Upon witnessing this, my stepdad said with a grin, "Is this the same girl who had trouble walking not that long ago?"

To which I replied, "This is the power of Jesus!"

So how then, could all the symptoms return two months later? After much contemplation, I concluded that the recurrence must be due to demonic influence. The resurfacing of symptoms had coincided with my family reunion, and I had evidence to suspect a generational curse on my father's side.

During my deliverance sessions, I had uncovered spirits of death and infirmity on my father's side, and I saw how this had negatively influenced the health of my family line for generations. Since I had received my healing incidentally through drawing closer to God, I wasn't sure how to get it back. I just knew it had been stolen away. John 10:10 (ESV) says:

"The thief comes only to steal and kill and destroy. I came that they may have life and have it abundantly."

The enemy had come to try to steal the health and life God had restored to me, and now I had to figure out what to do about it. Psalm 41:3 (ESV) says:

"The Lord sustains him on his sickbed; in his illness you restore him to full health."

I knew I needed God to get better again, for He is the source of life and the great Restorer. I spent the next few days listening to Andrew Wommack's teachings on healing. One of my friends from church had shared some videos from his ministry, and I intuitively felt he knew some key things about healing with Christ that I needed to learn.

Andrew teaches the importance of understanding authority in Christ as a believer. He states that when we understand the spiritual authority and power found in Jesus, followers in Christ can more effectively release God's healing power. Wommack teaches that healing is not just for a select few, but that it is available to everyone who believes. He bases his belief firmly on Scripture that testifies to God's healing power.

Andrew Wommack assures his listeners that we already have our healing, that it was given the moment Jesus died on the cross. He has a book called *You've Already Got it! {So Quit Trying to Get it}*. Andrew explains that God has already done everything necessary for our salvation, healing, and prosperity through the death, burial, and resurrection of Jesus Christ. He teaches we don't need to earn God's favor or blessings; we simply need to receive them by faith.

I contemplated this deeply, pondering the Scriptures which allude to Jesus already having healed me. 1 Peter 2:24 (NIV) declares:

"He himself bore our sins in his body on the tree, that we might die to sin and live to righteousness. By his wounds you have been healed."

This Scripture speaks of our healing in the past tense. *Maybe Andrew's teachings do make sense*, I thought to myself, *If my healing is promised, all I need to do is reach out and claim it.*

That night before bed, I was convicted to exercise my authority in Christ and stand on the truth of God's Word. I picked up Andrew Wommack's free booklet on healing and paced around my bedroom in my nightgown while reading the booklet out loud. While I read the selected Scriptures, I believed in faith in every word of the verses I read. While pacing around my bedside, with each step I took I imagined myself taking a step into the health and healing that God had already promised me.

My husband was lying in bed, agreeing with me on every Word of God that I was declaring out loud. Also inside the booklet were remarkable testimonies that I read while declaring that the same Spirit that healed the people in the stories can heal me. I spoke with increasing confidence, "The Spirit of God that dwells within me, strengthens and restores me!"

As those words shot out of my mouth with surprising certitude, the revelation of what I was saying finally sank in. I continued to walk as I spoke, my steps now becoming more of a rhythmic stomp around my bedroom. I took each step intentionally, my steps symbolic of my steps towards faith of being healed and restored by the Lord.

Wommack explains that our faith is not based on our feelings or experiences, but on the truth of God's Word. When we believe God's promises, even when we don't yet see them coming to fruition in our lives, we are releasing His healing power and blessings to operate within us. When we stop trying to get what God has already given us and simply receive it by faith, we can receive the healing from God that is already ours.

I persisted in my prayers and declarations that night for about forty-five minutes. As I neared the end of my prayers, I noticed that some of the pain and discomfort had subsided but wasn't fully resolved by the time I laid down. Instead of falling prey to doubt, I closed my eyes to sleep that night, resting in full faith that I was healed.

The next morning when I awoke, lo and behold, I *was* healed! The pain in my joints, swelling in my belly, neurological neck, and head pain had all completely vanished. *I knew it!* I thought to myself, a celebratory smile spreading over my face. *The enemy tried to steal my healing, but I stole it back!* I thought to myself excitedly. I immediately repented for any doubt I had been harboring that had opened the door for symptoms to return. I raised my hands in the air, praising and glorifying God for bringing another great miracle of healing.

It is the faith in believers that releases the healing power of Yeshua. As believers, we have been given the authority to cast out demons, heal the sick and raise the dead, but unbelief is the greatest obstacle. I was amazed how suddenly my healing was stolen, then how quickly it returned when I took a bold step of faith.

For all of my life, I viewed sickness as a fixed circumstance, perceiving it as a burden I must bear in life. Growing up, I was chronically sick with flus, colds, sinus infections, and respiratory infections. I sought remedies and found semi-solutions through natural medicine, yet there always remained something I was battling in my health.

One time, I listened to a testimony of a witch doctor from Africa who said when his patients came to him with an illness, he would simply exchange the illness for a different one. For example, if they had cancer, he would turn the disease into diabetes. This seemed to be the case with the healing work I studied for over a decade, although I was clueless at the time.

I "healed" migraines, then I got back pain; I "healed" back pain, then I got Lyme disease. The other practitioners I shared this path with convinced me that the reason for my sickness was due to the negative karma I had accumulated from different lifetimes. Now that I know the awful lie that was, I can see how the source of "healing" that drew from the realm of the fallen ones was providing results that looked like healing, but in reality, was producing even worse problems.

I am grateful to know now that God is the only true source of healing. Never again will I meddle with other "healers," I will turn to Jehovah Rapha, Yeshua, the Lord who heals. The problem with the lower realm's outward appeal is the hidden exchange of power that takes place. Many unsuspecting people, like me, don't realize the consequences of using sources of power for healing and inquiry that are not of God.

I was misled into believing I was plagued by a never-ending array of health issues, unable to see that my actual problem was seeking healing from the wrong source. This is one of the ways the realm of the fallen ones entices people into bondage, with false promises of healing. Meanwhile, the seed of the serpent is sown in the person in exchange for their miracle. The seed later gestates, giving rise to even greater challenges. This is not the kind of miracle to pursue. Every time one consults the shadow world for illegal power, they become more and more contaminated. This is the reason that someone like me, who considered themselves a highly spiritual being in the New Age, could be so covered with sinister spirits and ridden with health problems, despite my healthy diet and yogic lifestyle.

The reassuring reality is that God our Creator designed our bodies, and He knows how to heal them, with no strings attached. The same Spirit of God that touched my body and healed it is available to bring healing to yours as well. Experiencing triumph over the overwhelming symptoms that reoccurred was a significant milestone for me. The next time the symptoms showed up for me, I knew exactly what to do; stand on the Word of God and take the healing that was given 2,000 years ago with Yeshua's sacrifice.

The Holy Spirit taught me to rebuke symptoms as they arise. I've noticed that when I tolerated a small pain instead of addressing it right away, it would quickly escalate into more significant pain and problems. I found that exercising my authority over minor issues, such as headaches or colds, is essential so that I am better prepared when bigger health crises arise. By following this approach, I have made remarkable progress with chronic aches, pains, and illnesses.

Based on my understanding of Scripture, I have compelling evidence to conclude that as believers, pain and sickness have no rightful place in our bodies. Just as we are saved by the blood of Jesus, I am convinced that we can also be liberated from sickness.

From what I have witnessed in America, I strongly feel that believers could harness their authority in matters of health more actively within the mainstream church. I recognize each person has their own unique journey with healing, which may include various types of care in addition to prayer, but that should not discourage earnest stands of faith in Christ's healing potential. In acknowledging God as the ultimate source of life and healing, it seems crucial to seek the Holy Spirit's guidance to discern the most appropriate course of action for each individual circumstance.

Isaiah 53:5 (KJV) says:

"But he was wounded for our transgressions, he was bruised for our iniquities: the chastisement of our peace was upon him; and with his stripes we are healed."

This Scripture illustrates how Jesus paid the price for our peace and for our iniquities. I have tried so many approaches to healing, but nothing works as instantaneously and effectively as exercising my faith as a believer and claiming the health that is rightfully mine through Jesus Christ.

One day, I sat considering what Mark 16:18 (KJV) says:

"And these signs shall follow them that believe...they shall lay hands on the sick, and they shall recover."

So, believers just need to lay hands on the sick, and they will recover? I marveled.

I had some faith, having just witnessed what the touch of God had done for me, so I decided to try out what Mark 16: 17–18 said. I thought to myself, *I have to first believe, then lay my hands on the sick and they are supposed to recover. Hmmm, where am I to find a sick person?*

The next day, my neighbor was out in his yard. When I said hello and asked how he was, he said, "Oh, I am mostly good, except I pulled my back out and it's hurting."

Great! I thought to myself. Well, not great, but what a great opportunity to pray for someone. As my husband walked up and joined us, I asked my neighbor. "Can we pray for you?"

"Oh, sure," he said.

My husband and I laid our hands on him, and I said a simple prayer, something along the lines of, "Jesus, thank You for completely restoring him from head to toe."

A few days after we prayed, I received a text from my neighbor saying, "Hi neighbor, good news. I had a prostate problem that went away because of your prayers. Tell your husband. Praise the Lord!"

I was so excited. My first shy attempt resulted in success! I was merely praying for his back. I didn't even know about the prostate problem, nor did I want to ask that nice, elderly gentleman for all the details. I texted him back, saying, "Praise the Lord! God wants you well!" Then I sent him James 5:15 (KJV):

"And the prayer of faith will save the one who is sick, and the Lord will raise him up. And if he has committed sins, he will be forgiven."

My neighbor responded, saying, "Thanks for the prayers. I had the problem for years. Took a few days to realize the problem was gone, then I said, alright Lord, thank You."

I share this story because it is a great example of how simple healing can be if one is willing to apply themselves. Jesus told us to go and cast out demons, heal the sick, and raise the dead. Why not start now? We all have to start somewhere, and often the little wins quickly add up to big wins.

Something I noticed that can make a big difference in results, is the difference between petitioning for healing and commanding healing. For example, I could say, "please heal my wrist God, I know you can, and that you are good and mighty. Thank you." That would be a petition. Yet I found I get better results when I say something like, "Wrist, be healed, be restored, by the power of Lord Jesus, now! I release the healing power of Jesus into the muscles and tendons and command pain and inflammation to go! I command my wrist to operate under the authority of Jesus and come into alignment with the truth of the Kingdom of Heaven. Jesus is victor over my wrist! Praise the Lord!" That is an example of my commanding prayer.

As I made connections and started friendships within the Christian community, I came across many Christians who were not practicing their faith in this way. When I asked them if they believed in Jesus's power to heal, they responded "Yes," but after some time, I realized that believing in one's mind is different than believing in one's heart. I reckon one of the biggest obstacles Christians face when it comes to health is unbelief, even when they do believe. It is possible, and more common than not, to have both belief and unbelief simultaneously.

Mark 9:23–26 (NKJV) is a great example of a father who believes Jesus can heal (in his mind), yet still carries unbelief:

"Jesus said to him, 'If you can believe, all things are possible to him who believes.' Immediately the father of the child cried out and said with tears, 'Lord, I believe; help my unbelief!' When Jesus saw that the people came running together, He rebuked the unclean spirit, saying to it, 'Deaf and dumb spirit, I command you, come out of him and enter him no more!' Then the spirit cried out, convulsed him greatly, and came out of him."

Having come out of the New Age and occult, I had grown accustomed to witnessing the supernatural, to the extent that I had developed a habit of expecting results. Although at times I still harbored unbelief, I carried enough belief to counter my unbelief in order for progressive healings to occur. Belief and unbelief are two opposing forces, and when both are actively engaged, it can provide varied results.

I learned a valuable lesson in this regard when my husband and I prayed for my eyesight one evening. Due to spending long hours on the computer writing this book, I noticed my eyesight seemed to be deteriorating more rapidly. I discussed this with my husband, and together, we decided to pray about it. We took an authoritative position, saying, "Father God, in the name of Jesus, eyes, I command you to be restored. Vision, be completely restored in Jesus's name." We went to bed that night, keeping an open mind, but not entirely in faith.

The next day, I opened my laptop, put my glasses on, and began typing. After a few minutes, my eyes ached, and I noticed my vision was blurry. I had put my glasses on as a habit, but when I removed them, I realized that the prescription was now too strong.

My eyes had been healed! Well, *partially*, as I still couldn't see clearly without *any* glasses. Now I found myself in a predicament; I couldn't see with my normal prescription glasses because they were too strong, and my eyes were not healed enough to see on their own yet. It was a partial healing, from my partial faith. When I got home, I ended up reverting back to the first prescribed glasses I had received from over eleven years prior.

This same phenomenon happened a few times when I was praying for physical symptoms. For example, after being healed of chronic sciatic pain for several months, it returned. In response, I said, "Father God, in the name of Jesus, I rebuke the symptom of sciatic pain. Pain, get out! I command the sciatic nerve to be released and completely restored by the dunamis power of Jesus Christ, who dwells in me."

After that prayer, the pain resolved, partially. The improvement was undeniable, and yet some pain remained. My belief and unbelief were pulling the results in opposite directions. I had enough faith to experience improvement, but not completely resolve the pain.

As similar circumstances arose, I noticed a pattern. Prayer consistently resulted in an improvement of my physical symptoms, however my level of faith greatly affected how much healing power I was able to receive. I could have easily fallen into the mindset of thinking…well, it didn't work this time, so maybe it just won't work for me at all, losing faith or becoming discouraged.

However, I had just enough faith to be able to observe partial results, so I knew I was on the right track. Seeing evidence that my prayers at least had some effect gave me hope for what is possible. I know that it takes time and practice to become proficient in most skills, and I was willing to put in the work. In the decade I spent as an energy healer, it took many tries and years of study to see miracles. Eventually, after a significant amount of practice, I began to see results.

If I could get great results using an energetic system whose source was plugged into the dark realm of the fallen ones, how much greater the miracles could be with Christ as the source of healing! Being the determined person I am, I didn't give up. When I got partial results, I would pray more, and pray harder. Eventually, the pain I was experiencing would subside. My husband was convicted as he witnessed me in the exploration of using my authority in Christ and astonished by how my once debilitating symptoms could be overcome by faith in Yeshua and persistent prayer. Jesus is the Victor! He won at the cross 2,000 years ago, and He still wins today.

When Jesus said on the cross "It is finished" (John 19:30), that means that the battle ended there. One time when I was battling against a persistent stomach issue, I simply said over and over again, "Jesus is the Victor. It is finished. He broke the curse. The curse is lifted," I believed what I was saying, seeing the scene of Jesus's crucifixion replay over and over again in my mind. At first the pain intensified, and my abdomen shook every as I made each declaration. After about 30 min of speaking this truth over and over again, the stomach pain resolved. Persistence is key; many people exercising their authority in Christ give up too soon. I often find that right before my breakthroughs, things worsen as hell comes against my fight for freedom, but then I make it to the other side, and there is light; there is peace. There is resolution.

Whenever prayer is accompanied by even the slightest progress, I make it a point to celebrate the small victories because they confirm that I'm moving in the right direction. The more progress and miracles one sees, the greater their faith becomes. Seeking encouragement, I spent countless hours listening to testimonies and watching success videos to build up my faith in God's miraculous healing capabilities.

Hearing the testimonies of others can greatly stir one's faith. While some may argue otherwise, I firmly hold the belief that God's intention is for us to enjoy good health, even though sickness may occasionally arise to offer opportunities for spiritual growth and lessons during certain seasons of our lives. It is not only unbelief countering belief that can stifle our healing, sometimes there is a spirit of infirmity that is at the root of symptoms, as was the case with me.

I have noticed that many well-meaning and faithful Christians have the knowledge of God and His Word but haven't yet encountered the supernatural manifestations of His Spirit. Likewise, people like me in the New Age and occult often experience the Spirit of God and supernatural manifestations but lack the knowledge of who God authentically is. In both paths, people are diligently seeking God, but layers of deception prevent them from experiencing God without limits.

When we are able to combine the experience of the supernatural Spirit of the Lord with the knowledge of God's Word, we tap into the greatest power available to us. It is then that miracles, signs, and wonders manifest to confirm

His Word. As someone who operated in the supernatural and realm of the spirit in the New Age and occult, I was astounded to discover the even greater power and authority was available through Christ. The pillars of this world were built on the Word of God, and our Creator is the one true Master of it all.

John 1:1 (KJV) says:

"In the beginning was the Word, and the Word was with God, and the Word was God."

Also in the beginning, Genesis 1:3 (KJV) recounts:

"And God said, 'Let there be light,' and there was light. And God saw that the light was good. And God separated the light from the darkness. God called the light Day, and the darkness he called Night. And there was evening and there was morning, the first day."

When God released His Word, and said "let there be light," it was the catalyst of all creation. The Word of God is the foundation of this world, upon which all things were built henceforth. Since the Word of God is what upholds this world, when we stand on the Word of God, it is unshakable. Having faith in the Word, in Yeshua, and intimacy with the Holy Spirit allows us to walk in ultimate authority as sons and daughters in the Kingdom of God.

One day, while listening to a Sid Roth episode, there was a guest on the show who had been taken up in the spirit to heaven. He said that while he was there, he saw a building labeled "Unclaimed Blessings." Inside the building were various body parts. He said that he saw angels gathering the body parts to bring to believers in response to their prayers of faith for healing.

In the spirit, the man followed the angels and observed what happened on Earth when the angels arrived to deliver restored body parts for the person in need of healing. He said that the angels stood ready to impart healing beside each person, but due to unbelief, the miracle of a new body part could not be delivered.

This is a sad example of how people can carry both belief and unbelief at the same time. The people had enough faith to pray, but their unbelief blocked them from receiving their inheritance from the storehouse of heaven. The good news is that we can target our unbelief, and once we are able to chip away at it, it becomes less of an obstacle to receiving the gift of healing from God.

As I studied the great miracle workers such as A.A. Allen, John G. Lake, and Kathryn Kuhlman, I was considerably intrigued with the instantaneous healing that took place in the peak of their day. Considering their success, I realized that I carried an unconscious misconception that if I didn't see something great or magnificent happen right away, that the prayer didn't work.

The truth I found is that sometimes healings don't happen right away, and can manifest as a progressive healing, as was the case with me. In some instances, healing has happened and not yet been exhibited physically, so it is important to maintain faith and not allow unbelief to block the opportunity to receive healing. I have come to accept that any notable progress is evidence that I am headed in the right direction. I believe all things are possible with God, and with persistence and unwavering faith, every believer possesses the potential healing and power of God within them.

There is a fabulous documentary called *Christ in You: The Movie*. This movie features a fascinating discovery and hard look at what holds back believers from bringing hope, healing, and deliverance to the world. It contains remarkable interviews and demonstrations of ordinary Christians releasing the healing of Christ into their communities.

When I watched the documentary, I was entirely convinced to challenge myself. It stirred within me the determination to conquer my fear and unleash the power of Christ residing within all believers. The Word says that the same Spirit of God that raised Jesus from the dead dwells inside of born-again believers. The followers of Christ carry the resurrection power of Jesus, but the issue lies in the fact that many believers lack a complete understanding of how to release God's healing potential. Additionally, concealed unbelief can be a barrier that prevents the release of Jesus's power, even when faith is present.

In Acts 9:36–42, Peter prays for Tabitha after she dies, and then she comes back to life. In Acts 20:7–12, Paul throws himself on the dead body of a man who fell out of a window, and the man gets resurrected. If the apostles were able to walk in the resurrection power, we, as disciples of this era, can do the same. John 8:31–32 says:

"Then Jesus said to those Jews who believed Him, 'If you abide in My word, you are My disciples indeed. And you shall know the truth, and the truth shall make you free.'"

By abiding in His Word, we become His disciples. Through the experience of being born again, the very same Spirit of God that resided in Peter, Paul, and Jesus also indwells our bodily vessels.

It is the duty of true followers of Christ to preach the good news of the gospel, cast out demons, heal the sick, and raise the dead. However, that is not what I see in many Christian churches today. I see numerous followers of Christ who are intended to be vessels of glory, having faith in the Word of God, yet hesitating to act in accordance with their beliefs. Many possess enough faith to believe but lack the gumption to take action and step out in faith.

Religious beliefs that do not align with the Word can place constraints on what God can accomplish within churches and ministries. When God's abilities are confined by the flawed convictions of His followers, His power cannot be made fully manifest in His people. God desires to confirm His Word through signs and wonders, with His supernatural presence, but this relies on our belief in His Word, not just in our mind, but deep in our spirit.

When we wholeheartedly believe in our spirits that what He has declared for us as believers is indeed true, then God will manifest His glory within our surrendered and faith-filled vessels. It's high time we all get to know God without limits, and shed the limiting beliefs that hinder the manifestation of His power.

There are folks like me who experienced the void of God's absence in mainstream churches, as I once did. These individuals often perceive the study of the Bible as a rigid adherence to rules and standards because the supernatural presence of the Lord is not readily apparent to serve as a confirmation of the Word.

What the church needs today is a revival of God's Spirit and supernatural presence, free from the confines of religious dogma. Without the limits of religious assertions, the spirits of believers can be stirred to conviction through personal encounters rather than mere mental beliefs and knowledge about God. What the New Age and occult community require is a revelation of who God truly is; to recognize Christ is not a mere religious concept or a set of pious assertions; He is the living son of God, possessing unparalleled power and authority in all of the Earth realm.

The church can attain revival by shedding the layers of religious beliefs that limit God's power, and the New Age and occult can attain revelation by destroying the misconception that Christ equals religion. As the New Age and occult communities, along with the church, peel away these critical layers of confusion and deception, both groups will have the chance to get to know God without limits. When people see the uninhibited power of God moving in the church, they will be less inclined to seek the supernatural in inappropriate places, as I did for two decades within the New Age and occult communities.

If every Christian in the world ventured out into the streets, supermarkets, gas stations, or any other place once a day, faithfully and boldly releasing the resurrection power of Jesus as described in the Word, the world would undergo significant change. Sharing the Gospel doesn't have to involve intimidating rule-based preaching that repels people; it can instead be the release of light and life that is Jesus Christ. One soul in each of their prospective spheres of influence, releasing God's supernatural presence, can generate an unprecedented tidal wave of the restoration of Christ to our world. He will reveal Himself, for His glory.

In Acts 3:6–7 (NIV), Peter heals a crippled man by releasing what was inside of him:

"Peter said, 'Silver or gold I do not have, but what I do have I give you. In the name of Jesus Christ of Nazareth, walk.' Taking him by the right hand, he helped him up, and instantly the man's feet and ankles became strong."

Believers have something non-believers do not have; they are hosts to the Holy Spirit. God longs to demonstrate His power and love through His people in our ordinary, everyday lives. When followers of Christ regularly surpass the bounds of their comfort zones to touch the lives of other people with faith, an even greater move of God than what our forefathers have seen will begin to take root in God's people.

Jesus is the source of life, the way to the Tree of Life. In the beginning, God breathed the breath of life into Adam's nostrils. Genesis 2:7 (ESV):

"Then the Lord God formed the man of dust from the ground and breathed into his nostrils the breath of life, and the man became a living creature."

As believers, we possess the ability to approach God in faith, asking Him to breathe the breath of life into us, revitalizing and renewing our spirits. It can be that simple to experience a gentle, supernatural touch of the Lord. With God, and faith, all things are possible.

As a part of my regular spiritual practice, I take deep breaths, while anchoring myself on God's Word. While taking these breaths, I affirm, "Lord, that same breath of life that you breathed into Adam's nostrils, that breath that brings life and light, that is the breath of life, I draw into my nostrils right now. Your breath of life strengthens and restores my body." When I do this in genuine faith, I experience waves of invigoration and revitalization.

Romans 8:11 (KJV) says:

"But if the Spirit of him that raised up Jesus from the dead dwells in you, he that raised up Christ from the dead shall also quicken your mortal bodies by his Spirit that dwelleth in you."

I find that amazing; the Spirit of God living in believers *quickens* their mortal bodies. On dictionary.com, quicken is defined as "to give or restore vigor or activity to; stir up, rouse, or stimulate." We must know the rights and entitlements of being a believer! Satan will try to deceive you out of your full inheritance, but we can go to the Word, remember the truth, and receive the truth through faith.

There is so much potential packed in this revelation! In addition to claiming the light and life of Christ within my breath, I stand on the power and potential in the above Scripture by affirming, "The Spirit of God within me quickens my mortal body, strengthens, and restores me!" As I meditate on this Scripture and speak these words with unwavering belief in my heart, I notice a decrease in my fatigue, and find comfort in the assurance that I can draw strength from the Lord when weariness sets in.

◊ ◊ ◊

I faced a great trial when writing this chapter of the book, even amidst the wondrous results of my exploration of healing with Christ. The enemy aggressively targeted my health in an effort to dissuade me from spreading the good news of Jehovah Rapha, the Lord who Heals. Fortunately, through God's abundant mercy and grace, a way was made for me to again regain my confidence in God's exquisite healing capacities.

A few days before a family road trip where I planned to use the time we would be driving to write this chapter of my book, I was hit with a sudden, extreme headache. Within a matter of days, this intense headache escalated into an excruciating migraine accompanied by neurological symptoms, a condition that had been absent for the past three months in my newfound walk with Christ. Back when I was grappling with Lyme disease, these neurological migraine episodes were a frequent source of suffering for me, with an episode occurring almost every week.

As the pain intensified in the days leading up to my trip, I dedicated my morning prayer time to reading Andrew Wommack's collection of healing Scriptures. I declared these verses over my body and spoke authoritative prayers, demanding, "Pain go! In Jesus's name, pain leave! Father God, thank you for healing me completely of all neck pain, head pain, and neurological symptoms. I release the dunamis healing power of Jesus Christ of Nazareth over my head, my brain, my neck, and nervous system. Body, be restored, be healed in the mighty name of Jesus!"

Following my prayer, the pain would diminish in certain areas. However, when I would start my work for the day, the pain would slowly yet steadily return. By the end of my workday, the pain had intensified to the point that I again strongly contemplated taking pain medication to escape my symptoms.

I recall hearing a faint voice in my head saying, "It's ok, God doesn't mind if you take medicine. He doesn't want you to be in pain. You've done all you can with prayer, and now it's time to just rest and get relief from medication." Though I wasn't cognizant of it then, I have since come to recognize that voice as that of my enemy, tempting me into relying on something other than God to help me with my pain. God had specifically guided me to cease medication so he could manifest His good works in me.

Now, I know this may not be the path for everyone, but in my situation, God told me: "Hold on to nothing, and I will give you everything." A big part of my journey was letting go of supplements, medications, and certain ways that I was living in order for me to draw closer to God and trust Him for the healing I needed. If I listened to that malevolent voice, I would have come into agreement that the pain was mightier than God's power to heal me.

The day came for my family to leave for our trip, and I was terribly sick. That morning, I devoted an hour to battling against the pain and darkness that had befallen me. Although I made some progress, the pain that lingered left me in a barely functional state. When my husband arrived home, I lamentably shared with him the details of the situation, explaining I believed that I was under a spiritual attack from the enemy, who was attempting to hinder my efforts to write the chapter about healing in my book.

I sadly confessed, "I can't proceed with writing this chapter of my book about Jehovah Rapha, the Lord that heals, while experiencing an intense neurological migraine that I can't seem to get rid of."

"No!" he shouted. "We can't let this happen! We have to fight it." By this point, Gabriel had witnessed the mysterious disappearance and reappearance of extreme health issues on several occasions and knew from experience that prayer had the power to bring an end to symptoms.

We joined in a passionate prayer, rebuking the spirit of infirmity, the symptoms, and declaring God's healing over my body. Within ten minutes, I was already feeling a 40% improvement! It was enough of a result for us to know that we were on the right track, and that there was an unfavorable supernatural influence responsible for causing the physical distress. I had not yet been fully freed from the generational spirit of infirmity and death that had afflicted me throughout my life, and it continued to manifest bouts of undesirable symptoms.

We needed to get on the road, so we packed up the car and headed out. As we drove, I endeavored to do some writing during our drive. To my surprise, the moment I attempted to write about the healing I had experienced from God, the pain increased tenfold into piercing, mind-boggling pain. My vision blurred and waves of terrible nausea swept over me.

I cried out in distress to Gabriel, barely getting out, "I don't think I can do this anymore. The pain is becoming unbearable, and I might need to take medication. Yet, I also fear that the enemy might be deceiving me."

"Let's pray," he said. He started by speaking in tongues, making declarations of healing over my body. He rebuked all the symptoms, one by one, then released Jesus's healing powers into the affected parts of my body. After fifteen minutes of focused prayer, I experienced a remarkable improvement, feeling approximately 80% better! With a heart full of gratitude, I again praised God for His grace and felt deeply thankful for every single one of my prayers that He had answered.

That evening, I was able to enjoy a fun time with my family on the first day of our trip, free from the burden of overwhelming symptoms. Yet, as bedtime approached, the severe head pain returned with a vengeance. Tired as we were, Gabriel and I merely said a short prayer of faith before bed, together declaring and agreeing that when I awoke, I would be fully restored.

The next morning, upon awakening, I felt amazing! I felt even better than I had in years, as if a great weight had been lifted. I turned to my husband and exclaimed, "God healed me! I'm all the way healed! All the pain and symptoms are gone. We won!"

He smiled, as if he knew something I didn't, then said, "Yes, He did, my dear...and He used me to do it!"

"What do you mean?" I asked curiously.

He said, "I woke up in the middle of night to an overwhelming presence of the Lord, and He instructed me how to break strongholds on your health."

How interesting, I thought. My son walked in asking for breakfast, so we didn't have a chance to discuss it further until later that morning.

Given the remarkable nature of this healing testimony, I will share Gabriel's journal entry from that day:

October 28, 2023

Bri had been well for months, and it seemed that her health issues had resolved. However, on our drive to San Francisco, she became afflicted with migraine symptoms, nausea, weakness, and blurry vision. The symptoms made it impossible for her to write the chapter of her book titled "God the Healer."

The pain was so intense that she felt tempted to take migraine medication. We knew she was fighting a spiritual battle because the symptoms would dissipate every time we prayed intensely.

I awoke in the early morning hour, long before the sun. As I gained awareness in that moment, I identified more with my spirit man than my body and personality. My spirit man is awesome. He is confident, powerful, wise, and takes no nonsense. A messenger angel appeared and shared an insight that Bri had 11 interfering spirits, and my task was to remove them.

While the Holy Spirit led me to work on her, I found it amazing that Bri stayed asleep as I battled demons on her behalf, as she has always been a light sleeper. It gave me hope that perhaps I could have a sleepover with my stepson and wage war on the spirits afflicting him. By the holy presence, I was guided to address each spirit of affliction individually.

First, I was to evict the spirit of idolatry. It looked like a hodgepodge of different Eastern gods with scorpion legs and a tail. As my spirit man engaged in battle, it was clear that there was no contest. My Christ-filled presence was not attacked. The only tactic the evil spirit employed was to attempt to cling and try to hide.

In response, my spirit man used blue swords to battle it. Rather than swinging them around, these swords seemed to materialize out of thin air in the place they needed to motivate the demons to leave of their own accord.

Second was the spirit of pain, which appeared in the spirit realm as a large black scorpion. The third was a spirit of despair, and manifested as a heavy dense, soggy grub filling up cavities in her spirit and spawning more like it. The swords materialized, which repelled the grubs, flinging them out of her system with ease.

The fourth was a demon of hell. God guided me deeper into the core of Bri. I reached a point where the bottom dropped out, as if it fell away into an infinite darkness downward. I spotted an enormous demon that looked like the classic devil, with horns and reptilian eyes. Even though this demon was powerful, it instantly knew I had the authority to cast it out and left in obedience, up and out of the cavern and out of her body.

The fifth spirit was a spirit of fear. The Lord took me into a smaller and smaller perspective until I was the size of a cell and inside her bones. I felt guided to point my spirit sword at the bone cell and command what was in there to come out. What burst out of the cell was a wispy shadow. I suddenly noticed a deep fear that wasn't mine.

This cell represented all bone cells, and a torrent of terror emerged from the cells, creating a whirlwind of shadow and the bristling of fear. Bri convulsed in her sleep, and the shadows disappeared. A peace filled the room, and I felt emboldened and victorious.

The sixth spirit was a spirit of death. My courage was tempered by the next foe. My sword poked death, and it responded aggressively, descending over me, darkening my view in the spirit realm, and filling the room with a demonstration of dark power. I responded by becoming humble, leaning on, and yielding to the Lord. From my surrendered vessel, God took over, and it was instantly gone.

The seventh spirit was a spirit of infirmity. I perceived in the realm of the spirit, a gray goo that covered Bri's body. Everywhere it stuck to, it caused physical dysfunction, physiological confusion, and disease. It was easily dispensed of, but I sensed that the forces of that spirit were actively degrading the physical body of many others in our world. I felt sadness for all the people suffering under its influence.

The eighth spirit was a spirit that hinders love. This spirit had a hold in both Bri and I, similar to the spirit of infirmity, except the target of dysfunction was focused primarily on relationships instead of physical processes. It appeared in my inner vision as hundreds of bats clinging to the inside of our hearts. When they were chased and flew out, I felt our hearts *effortlessly pulsing in the same sacred movement, God becoming one with us in a great harmony.*

The ninth spirit was a spirit of control. The spirit was small but insidious. It was attached to the brainstem and stretched through the optic nerves. It took time to surgically remove it.

The tenth spirit was a spirit of OCD. This was a web-like substance that was woven throughout the tissue in the brain, subtly influencing Bri to follow habits and obsessions that it wanted to fulfill. Extracting it took a lot of energy and gentleness because the spiritual removal was such a delicate process.

The eleventh stronghold was a group of seven white snakes. My sword extended and caught them by the neck. I paused, and when the snakes saw what would come of them if they stayed, they left. Then thousands of tiny snakes and eggs were vacuumed up and out. As this occurred, I sensed the Holy Spirit fire making its way up her spine. She gently shook in her sleep, sighed, and then again fell still.

I was struck with awe as I listened to Gabriel read the journal entry of his middle-of-the-night encounter with the Holy Spirit. A surge of gratitude entered my heart as I marveled at the unique and creative ways that God uses people to bring restoration. That entire rest of the day, I was overflowing with incredible joy, energy and stamina, my body restored by the divine touch of God.

I acknowledge that each person's journey is unique and may differ from mine, but I encourage you to explore what is the width and depth of God's love and desire in healing you. Ephesians 3:16–21 (NKJV) says:

"...that He would grant you, according to the riches of His glory, to be strengthened with might through His Spirit in the inner man, that Christ may dwell in your hearts through faith; that you, being rooted and grounded in love, may be able to comprehend with all the saints what is the width and length and depth and height—to know the love of Christ which passes knowledge; that you may be filled with all the fullness of God."

When I read Scriptures related to healing, I believe what is written, despite certain religious individuals who may argue otherwise. James 5:15 (NIV) says:

"And the prayer offered in faith will make the sick person well; the Lord will raise them up. If they have sinned, they will be forgiven."

By embracing faith and exercising the authority granted to believers over illness and affliction, followers of Christ transition from mere cognitive belief to spirit- and action-filled faith. If you are a devoted believer who is filled with the Spirit of Christ, you can take authority over headaches and/or backaches; assertively command pain to leave, persisting until it yields, then release God's healing power in its place. I have done this exercise many times for myself and others, and there is noticeable improvement in pain levels when applied faithfully.

At a time when I was questioning how to help people walk in their full potential as vessels of God's glory, I received an incredible insight from Jesus. One night at the Emerging Prophetic Voices group at my church, I had a vision during our prayer time.

When I closed my eyes and began to pray, my spirit was transported to another dimension. I saw myself standing on a cloud-filled landscape, clothed in a long, white wedding dress, complete with a veil. Beautiful light streamed in all around me, glowing warmly in a golden sunset. In the vision, I saw myself walking down the aisle towards a man in a long, white robe, his back turned towards me.

As I approached, the man turned to face me. It was Jesus! He reached His hand out to me and said, "Will you be my spiritual bride?"

"Of course," I said, "I want nothing more!"

He turned to face the golden heavenly sunset again, and said, "It's time." Right after He said that a golden chariot arrived, and I hoisted myself inside. The chariot carried me over a golden bridge until we arrived at two enormous doors. As we drew closer, the colossal doors swung open to allow us in.

When I got out of the chariot, I saw many people, all in wedding attire, men in tuxes and women in bridal gowns. They were gathered there, awaiting a wedding banquet, anticipation hanging in the air. At first, I was a bit bashful, feeling undeserving to be there.

I began a slow stroll around the area, relaxing as I took in the striking beauty of the rich scene. I walked delicately over a footbridge and stared dreamily into a river that glistened with light reflecting off gemstones. The air was vibrant and full of life, sweet to my mouth. As I drew in a deep breath, deep peace washed over me. I saw Jesus approaching me on the footbridge. When He stood in front of me, He said, "What do you think?"

Timidly, and with reverence, I said, "It's absolutely stunning and gorgeous." Some part of me felt slightly sad, knowing that there were people who wouldn't make it to Jesus's banquet. "It's just... I want everyone to experience this. How do I help everyone be able to attend the banquet?"

Jesus replied, "Teach my people that I am inside of them." He touched my hands, and I could then see a glowing light inside my palms. I understood He was revealing to me His light that resides inside of me. "It is from My Spirit inside of them that a great banquet of glory and miracles can come."

He said, "Obedience equals glory. It is My will inside of My people that manifests the glory of God, not their will. Unsurrendered vessels cannot hold the glory of God, they are like leaky cisterns that cannot contain holy water."

A cistern is a tank or container that traditionally holds water; our bodies are like cisterns built to hold the glory of God. The wisdom in Jesus's words resounded through the silence, the profundity of what He said rippling through me. The vision ended abruptly, and I found myself back in my body, covered in goosebumps. A blanket of sacredness and peace remained with me for some time afterwards.

Further revelation on this vision came later, as the Holy Spirit helped me understand that the banquet symbolized the partaking of God's glory and the accessing of the full inheritance of God's Kingdom. I realized that there were occasions when I had been ministering to people for healing or miracles, but my actions were not in total alignment with God's will, and the interference of my own will had prevented the full manifestation of God's glory and grace.

From this insight, I gained understanding that if believers fail to fully surrender their vessel to God's will while seeking God's will over their own, they become leaky cisterns incapable of holding the glory of God. If believers can't contain the glory of God within their vessels, they may miss out on the wedding banquet He has set aside for His bride. Therefore, followers of Christ must marry their will to His will in order to become His spiritual bride and feast on His glory.

It is the realization that Jesus is inside us, that releases the light and life of Christ from His dwelling place within us. That is what Jesus was showing me when He touched my hands and I saw His light glowing from inside of me. If we can put our focus on Jesus being inside of us instead of picturing Him outside of us, then we obtain access to the banquet of health, happiness, peace, and goodness from Him within ourselves. When we become more and more aware of His life-giving power within us, then Christ's strength can more easily flow into those whom we lay hands on and minister to.

Mark 16:20 (KJV) says:

"And they went out and preached everywhere, the Lord working with them and confirming the word through the accompanying signs. Amen."

By having and exercising faith in the Word of God and coming to understand that Christ Himself dwells in us, the Lord is able to work from within us to confirm His Word with signs and wonders.

For those who are in need of a miracle or healing, God's message is that we must know the Word of God and recognize it to be the will of God. Once that recognition takes place, the next step is to fully understand that the Spirit of God is indeed within us, and that by surrendering our will to His, He will confirm His Word with signs. To walk in healing and miracles, one must first walk in a surrendered vessel. This is the prerequisite to host the magnificence of God here on Earth and to partake of His glory banquet.

This is the prayer I pray: "Heavenly Father, I surrender my will to Yours, and recognize that Your will is the Word of God. I have faith that Your Word is Your will and align my will with Yours. Lord, manifest Your will in and through me, and confirm what is written. My Lord, I surrender my bodily vessel unto thee as a living sacrifice, that it may hold all of Your radiance."

Romans 12:1 (NIV) says:

"Therefore, I urge you, brothers, in view of God's mercy, to offer your bodies as living sacrifices, holy and pleasing to God—this is your spiritual act of worship."

My hope for all believers is that they boldly offer their body and lives as a living sacrifice, not solely in their mind, but also through their actions. Putting belief in action entails doing what is written in the Word, rather than keeping it hidden away as a mere notion in our minds. In a time such as this, the world desperately needs sons and daughters of the Kingdom of Heaven to walk out their full inheritance of the glory of God.

God is calling His people to unprecedented greatness, for when His people are clothed in His glory, it will lead many souls toward salvation. Will you heed God's calling to walk in the fullness of His glory, to be a representative of the Kingdom of Heaven, and a true son or daughter of light?

18

God's Miracles, Signs, and Wonders

Delighting us with signs, wonders, and miracles is part of God's divine plan. In Acts 2:22 (ESV), Jesus says:

"Unless you see signs and wonders, you will not believe."

While faith alone suffices for some, for others, it takes a sign or miracle to stir belief. God is glorified through His works in His people, and the testimony of His miracles are often just what someone needs to hear in order to turn more fully towards the embrace of God.

One evening while lying in bed, in an in-between state of sleep and wakefulness, I received a vision from God. In the vision, I saw gold being poured over my teeth, filling cavities and the space in my bottom left jaw where a tooth is missing. What I saw filled me with excitement; I interpreted what God had just shown me as a promise of restored teeth.

I had dental problems for much of my life. By the time I was eleven years old, I already had ten cavities. Some of the fillings I received in my youth were toxic mercury fillings that I had removed as an adult. My teeth were prone to cavities, even in adulthood.

I had recently switched dentists. Much to my dismay, my new dentist found nine new cavities. I was so disheartened when I got this news, feeling helpless against the onslaught decay in my teeth. Despite my great oral hygiene efforts and low-sugar diet, I somehow ended up with an exorbitant number of cavities. The dentist I found was a two-hour trip away, and he said that he could only do one filling per visit because of my insurance. That meant nine trips for nine cavities!

In addition to cavities, for the past several years, I had been experiencing excruciating tooth sensitivity. Nothing seemed to help, no matter what sensitive toothpaste or mouthwash I tried. Some days I could hardly eat and sometimes would have to blend my food in order to eat. I desperately needed God's gift of restored teeth. Even if I were to get all the cavities filled, there was nothing the dentist could do about my high level of tooth sensitivity.

Once again, I faced my biggest obstacle: unbelief. I'd heard of dental miracles, but I had never met or spoken with someone who had received one. My faith was not yet strong enough to receive what God was showing me was possible.

For some reason, receiving miracles with my health seemed more conceivable than receiving miracles in my teeth. Teeth are so…solid. I wanted to believe, but ultimately my disbelief was far greater than my faith.

In John 11:40 (KJV), Jesus said:

"Did I not tell you that if you believe, you will see the glory of God?"

When I read that verse, I believed what was written. I knew that unbelief was my greatest obstacle, not faith. I had so much success with God healing my health ailments, why not my teeth as well?

I decided to start by dismantling the lie I believed—that teeth can't be healed. What a lie that is! It is a corrupt lie that prevents us from receiving God's glory in our teeth.

For the first couple months, I challenged myself to become more and more comfortable with the idea of dental miracles. I focused my efforts on tearing down the mental framework that kept me trapped in a matrix of lies around my teeth. To make progress, I needed inspiration, and I required confirmation to stir my faith.

One day, I went on YouTube and searched "dental miracle videos," and lo and behold, there were many! Listening and watching the testimonies, I discovered, was a necessary ingredient for me to grow my faith in dental miracles. The videos and testimonials of people who received miracles captivated me. I found much delight in seeing people joyously and miraculously receive golden fillings and crowns from God.

When one woman received her gold tooth, she became intoxicated under the glory of God's touch, laughing and stumbling, seemingly drunk, while attempting to hold her mouth open to show off her new tooth. The teeth God gave to the people in the videos were beautiful! The gorgeous golden crowns shone brilliantly with God's splendor, the recipients beaming with elation upon receiving such a precious gift from God.

Well, if they can receive a dental miracle, why not me? I reasoned. I felt deeply convinced. I finally felt I had sufficient faith to start praying for my teeth. I prayed constantly for several weeks, working diligently to overcome veiled unbelief.

One night, the Holy Spirit came upon me, rousing me from slumber. I could sense the holy presence surrounding me. My attention shifted toward my teeth, and I concentrated my prayer there. As I prayed, I heard popping sounds in my jaw and gums, as well as sensations in and around my teeth. This continued for some time, and eventually, I drifted back to sleep. When I woke up later, the first thing I did was run to the mirror to see if anything had changed.

When I peered into the mirror at my teeth, I was surprised to see my teeth appeared to be unchanged. *How could that be?* I wondered to myself. I knew that the Spirit of God had certainly come in the middle of the night, and I had sensed supernatural activity in my mouth. I found it challenging to avoid slipping into disappointment and disbelief, still operating under my misconception that the miracle should happen instantaneously, yielding immediate, tangible results.

I fought to maintain my faith, struggling to hold back the impending discouragement. In Mark 11:24 (ESV), it says:

"Therefore I tell you, whatever you ask in prayer, believe that you have received it, and it will be yours."

I didn't want to give up. If other people were receiving dental miracles from Lord Jesus Christ, I desired to be a part of it. So, I returned to my efforts of eliminating disbelief and fortifying my faith.

A month later, I was in prayer with my mother, Teresa. In our sincere praise of the Lord, the Spirit of God fell upon us. As God filled the atmosphere of my little prayer room, we unexpectedly became intoxicated by His presence.

We joined together in prayer, petitioning God for help in several family matters. After a moment of silence, we then said a prayer over my teeth. As prayer was released, my teeth began to chatter uncontrollably.

This must be it! God shakes what He is healing, I thought to myself. I remembered the times that God had healed or touched my body, and how intensely my body shook under God's power. I made an attempt to stay relaxed and receptive, trying to keep from interrupting what was happening.

I perceived a great presence of the Lord in the room, draped over us like a heavy blanket. *This is the perfect atmosphere for miracles*, I thought, *God's glory is upon us.*

When our prayers came to completion, I ran my tongue over my teeth, and it felt smoother in some places. That must be my new gold filling! I thought excitedly. I was pretty sure I had just received the dental miracle that I had been waiting for.

I went to the mirror and peered inside. Much to my disappointment, I saw no change. I felt confused. This was the second time that I felt certain God had done something to heal my teeth, but my teeth seemed unchanged.

At this point, I was unable to hold back my doubt and defeat. After that day, I had to put the idea of teeth miracles out of my mind for a while, until I felt ready to return to it.

During the time I made the petitions for healing for my teeth, I ended up getting four of nine cavities filled by my dentist. When I went in for the fillings, something felt so inherently wrong about the whole dental office scene. I knew God could heal, so why is there such a heavy reliance on doctors and dentists as our primary source of treatment?

I felt deeply unsettled after undergoing the four fillings, so I decided to take a two month break from the dentist's treatment plan. I needed time to attempt to figure out how to utilize God's healing power for my teeth. Every day, I persisted in my efforts to both fortify my faith and eradicate unbelief. After weeks of pounding away at unbelief, once more I felt ready to trust in God's ability to restore my teeth.

Eventually, the doubt I harbored began to dissolve. I developed a practice of keeping my focus on Jesus, maintaining my attention on Him constantly. As I would fix my inner gaze on Him, tremendous love, peace, and overflowing gratitude would arise. I thanked Him over and over again for what He was doing for my teeth. Even if I didn't see results, I believed in them.

As my prayers became more sincere and faith filled, I noticed the pain and discomfort in my teeth began to diminish, which I attributed to the prayers I had been saying for the restoration of enamel on my teeth. In addition to the overall ache of my teeth disappearing, my teeth were no longer sensitive to cold and hot. Interestingly, I hadn't made any changes in my oral hygiene routine or eating habits; it was evident that God was at work in my life.

I found myself able to resume eating items such as chips, which had typically been too painful to eat. Thanks to God's divine intervention, I was finally making progress! Each victory God bestows is reason for celebration, and I am ongoingly amazed how miraculous His ways are when we simply allow Him to work without interference. After I experienced the decrease in pain, the idea of cavities being healed by God's touch became easier to grab ahold of.

As part of the healing process for my teeth, I repented to God for every foul word that ever left my lips, for every time gossip was on my tongue, and for any time my mouth was used in acts of sexual immorality. I repented for using my teeth to eat in ways that weren't good for me, for any time my tongue flicked my teeth in criticism and everything else I could think of where my mouth was used in unholy ways. I rebuked the tooth pain, the cavities, and the missing teeth. I poured my heart out to God, telling Him how I intended to use my mouth for good, for praise, for prayer, to speak His Word and carry His glory in my mouth.

I surrendered. I let go. I said, "God, Thy will be done, on Earth as it is in heaven. Lord, I pray that You may be glorified through the works You do in me, and that with the glory You lay on my teeth, that I may inspire many others and advance the Kingdom of God on Earth." I praised His magnificence, bowed in reverence, and celebrated His goodness.

After the two-month break from the dental treatment plan of my dentist, the day came for me to return for my follow-up appointment. On the drive, I was both anxious and excited about what my dentist would find. When I arrived, I joyfully reported to my dentist that the pain in my teeth had disappeared, sharing that I believed God had healed my teeth. I requested a new X-ray, which, by grace, my dentist agreed to.

The results came in that day, and I am thrilled to report that three out of five remaining cavities were miraculously healed! Woohoo, go, God! The fact that not all five cavities were healed didn't matter much, as I was elated that three were gone. It is with joy that I can now declare that not only is God a great physician, He is also a great dentist!

I left the dental office that day feeling inspired and thankful that my efforts had been greatly rewarded. The following weekend, I found out about a worship concert happening in my local park, so I decided to attend and check it out.

It was a sunny, warm afternoon at the end of summer. As I walked up, I noticed a large crowd of people gathered on the lawn, singing and dancing their praises to the Lord. Banners and bright flags were strewn about, smoke rising from a BBQ nearby. My eyes scanned the scene, and in the distance, I spotted a pop-up tent that immediately caught my attention. I gravitated towards it, squinting to make out the letters on the sign in front of the tent.

The sign read "PRAYER TENT." *Oh perfect*, I thought to myself, *I am going to go over there and ask these prayer warriors to agree with me on healing the rest of my cavities.*

I walked up to the booth and waited until a woman came to greet me. She said, "Would you like prayer?"

"Why yes, I would," I said cheerfully to her. She led me to some chairs at the back of the tent where another man joined us.

"What would you like to pray for?" the man asked.

I replied, "Well, God gave me a vision of restored teeth. I am here because I would like the two of you to agree with me on God healing my missing tooth and cavities."

As I spoke, I held firmly to my faith in God's Word, written in Matthew 18:20 (ESV):

"For where two or three are gathered in my name, there am I among them."

I could tell by the look on their faces that what I was asking for wasn't what they were expecting to hear. After a moment of silence, the man said, "Okay then... let's pray for your teeth." The three of us joined together in prayer, and the moment they began to pray, I felt a whoosh of wind blow over my face, even though it was a still day. Within the gust of wind, I sensed a holy presence.

Just before the breeze came, I heard the man pray for supernatural whitening of my teeth. *Hmm, not what I was asking for, but why not?* They made sure to include in their prayer "the restoration of my teeth." I thanked them and went about enjoying my day at the concert. That evening when I got home and smiled at my husband, he said, "Wow, your teeth look so white."

"What? Really?" I asked incredulously. My husband had no idea where I had been or even that I had received prayer, so I was shocked when this was the first thing he said to me. I hadn't even thought to look in the mirror and check after the prayer earlier that day. I told him I had been at the worship concert, and that someone had prayed whitening over my teeth.

"No way! That is so awesome," he exclaimed. We both praised the Lord for His wondrous demonstration of power and love. For me, it is essential to celebrate every win, even if the miracle you are hoping for shows up differently than anticipated.

A few nights after the miracle, the night after we watched *Christ in You: The Movie*, I was feeling especially convicted of the power of Christ within me. When my husband and I were going to bed, he again commented on the whiteness of my teeth, amazed at what God had done. When he said that, a great boldness arose in me, my faith freshy stirred from watching every day Christians do miracles in the documentary.

"Do you want your teeth whitened too?" I was surprised that it came out of my mouth, but God's Spirit was alive in me.

He paused and thought for a moment, then said, "Okay, why not?" His teeth had been yellowed in certain areas, and I had seen him try different whitening products in the past. I felt strongly that God would do it, not for his vanity, but to increase Gabriel's faith and trust in the Lord's power.

I placed my hand on his face and said, "In the mighty name of Jesus, I release supernatural whitening over your teeth." As soon as the words left my mouth, I instantly saw the result manifest on his teeth. It was as if a wave of power left my lips and flooded over his teeth, turning his teeth several shades whiter. It was the first time I saw something happen instantaneously with the power of God.

"Wow!" I exclaimed. "Your teeth just changed shades right before my eyes!" I blinked a few times, wondering if I imagined it.

He didn't want to look right away, but when he did, he said with surprise, "Wow! They really are whiter! God is amazing!" He couldn't stop smiling.

It seemed like such a silly thing to ask for, but when I consider the value of a growing faith in God, such sweet little miracles can really help build confidence in God's abilities. When Gabriel and I had a radical encounter with the Lord the night he was saved, we both had visions of us serving in ministry. In the vision, we were ministering to huge crowds of people who were falling under the power of the Lord. I felt God's wisdom in the granting of this little miracle of faith because I understood it to be a preparation for greater days ahead.

As believers, we are called to hold the glory of God, yet the obstacle of limiting beliefs often stifles the exercising of faith in action. Though we may not be great miracle workers yet, we can practice stretching our faith with little things, until one day healing cancer or lifting someone out of a wheelchair doesn't feel like as much of a stretch of faith as when we first started exercising our authority as believers.

◊ ◊ ◊

Some months later, Gabriel and I had the honor of experiencing another sign and wonder of God. One night, as we drove home after the Saturday evening service at our church, we became passionately engaged in intercession. There was a young woman in our backseat who had been struggling with deliverance, and we were using the time we had on our drive to pray for her. Our fervent prayers for her lasted the whole forty-five-minute drive to our house.

Just as we pulled up to her vehicle to drop her off, I noticed dozens of shiny specks glistening on the dashboard of my car. I leaned in to study the phenomena. "Look!" I exclaimed, attempting to grasp what my eyes were seeing. "I think it's glory dust."

"No way!" my husband said, beginning to inspect with me. The woman sat in the backseat with her arms crossed, reasonably skeptical. "Yes, for real! Look, it's everywhere!" We turned the car lights on and began to study other surfaces in the car. At first, I thought, maybe some glitter got in here somehow. But how? I hadn't brought any glitter in the car, and there was no logical explanation for it to be so evenly spread across every surface as we were witnessing. I had heard stories of "glory dust" falling in churches, but I had never been privileged to witness such an extraordinary manifestation of God's power.

Not only did we discover "gold dust" on the dashboard, but it was also on the door panels, the center console, the steering wheel, and even in the crevices of the gear shift. After inspecting the car and finding the golden sparkles evenly distributed throughout the front of the car, we were both perplexed and humbled by what had just transpired. Despite the physical manifestation, the woman we had been praying for remained skeptical, suggesting that we must have spilled glitter in the car.

I think I would probably know if I had brought glitter in my car, and meticulously spread it over my entire dashboard, door panels, steering column, and center console area, I thought to myself. The woman had been struggling with her faith, and I felt like this could have easily been a manifestation for her specifically. Yet, she didn't have the openness or eyes to see what was in front of her, suspecting we had set her up or managed to spill glitter everywhere without knowing it. *How many times is God manifesting His glory for me, and I don't have the eyes to see or ears to hear,* I wondered. This was a good lesson and reflection for me.

My son came home a few days later, in addition to a visit with my four-year-old niece and six-year-old nephew, who joined us for a sleepover. My husband and I excitedly shared the story about how we believed God had manifested glory in the form of golden sparkles inside my car. Being the curious children they are, they asked if they could see it. "Sure!" I said.

I hadn't driven my car since the night the gold specks appeared, so I assumed we would still be able to see at least some of it. When we all reached the car, the kids began to inspect all the surfaces. The "glory dust" was still there!

In the daylight, the sparkles took on a new dimension of beauty, and we noticed for the first time that it was not just golden dust, it was also purple and silver! We did our best to collect some samples, but the dust was so fine that it was difficult to capture. When we got back to our living room, the kids said, "We want God to give us glory dust!"

Suddenly, I was overcome with boldness, and said, "God will give us glory dust if we pray for it." Did I really just say that? Just like the night of my husband's teeth whitening, I was surprised by what I said. I didn't feel like I could pray for glory dust on demand; it had just seemingly been a magnificent side effect of a heartfelt prayer we said for a woman in need of ministry and faith.

The kids stared at me expectantly, so I said, "Ok, gather around and join hands. Let's see what God does. If you want to see the glory of God, let's pray harder than we ever have before." I knew God is not a God of tricks and stunts on demand, but I also knew that it is the will of God for those children to come to faith. Not one of them earnestly believed in God or had ever had a personal encounter with Him. Ever since I had been radically encountered by God, it had been a point of contention between my son and I; he did not believe in God.

I began to lead the children in prayer, keeping my focus on God and His will for the children to know Him. I aligned my will with God's will, and pressed in. I thanked the Lord for blessing us in His glory. I urged the kids to pray harder and long to know Him.

After about five minutes of prayer, we thanked God for His presence, for receiving our prayers, and opened our eyes. The kids spotted some sparkles right away. They had them on their pants, shirts, and hands. It was the tiniest amount of sparkle dust, but enough to inspire faith. *Could it be sparkles they picked up from the car?* I pondered.

We discovered a more concentrated pile of sparkles underneath my son's legs, what looked like purple amethyst dust. My heart turned in reverence towards God. Was this just the touch of God that my son needed? After that day, the tension with my son about God and church lessened, coming as great reprieve to our family dynamic. Whether the sparkles were from the car, or new manifestations from God, I cannot say for certain. What I can say is that God touched our family that day.

God's ways are mysterious, and I am just getting to know Him. There's a lot I don't know, but what I do know is that the Creator God of heaven and Earth loves us. He longs to be close to us and wants for us to seek Him. 1 Thessalonians 1:5 (KJV) says:

"For our gospel came not unto you in word only, but also in power, and in the Holy Ghost, and in much assurance."

I am much assured by God's signs, which have brought great comfort and resolve in my journey towards Him.

One of the names of God is Jehovah Jireh, which means "The Lord Will Provide." We are His sons and daughters, and God's promise is that He will provide for us. Romans 8:17 (NIV) says:

"Now if we are children, then we are heirs—heirs of God and co-heirs with Christ, if indeed we share in his sufferings in order that we may also share in his glory."

He is faithful, He is the Provider, and we are co-heirs with Him in the inheritance of His glory.

19

God Is Calling You

One night, as I was lying in bed trying to fall asleep, I became aware of a holy presence in my bedroom. From out of the stillness of the night, I heard a startling ripping sound, followed by a vision of Jesus ripping the veil between heaven and Earth. In my sleepy confusion, I cried out to my husband, "Honey, Jesus just ripped the veil between heaven and Earth!"

He turned slightly, and said, "Hmm, okay dear," then turned over to go back to sleep. For a moment, I thought Jesus was ripping the veil right then and there, but then I thought of Matthew 27:51 (NASB):

"And behold, the veil of the temple was torn in two from top to bottom; and the Earth shook, and the rocks were split."

Before Jesus' death and before the Holy Spirit descended on believers at Pentecost, God's Spirit resided in the Holy of Holies of the Temple. When Jesus died, a physical veil in the Temple was torn in two, symbolizing God's granting of access to His presence through Jesus's sacrifice. When Jesus's flesh was torn, the veil between God and humanity was also torn.

This opened a doorway between heaven and Earth. Hebrews 10:19–22 (NASB) says:

"Therefore, brethren, since we have confidence to enter the holy place by the blood of Jesus, by a new and living way which He inaugurated for us through the veil, that is, His flesh, and since we have a great priest over the house of God..."

Yeshua is calling us to enter the doorway He opened for us; He is calling us to righteousness and a goodness that can only be found in the Kingdom of God. Whether you have already asked Christ into your life, or you are still finding the courage to seek Him, there is a new level of glory and deeper intimacy with Christ that awaits us all.

Hebrews 14:6 (NKJV) says:

"Let us therefore come boldly to the throne of grace, that we may obtain mercy and find grace to help in time of need."

Believers have the authority to walk boldly to the throne of grace and are entitled to receive the resources they need from the storehouse of heaven. Whether you need justice in the courts of heaven, a new body part, or the dispatching of warring angels in difficult cases of deliverance, you have a right as a citizen of heaven to access the unmatchable power of God our Creator.

There is a whirlwind of delusion in this world meant to distract us from finding the way to heavenly realms. Philippians 3:20–21 (NIV) states:

"For our citizenship is in heaven, from which we also eagerly wait for the Savior, the Lord Jesus Christ, who will transform our lowly body so that it may be conformed to His glorious body…"

The fallen ones have constructed an intricate matrix of lies designed to keep humanity from knowing their true inheritance granted through the death and resurrection of Jesus Christ.

For non-believers, the matrix of lies prevents them from knowing that Yeshua is the doorway into the Kingdom of Heaven, not realizing they could be robbed of their chance to enter the realm of heaven. For some believers, the matrix of lies has kept them in fear or doubt of doing what Jesus wants to do through us: spread the Gospel, cast out demons, heal the sick, and raise the dead.

In the church, there exists a religious spirit that often suppresses believers from exercising their full authority in Christ, leaving Christians vulnerable to all sorts of attacks in their health, marriages, finances, and other areas. Jesus's teachings emphasized practical acts of love and service over theological debates. It's easy to get caught up in doctrinal disagreements and miss the call to love our neighbors as ourselves, help sick people recover, and free those oppressed by the devil.

In the Bible, the Pharisees are a great example of how their devotion to God through their religion clouded their hearts and minds and kept them from seeing Jesus for who He is—their long-awaited Messiah. Jesus called his followers to embrace radical change and follow him on a path that often contradicted societal norms. Christ's example encourages us to move beyond comfortable and established religious practices and be open to the challenge of a growing and evolving faith that is Holy Spirit led.

If you are someone who hasn't yet had your come-to-Jesus moment, *why not now*? What better example than Jesus is there to become a better human in a fallen world? Why wouldn't you want an alliance with the strongest force in all heaven and Earth? If you have yet to take that step, let not another day pass by without Yeshua as your personal Lord and Savior. You can simply say, "Jesus, I want to know You. Come dwell inside me. I realize I have not lived according to God's divine laws, and I repent for living in sin. Through Your sacrifice, Jesus, I believe Your blood cleanses me from the wages of sin, which is death. Thank you, Jesus, that I am now under Your divine protection and covering of grace, goodness, and light. Let it be so, Amen."

If you are already saved, *why not ask* Jesus to take you into a greater cycle of glory? God is calling His people to a new level of walking out the authority of Christ. If you are not already doing so, lay your hands on the sick, command illness to leave, and know that the Spirit of the Lord who dwells in you has power and authority over all sickness and disease. If you see someone afflicted by a malevolent spirit, cast out demons in Jesus's name! If a person dies at the hands of the enemy, pray to God, read Scripture on resurrection, and raise the unrightfully dead in the name of Jesus. The world needs to see and experience the power of God, and it is through His disciples, that His glory can be known.

Above all things, seek God unceasingly. It is in Him that we will find all that we seek, not by selfish desire, but through wholehearted surrender. God *is not* a cosmic vending machine; He wants intimacy with us. He wants a relationship.

Coming from the New Age, one of the first things I noticed in the church was a lack of discipline in spending extended time with the Lord. In my previous spiritual practices, one of the ways I became proficient in the spiritual realm was through hours and hours of meditation practice. I used to participate in numerous intensive retreats each year, one where I would meditate from 4 a.m. until 10 p.m. with minimal breaks.

I do not boast as if this is my own doing; rather, I am grateful God set me up to have consistent spiritual habits before He revealed Himself to me. Had I grown up in the church, so much of my story would not have happened, and chances are, I would not spend as much time in prayer and worship.

Why is it that not many Christians I know are seeking God that fervently? I don't hear of or see people in mainstream churches going on silent Christ retreats for eleven days without speaking, as many people involved in the occult do regularly with Vipassana retreats. I believe the church can bring God's people to new levels of glory by putting believers in immersive, intensive experiences like is done in Eastern religions, New Age, and occult practices.

I remember one night in India, I heard a group of people praying and worshiping their god for twelve hours through the night, without ceasing. What if, in addition to the nice compact Sunday service, Christians were challenged regularly to seek God with discipline for prolonged periods of time? What if the same intensity of seeking spiritual experiences that can be found in the New Age and occult could also be found in the bulk of mainstream churches?

My most intense encounters and intimacy with the Lord always came out of periods of extended prayer, worship, fasting and meditating on the Lord. I think there is much room in the church for the development of more serious spiritual discipline in a way that brings greater glory and transformation to God's people. Extended periods of surrender, worship, and fasting within congregations have the potential to advance God's Kingdom on Earth like never before and initiate the next wave of revival.

God's greatest gifts and mysteries are revealed in the stillness of union with Him. The closer we draw to God, the more we can become a fortified vessel of His glory. It's one thing to believe in God and abstain from sin and another to go after Him constantly and continuously lay down your life for Him.

If you have fallen into sin, there is no better time than the present to confess and repent. By doing so, it opens the door for God's mercy and grace to pour over you and heal even your deepest wounds. Acts 2:38 (ESV) says:

"Repent and be baptized every one of you in the name of Jesus Christ for the forgiveness of your sins, and you will receive the gift of the Holy Spirit."

God lovingly receives all who come to Him in humble repentance and have a need for healing.

The enemy seeks out places where our covenant with God has been broken; the dark realm has the right to enter and attack our lives and families when we are in sin. Don't make the mistake of leaving unconfessed, unrepented sin unattended—for when you come face to face with darkness, it will be an opening through which it can enter.

A few months after my husband and I were married, we attended the one-week deliverance conference that my church hosts twice a year, called the Isaiah 61 Conference on Deliverance and Spiritual Warfare. At that point, I had the honor of joining the deliverance team at my church and spent many hours each day helping to set God's people free.

The week was both incredibly insightful and unavoidably intense. My husband was still fighting to get free from demonic strongholds, and his battle manifested physically throughout the conference. It was thrilling to be involved in back-to-back deliverance and helping set people free for many hours, many days in a row, but by the end I was ready for a period of stillness, rest, and rejuvenation.

At the time, my husband's parents were visiting from out of state, and staying at a cabin on Mount Shasta. We had plans to visit them the weekend following the deliverance conference, since it was the only weekend we could do so before they headed back East. Straight from the intense week-long conference, we made the four-hour trek up the mountain to see my in-laws. On the way, I was fantasizing about a nice cozy rest in their cabin in the woods, eagerly anticipating a good night's sleep after many late nights and early mornings that week. Little did I know what lay ahead that evening.

When my husband and I tucked into our room for the night, instinctively I began praying over the room, the bed, and calling in the presence of God. Once I was satisfied with my prayers, we laid down to rest. I quickly drifted off to sleep but was not asleep for long before being abruptly awoken. As my consciousness drifted back into awareness, I discovered with surprise that my body was being used for intercession. I felt as if I were disconnected from my body as my mouth spoke in tongues and my hands made distinct motions through the air without my conscious consent. *What is going on here?* I thought to myself.

Then, from my mouth came forth declarations over the territory in and around Mount Shasta. Words poured out, fervently proclaiming, "I break the power of principalities and rulers of darkness over this region! I call forth the Kingdom of Light and plead the blood of Jesus over every dark altar. I pray against every stronghold in this region, in the name of Jesus!" A strong and holy presence coursed through me, and I could feel the power and impact of my intercessory prayer surge through the atmosphere.

What a strange phenomenon; the Holy Spirit was using my body for intercession while I was asleep, and I had awakened in the midst of it. I had never engaged in intercession over a territory in that manner before, nor would I have thought to wake up in the middle of the night with such concentrated prayers and precise hand motions. I had

303

heard that certain areas or regions have territorial dark rulers assigned to them to cause mayhem but would not of my own accord have considered challenging them. I was way out of league, but I sensed God's holy presence in and around me. Each time I made a declaration and my hand dropped towards the ground; I sensed a shaking in the spirit world. Clearly, something significant was unfolding, and God was using me to do it.

After awhile, I drifted back into sleep. Not more than an hour passed by before I was abruptly awakened once more. I sensed the Holy Spirit influencing my body, again speaking through me, saying, "I command the dispatch of warring angels from the Kingdom of Heaven into this land. I call forth the Kingdom of Light and declare dominion over darkness. I cover this territory in the blood of Jesus and cleanse the forces of darkness and evil from this area." Following these declarations, I continued praying fervently in tongues, until once again I dozed off.

This time, not more than 30 minutes went by before I was roused in the same manner as the first two occasions, guided to persevere with potent intercessory prayers. I sensed a pervasive darkness enveloping the area. In the spirit realm, I became aware of blood sacrifices being made, and of the buzz of witchcraft in the air. It was then I began to realize the gravity of the spiritual warfare I was facing. It must have been about 2 or 3 a.m. at this point, and fatigue was setting in. After exerting myself in prayer and spiritual combat, I finally yielded to the need for rest.

The fourth time I awoke, I was startled to find the room filled with dark entities. As I attempted to pray, I felt an unseen force sealing my lips shut and paralyzing my body. It was an ambush. I found myself surrounded by a horde of heinous spirits. *Busted*, I thought, *I guess they figured out where the inference to their dark agenda for the evening was coming from.* For a moment, fear gripped me, then I thought to myself, *Jesus Christ is my Lord, and He has authority over all heaven and Earth, darkness, and all principalities; what do I have to fear?* God wouldn't use me for such intense intercession and then abandon me with all these sinister spirits.

The moment I remembered my authority in Christ, I screamed Jesus's name silently inside my heart, and instantly, I broke free from the body paralysis. With my lips now free, I yelled, "I rebuke you, Satan!" my arm flailing sideways and hitting my sleeping husband in the face. Amazingly enough, he had stayed asleep during the whole night while I was interceding. I didn't need to provide him with an explanation, because as soon as he opened his eyes, he saw in the spirit realm that hell had broken loose. There, before us stood a powerful group of demonic entities encircling our bed.

With wide eyes, he yelled, "I got this!" and then a rush of tongues erupted from our mouths in unison, unleashing a great burst of light that slammed against the encroaching darkness in our room. I had never heard my husband pray with such fervor before. He began repenting for a multitude of sins from his past. *What an interesting time for a life review of past wrongdoings,* I thought. Yet in the way he was crying out to Jesus, I sensed a deeper surrender, allegiance, and loyalty being established in Gabriel, more than ever before. Nothing like a pack of nightmarish demons to inspire him to get right with God!

At one point in the spiritual battle, I caught sight of Gabriel wrestling around with an entity that had him pinned. Later, when he recounted his experience, he shared, "When I woke up, I saw demons standing around our bed, it being the largest group of dark entities I had ever encountered. The oppressive presence of darkness drove me to seek

Jesus with an intensity I had never felt before, knowing that victory was impossible without the power of Christ. Then, a demon appeared that looked like an evil bear. It meticulously scanned me, looking for an entry point through my sin and transgressions. That's when I started repenting and calling for Jesus."

We learned an important lesson that night; any unrepented sin we carry becomes an open door, leaving us vulnerable to attacks from the Kingdom of Darkness. That night, the Holy Spirit convicted Gabriel of his sins, leading him to repentance. The act of repentance restored his hedge of protection and granted him safety from the onslaught. Repentance is the key to deliverance; if there is no repentance, the door remains open for the enemy to torment even a believer.

The good news is that Jesus is the victor, and He won the battle at the cross 2,000 years ago. If we repent and cover ourselves in the blood of His sacrifice, we are freed from the bondage of darkness. When Gabriel and I stood together in our faith in Yeshua, we were able to overcome some of the most fearsome demons we had ever encountered. (I don't recommend trying this or ever challenging dark rulers or principalities without the guidance and covering of the Holy Spirit. I have since learned how dangerous it can be to contend with principalities of regions. In my next book, I will cover the strategy that the Holy Spirit gave me to gain territory and leverage against principalities without putting yourself at risk.)

The dark rulers of the region of Mt. Shasta were not happy about the intercession the Holy Spirit did through us to break demonic strongholds in their territory. The significance of that night for the Kingdom of Darkness became apparent to me when I realized there were some pertinent details I had overlooked before embarking on my journey. The next morning, it dawned on me that it was Friday the 13th, on the eve of a solar eclipse in Mount Shasta, California, a known epicenter of witchcraft.

Many witches and warlocks hold the belief that Friday the 13th is a day of special power and utilize it as a day for rituals, magic, or sacrifices. Eclipses are also viewed as a time of heightened power, often leveraged by more malevolent witches for the practice of dark magic. Dark magic typically involves using magical practices with malevolent intentions, such as causing harm to others or casting curses. It is said that during eclipses, when both the sun and moon are obscured, dark magic's effectiveness increases due to the thinning of the veil between worlds.

It's no wonder I sensed witchcraft all through the night! I thought to myself. The realization of the significance of the events was a profound confirmation of what I had sensed in the spiritual realm, especially the offering of diabolic blood sacrifices that were defiling the land. After putting it all together, I spent the morning continuing to intercede during the solar eclipse, until the moment light burst forth on the other side.

Whether you realize it or not, there is a Kingdom of Light and a Kingdom of Darkness, and they are at war. This spiritual battle has ensued for centuries and has not yet reached its apex. Both kingdoms are contending for your allegiance. The Kingdom of Darkness operates through a matrix of lies, meant to deceive the uniformed from recognizing its true origin and nature.

My personal journey serves as a testament to this reality. For many years I was deeply entrenched in white witchcraft, mistakenly convinced I was serving the Kingdom of Light. It wasn't until God pulled back the veil that I could grasp the true nature of my involvement. In the lower realm, there are varying degrees of what appears to be light, some seemingly brighter than others, yet all of their power originates from the realm of the fallen ones.

Be cautious not to be deceived into seeking power from the wrong source, as I once was—seek only Yeshua, He is the way into the Kingdom of Heaven, and under His covering, you will find protection. In John 14:6 (NIV), Jesus said:

"I am the way and the truth and the life. No one comes to the Father except through me."

For those of you still contemplating on whether to invite Jesus into your lives, it's essential to recognize that delaying a decision is, in itself a choice. If you are already walking with Yeshua as your Lord, be vigilant not to let worldly matters take precedence over your relationship with God. Strive for obedience and follow Jesus's teachings, not religious customs. Nothing from this world will go with you when you leave, but the Kingdom of God is eternal.

God is calling us into deeper intimacy with Him. True glory is found in surrendering to Him and laying down our lives for His purpose. Instead of getting lost in entertainment, scrolling through social media, or frequenting social gatherings, set aside time to study the Word of God and seek Him in hours-long sessions. It's one thing to talk about the teachings of Yeshua, but it's another to walk them out. This world needs more people on fire for God; create the time necessary to be still and attune yourself to His guidance.

A week after my vision of Jesus's banquet, during prayer in my prophetic class, the Lord blessed me with another revelation. In it, I beheld the Spirit of God contained within a large cloud. The cloud that was filled with the Spirit of God then blew a storm over the nations. I watched anxiously as the foreboding storm descended over the entire Earth. *Oh no*, I thought, *this isn't good.* Heavy rains swept over the land. Then, the Holy Spirit reassured me, helping me to understand that these rains were holy waters sent from the storm of God, intended to sanctify the lands of the Earth.

From the rainfall of God's storm, I witnessed the birth of new life and the emergence of fresh vegetation. Then God said, "The destruction of the storm is necessary for cleansing, and it will bring new life and growth." I sat in silent contemplation, allowing the profound vision to soak in.

God brought to mind the vision from the previous week, when Jesus had said, "Tell my people that I am inside of them," and then proceeded to reveal His light within my hands.

God spoke then, saying, "Tell my people that I want them to be lampstands in the storm, that I am the Light and I will fill them. I will fill them with an oil that won't burn out. Nor will the wind be able to tip the lampstand of My people. These lampstands will be a light unto the world during the great storm, a place of refuge and warmth, when the Earth is in darkness."

God is calling you to be a lampstand onto this world, at this very moment in time. Matthew 5:14–16 (NKJV) says:

"A city that is set on a hill cannot be hidden. Nor do they light a lamp and put it under a basket, but on a lampstand, and it gives light to all who are in the house. Let your light so shine before men, that they may see your good works and glorify your Father in heaven."

To become a usable lampstand, one must surrender to the Lord and present oneself as a living sacrifice. Unsurrendered vessels are incapable of containing the full radiance and wonder of God that we are meant to bear. In Revelation 2:5 (NKJV) God says:

"Remember therefore from where you have fallen, and repent and do the first works; or else I am coming to you swiftly, and will move your lampstand out of its place, unless you repent."

Then Mark 1:15 (NKJV) says:

"The time is fulfilled, and the Kingdom of God is at hand; repent and believe in the gospel."

God is inviting us to wear the cloak of His glory, to be covered in His goodness. Joel 2:28–29 (KJV) says:

"And it shall come to pass afterward, that I will pour out my spirit upon all flesh; and your sons and your daughters shall prophesy, your old men shall dream dreams, your young men shall see visions."

By shifting our focus away from the world and directing our attention on God, we become co-heirs with Christ, entitled to share in the glory and riches of the Kingdom of Heaven. When we surrender ourselves to God, He pours out His Spirit, enabling the Holy Spirit to exhibit the power of God that confirms His Word. May God help us all to properly discern the deceptions of the matrix of lies and religious barriers that can prevent us from claiming our full inheritance through Christ.

Let's rejoice in the goodness of God and proclaim the message of salvation and liberation from the bondage of darkness to all people. 1 Chronicles 16:23–25 (ESV) says:

"Sing to the Lord, all the earth! Tell of his salvation from day to day. Declare his glory among the nations, his marvelous works among all the peoples! For great is the Lord, and greatly to be praised, and he is to be feared above all gods."

God is gathering His sheep unto Himself to build a great and mighty army of righteous ones. Here are several attributes that characterize the prophesied end-time army of the Lord:

✝ John 3:30 – They will be surrendered vessels

✝ Psalm 110:3 – They will offer themselves willingly

✝ Isaiah 60:1 – They will usher in the glory of the Lord

✝ Isaiah 60:2 – The glory of the Lord will appear on them

✝ Matthew 21:21 – They will move mountains with faith

✝ Luke 9:1 – They will drive out demons and cure diseases

✝ Psalm 104:4 – They are ministers of flaming fire

✝ Matthew 24:14 – They will preach the Gospel

✝ Mark 16:20 – Signs, wonders, and miracles will confirm their preaching

✝ Matthew 22:37 – They will love God with all of their hearts

✝ Matthew 22:39 – They shall love all people

✝ Joel 2:7–8 – They will work in unity

Will you be a lampstand unto the nations? Will you accept God's invitation to be a representative of the Kingdom of Heaven? Will you carry the illuminating light of

Christ within you and step into your full inheritance as a beloved child of the Most High? Will you place your faith in God, *without limits?*

God is summoning *you*. This book is more than just a story; it is a revolution, a call to your spirit, a call to action. Will you heed the call to serve the Kingdom of Light in a world shrouded in darkness?

Afterword

As with most things in life, this book has come to an end, yet God's Kingdom remains eternal. Thank you for journeying through my story and bearing witness to what God has asked me to share. If you have enjoyed this book, you may be pleased to know that God has revealed to me that there will be a sequel.

If this book has inspired transformation in your life and you wish to share, I would love to hear your story. You can send your story or testimony to godwithoutlimitsbook@gmail.com, and please include "GWL Book Testimony" in the subject line.

If my story has uplifted you, I encourage you to share it with someone you believe could also benefit. Through God's grace, this book has come into existence, and I have faith in its ability to guide lost souls to salvation and elevate the oppressed, leading them towards a new era of glory.

In the concluding pages of this book, you'll find a simple deliverance prayer for those in search of freedom, along with references to the resources mentioned throughout the story. Additionally, there are links to other valuable resources for healing and deliverance.

Deliverance Prayer

Here's a deliverance prayer for anyone seeking freedom from bondage. Deliverance from certain strongholds can happen instantaneously in some cases, while for others, it's a gradual journey. Personally, I view deliverance as an ongoing process. Whenever we align with anything contrary to God, we risk inviting demonic affliction into our lives.

I realize that there are differing opinions, but I believe that even Christians can experience affliction from demons. With Jesus's assistance, I have personally aided in delivering many Christians from the grip of malevolent spirits. Just one open door is enough for a demon to gain a foothold, and the world can be a deceiving place.

There are numerous methods of deliverance, and I encourage you to discover what works best for you. One powerful way to ward off demons is to praise God with all of your heart and soul and focus on the light of Christ within you. In my quest towards freedom, I discovered that the deeper my understanding of my identity in Christ, and the more intensely I praised God, the more rapidly demons fled from my presence.

Be sure to speak the words of this prayer aloud. This prayer can be recited alone, or ideally with a fellow believer to stand alongside you in agreement.

WARNING: It is better to wait to say this deliverance prayer until you are ready to invite Jesus of Nazareth the Messiah as your Lord. If demons or evil spirits are expelled and you're not yet saved, they may return stronger. Having the hedge of protection from faith in Jesus is essential to fill the void left by the departure of evil spirits from within you.

Deliverance Prayer

Lord Jesus, my soul cries out to You. I long for You. I accept You as my beloved Lord and Savior. God, I welcome Your Spirit to fill my heart and soul. Holy Spirit, touch me with healing grace. Cleanse me with Your presence.

If there is anyone or situation in my life that I have not forgiven, Lord, I take this opportunity to forgive all who may have knowingly or unknowingly trespassed against me. I forgive every person who has ever harmed me. Your forgiveness empowers me to forgive others, and any unforgiveness in my heart is a doorway for darkness to enter. I now close that doorway to darkness by forgiving all people and situations in my life, including myself.

In the name of Jesus Christ, I now take authority over every demon in or around me and my home. I command any demon, any leviathan, any serpent spirit, any scorpion, or snake spirit to leave now in the name of Jesus! I release the cleansing fire of God into my body and home. (Imagine Jesus inside of you as you release these commands.)

Lord, I stand on Your Word, knowing that in Luke 10:19, You said, "I have given you authority to trample on snakes and scorpions and to overcome all the power of the enemy; nothing will harm you."

Beloved God, I come into agreement with the power and authority You have given me to trample on snakes and scorpions, and by the blood of Jesus, I command every unclean and unholy spirit to leave me. Leave now!

ALL unclean, unholy spirits, leviathan, demons, succubus, incubus, and mind control spirits, leave now by the authority of the name given in Jesus Christ of Nazareth! You must YIELD to the name of Yeshua, beloved Son of

God, for He holds ALL authority and dominion in this world. (Focus on the truth of your authority in Christ.)

I release the Kingdom of Light, the Kingdom of God, the Kingdom of Heaven, the power of God Almighty over me and my home. Thy Kingdom come Lord, Thy will be done in me and my home, as it is in heaven. Lord, I ask You to take spiritual authority over my life, my home, and my family.

I command every spirit of anger, frustration, sadness, grief, misery, impatience, loneliness, despair, hopelessness, suicide, death, confusion, rejection, depression, torment, doubt, unbelief, guilt, and shame to leave me, NOW!

All spirits of leviathan, of evil, of witchcraft, of sorcery, voodoo spirits, fortune telling spirits, spirits of astrology, clairvoyance, and demons of necromancy, I renounce you and break you off of me and my life, in Jesus's name! I command you to leave my body, my mind, and my life. All occultic demons, you are evicted! By the blood of Jesus, I am now set free.

All spirits of pain, spirits of affliction, spirits of infirmity, spirits of death, spirits of torment, symptoms of disease, I rebuke you, leave in Jesus's name! Sickness, I command you out of my body. (See Christ inside you, glowing in His light, restoring your body and mind from the inside out.)

In the name of Jesus, I break all hexes, all curses against me, my family, and my home. I plead the blood of Jesus, over my bloodline. I plead the blood of the lamb, over every doorway and window of my home. I draw a bloodline of Christ's blood around the perimeter of my house and cast all demonic presences out. I drive the enemy out of my camp, now! Fire from God against enemies in my camp! Holy Fire, now! Satan, I rebuke you! You leave me and my home, in Jesus's name. (Take deep breaths, pushing out any heaviness.)

Demons of false religion, of false Holy Spirit, I command you up and out of my body, you leave me now in Jesus's name. Demons of eastern religions, leave now! I command spirits of Eastern religions to come out of me right now. I demand all the demons of Buddhism and Hinduism, demons that entered through transcendental meditation, the Kundalini spirit, Yogic spirits, Tantra spirits, Krishna spirits, Christian Science demons, Mormon demons, demons of Catholicism, and Scientology demons to get out! Leave my body now!

Thank you, Jesus, for dispatching warring angels of God on my behalf. At the command of Jesus, I release angels of warfare into my home and family and ask God, the judge of all, to execute judgment on every foul spirit in my domain.

Nightmare demons, fear of the dark demons, get out! Night terror demons, come out of me and my home! Demons of anxiety, leave me now! Fear, go! Paranoia and schizophrenia spirits, get out in Jesus's name. Spirit of insanity, dementia spirits, go! I command you by the authority of the blood of Jesus Christ, move out right now!

Thank you, Father God, for releasing the Holy Spirit's fire. I command the release of fiery arrows from heaven against every demon in or around me and my home, in Jesus's name. Fire, holy fire, against every spirit of darkness in or around me!

All spirits of wrath, hatred, bitterness, rage, animosity, all demons of anger, frustration, irritability, and violence, leave in the Holy Name of Jesus! Lord, I repent for the ways I have come into agreement with anger, irritability, and rage, and I renounce it now. I renounce frustration. I permanently close the door to rage by inviting the love of Christ to dwell in my heart. Come into my heart, Jesus, come. God, let that righteousness reign in me.

All spirits of perversion, of pornography, molestation spirits, spirits of sexual immorality, sex addiction, and spirit of Pan, I command you to leave me by the blood of Jesus! I repent for any and all sexual immorality and command all demons to leave now. I ask the Holy Spirit for cleansing of my memories, experiences, and transgressions, that I might be cleansed and sanctified by the Lord's grace.

In the name of Jesus Christ, I come against every spirit of addiction, addiction to food, addiction to nicotine, addiction to sex, phone addiction, addiction to drugs, alcohol, marijuana, meth, ecstasy, oxy, diet pills, pain pills, cocaine, and video games, in the name of Jesus! Come out! I repent for damaging my vessel with any drug or alcohol use and ask that the blood of Jesus cleanse and restore any negative side effects.

In the name of Jesus Christ, I declare that I am delivered from the Kingdom of Darkness right now! I pledge my allegiance to the Kingdom of Heaven, the Kingdom of Light, and Jesus Christ. I now surrender my vessel to Yeshua, to God Almighty, to serve as a holy instrument in God's Kingdom.

I release life and light from Jesus into every cell of my body, into every part of my mind, into every hidden place of my spirit. I release the resurrection power into every part of me that has been wounded by the enemy. (Draw in several deep breaths while visualizing Jesus's light inside you growing brighter). I seal every demonic doorway shut with the blood of Jesus.

I call forth to enter me and my home, the God of all creation. I call upon the names of God, El Elyon, God of the Most High! Jehovah Rapha, the Lord that Heals. Elohim,

Supreme and Mighty One! Yahweh, my Lord. Abba, Father! El Shaddai, God Almighty. El Olam, the Everlasting God. I dedicate my body, my home, and my life to the Lord, and the name above all names, Yeshua of Nazareth! Come, come in a tsunami of grace and glory, come wash over me, Holy Spirit.

I thank You Lord God, for Your mercy, for Your grace, for Your protection. Thank You for completely restoring me mentally, physically, emotionally, and spiritually. The Spirit of God within me, is now restoring, refreshing, and revitalizing me. I release the light and life of Christ into every part of me. Thank you, Yeshua.

I ask you Father, that my fiery hedge of protection is reinforced. Thank You for making me whole again, for stirring my destiny, and making me a mighty man or woman of God! Amen!

Please Note: If you have been involved with the New Age, occult, used chakra systems, done yoga, or been involved with witchcraft, deeper deliverance may be required. Please refer to the resource section for the "Prayer for Repentance of Kundalini" and complete the full renunciation. This prayer is essential for anyone involved in New Age practices.

Resources

Additional resources can be found on my website at: http://GodWithoutLimitsMinistry.com

Additional copies of this book can be purchased on Amazon.com. If this book has touched you, please share the message with someone else.

▶ MUST WATCH VIDEOS

God Wants You Well Series by **Andrew Wommack**

Series of 22 free videos on how to take authority and heal sicknesses.

https://www.youtube.com/watch?v=XwKLXl9dYgk&list=PLOER0yhdOW6Di5bw3hJ7qxvm52CDgkaLL

Description: Learn how to walk confidently in the health and healing that God has already provided for you and see your way of thinking about pain and sickness radically transformed.

Signs and Wonders: 2 Hours of Prayer and Intercession

Powerful fire prayers for signs and wonder.

https://www.youtube.com/watch?v=ZDiyoSTUTW0&t=2654s

Description: Stephen A Garner Ministries leads through 2 hours of potent prayers for signs and wonders. For the best results, pray along!

Vlad Savchuk Deliverance Session

"Prayer of Deliverance from Occult, Fear, Wrath, and Addiction"

https://www.youtube.com/watch?v=n-p_8M4cj9M

Description: Here is a powerful prayer of deliverance! If you or someone you know needs deliverance, they have to watch this!

Contending in the Courts of Heaven by James K.

Guided instruction on Courts of Heaven

https://www.youtube.com/watch?v=N1Qu-sRINPY&t=4491s

Description: Follow along with James Kalawya as he leads you into the courts of heaven and teaches you how to use the courts for tough cases of deliverance.

Courts of Heaven by Robert Henderson

Incredible series on The Courts of Heaven.

https://www.youtube.com/watch?v=A-MANcuJwVo

Description: Super insightful information on how to use the Courts of Heaven as believers.

8 Steps to Self-Deliverance by Vlad Savchuk

Excellent follow along process for self-deliverance.

https://www.youtube.com/watch?v=mm0842iyFNg&t=283s

Description: These 8 steps to self-deliverance are very helpful in getting free from demonic strongholds and afflicting spirits.

DELIVERANCE From Serpents, Witchcraft, & Idolatry by Katie Souza

https://www.youtube.com/watch?v=elAWKjEjJ2E

Description: GET DELIVERANCE from serpents, witchcraft, and idolatry, along with the audience.

Deeper Deliverance with Alex Pagani

https://www.youtube.com/watch?v=EQaBMs6KloU

Description: Apostle Alexander Pagani shares a message about the depths of deliverance and how you can dive deeper into your own personal deliverance.

Isaiah Saldivar Podcast (Ep. 140)

Richard Lorenzo Ex Warlock on Satan's Agenda
https://www.youtube.com/live/gQxV5M5AwxM?feature=sh are

Description: Pastor Rich was once a drug lord, a womanizer, and a warlock working with voodoo and Santeria. He had even described himself as an apostle of the devil. He had the money, women, and life experiences that many chase today for fulfillment. You have to hear what happened when Jesus revealed Himself to Rich and took him from being a warlock to now a senior pastor.

Alexander Pagani on Witchcraft

Informative video on witchcraft in church.

https://www.youtube.com/live/fz9k8cOhHJ0?feature=share

Description: Great insight in this video on witchcraft strongholds.

 WEBSITES

Andrew Wommack

God Wants You Well Resources

www.AWMI.net

Curry Blake

Amazing resource for healing in the authority of Christ: DHT: Divine Healing Technician Training Course.

https://www.divinerevelations.info/documents/healing/jgl/jgl_ministries.htm

Pastor Vlad

Amazing resources for healing, deliverance, and Holy Spirit encounters.

https://pastorvlad.org/

"Prayer for Repentance of Kundalini"

Adapted by Diane Hawkins from "The Serpent and the Tree of Knowledge" by Amanda Buys of Kanaan Ministries. A 40-page renunciation for New Age and Occultism, severing of serpent power, and closing of gateways.

https://www.rcm-usa.org/PDF%20Files/Kundalini%20Renunciation_July-2018.pdf

Church of Glad Tidings

Extensive archive that includes lots of resources on deliverance.

https://churchofgladtidings.com/livestream-archive

 RECOMMENDED READING

Treasures of Darkness III Part 1: Foundations of a Transcendent Life by Joseph C Sturgeon II

https://www.amazon.com/Treasures-Darkness-III-Part-Transcendent/dp/0620786949

Description: Foundations of A Transcendent Life covers such aspects as accessing the overshadowing presence, abiding intimacy, the capacity to receive love, and positioning yourself in the presence of God. This book lays a practical foundation for the interworking of God's interaction with humanity in order to bring our hearts into perfect alignment with His.

The Serpent and the Savior

By Dave Bryan

https://churchofgladtidings.com/store/the-serpent-and-the-savior

Description: The Serpent and the Savior is Dave and Cheryl Bryan's dramatic and controversial eyewitness account of one woman's rescue from the macabre maze of satanic ritual abuse and the Crowleyan "Rituals of Defilement" into "the glorious liberty of the children of God!"

Fire Prayers

By John Ramirez

https://www.amazon.com/Fire-Prayers-Building-Arsenals-Kingdoms/dp/163641155X/

Description: Fire Prayers will equip you with a spiritual warfare arsenal that will leave Satan and his kingdom trembling and unable to manipulate, control, or dominate you; hinder your relationship with Jesus; or thwart your destiny.

Demon Hit List

By John Eckhardt

https://www.amazon.com/Demon-Hit-List-John-Eckhardt/dp/1629117900

Description: This is an excellent deliverance thesaurus to help believers know the specific names and attributes of demons so they can become more successful in casting them out.

You've Already Got It! {So Stop Trying to get it}

By Andrew Wommack

https://www.amazon.com/Demon-Hit-List-John-Eckhardt/dp/1629117900

Description: If you are in need of healing, this is the book for you! Andrew teaches us how to receive the blessing, deliverance, healing, and prosperity that God has already given us. If you've prayed and tried to get well but haven't found healing, this book will help you develop a fresh perspective on how to obtain God's promised healing.

MOVIES

Come Out in Jesus Name

https://www.imdb.com/title/tt27002406/

Description: Following a startling chain of events, the most controversial pastor in America, Greg Locke, took a 180-degree turn from his mainstream religious traditions and led his church into full blown revival. He and a diverse group of unconventional preachers then began to spark the most important awakening in the history of the Christian Church through the most unlikely means—by casting out demons.

Christ in You: The Movie

https://www.imdb.com/title/tt6872310/

Description: We owe the world an encounter with God. This movie features a fascinating discovery and a hard look at what holds us back from bringing hope, healing, and deliverance to our environment. Amazing interviews from the heroes of the faith of today and on the street demonstrations by ordinary Christians will teach you how you can step out, overcome your fear, and use your God-

given gift to change the lives of the people around you. *Christ in You: The Movie* presents an inspiring and challenging vision that could change the course of world history.

LOCATION

Glad Tidings Church

Yuba City and Grass Valley, CA

https://churchofgladtidings.com/

Description: Spirit-filled inter-denominational Pentecostal church that teaches deliverance, the supernatural, and many other amazing topics. The Spirit of God moves in this church in miraculous ways. Join for the online streams, or the annual Isaiah 61 conference on Spiritual Warfare & Deliverance by Pastor Dave Bryan.

About the Author

Bri Griffen-Moss is a dedicated follower of Christ, as well as a loving mother and devoted wife who has recently embarked on a new journey as a self-published author. Her mission is to reach the hearts and souls of those trapped in unknown bondage. After her first encounter with the Holy Spirit, she made the decision to leave behind a decade-long career as a practitioner in the healing arts and New Age Spirituality to embrace a new path—following Christ.

Her book marks the beginning of a series detailing her extraordinary encounters with God and His miraculous nature. In place of the practices she left, she now offers prayer, deliverance, and counsel to those seeking to cultivate a relationship with the Holy Spirit and Yeshua. She joined the deliverance ministry at her church and has plans to travel as a guest speaker and share the insights she has learned through her spiritual journey. She has initiated an online ministry called "God Without Limits" that provides content and resources on topics covered in her book.

For those who desire to connect with Bri, please send all questions, comments, reflections, or testimonies to: godwithoutlimitsbook@gmail.com. For interview requests for podcasts, talk shows, or social media channels, you can find a contact form on her website.

To stay updated on new book releases, upcoming events, and more, sign up for her mailing list on her website. If you are interested in inviting Bri Griffen-Moss and her husband Gabriel Moss to travel to you to share on topics covered in this book, to offer their ministry services, be a part of workshops or retreats, you can utilize the contact form found on her website.

Stay Connected to God Without Limits Ministry:

GWL Website: https://GodWithoutLimitsMinistry.com

Facebook: https://www.facebook.com/GodWithoutLimitsMinistry

YouTube: https://www.youtube.com/@GodWithoutLimitsMinistry

Twitter: https://twitter.com/BriGriffen

TikTok: https://www.tiktok.com/@brigriffenmoss

Instagram: https://www.instagram.com/bri.griffen.moss

GWL Bookstore: https://thehealingservicebybri.com/books/

Acknowledgments

To God…

Who asked me to write this book and breathed it to life through my devotion. Whose very Spirit and essence enliven every page and every word. Who carried me every step of the way, giving me strength, resilience, and endurance to see it to the end.

To my beloved husband, Gabriel…

Your support, love, and belief in me have been an essential part of the completion of this book. Your patience and understanding through endless hours of writing has made the long journey to publishing more enjoyable.

To my mother, Teresa…

For your unwavering compassion, understanding, and support as my mother. For never giving up on me and praying me into redemption. Your strength and grace have shaped my life and this journey in ways words can scarcely capture.

To my son, Takoda…

For all your patience, as I wrote this book. Your support and understanding in allowing me the time to pursue what God called me to do has been invaluable.

To Cheryl Bryan…

You have been an amazing mentor and are a cherished friend who has shown me the true essence of love and surrender to Christ. Your guidance has been a light on my path, illuminating the way with grace and wisdom.

To Tina King...

Thank you for your steadfast pursuit of God and for extending your steady hand as I navigated my escape from the matrix of lies. Your strength and devotion have been a guiding force in my spiritual journey.

To Kathy Hurlin...

I am grateful for your many years of friendship. Thank you for opening the door to my redemption and being a steadfast alliance in my spiritual journey.

To Deanne Hansen...

Thank you for being a true friend in Christ when I needed it the most. Thank you for believing in me and supporting me with Holy Spirit-led wisdom. Your friendship has been a source of comfort and strength in this journey.

To Pastor Dave Bryan...

An incredible force for God in a world desperately needing leaders like you. You have shown the light of Christ and provided a spiritual haven for many, including me. Thank you for believing in me, loving me, and giving me a place to call my spiritual home.

To Lee Baker...

For being the person who inspired the three-hour prayer that changed the course of my life. For creating space and sharing the wisdom that has helped me learn to grow and move in the prophetic.

To Jess Parker...

For your mentorship in the art of deliverance and fighting with me for the freedom I had yet to gain. I am grateful for your wisdom and support.

To Peggy...

Thank you for your wisdom, generosity, and grace in discovering the deeper levels of deliverance I needed; for being a friend and ally in the Kingdom.

To the Church of Glad Tidings...

For creating a sanctuary of God's presence that set me free from a lifetime of bondage. For every person that raised their hand in prayer and fought for me when I was weak. For giving me hope and showing me the love of Christ. This community has been a beacon of hope and transformation for my life.

...And for all the hands who have helped me along the way.

Colophon

This book, *God Without Limits: Escape from the Matrix of Lies*, was carefully crafted to bring the author's vision to life. The first edition was published in 2024.

Book Design

The cover of this book was designed by Veniamin Mykhalynchuk from Spain, whose patience, skill, and dedication brought the book cover to life. His expertise in design excellently captured the book's theme of escaping limitations and discovering truth in God.

Editing

Developmental Editor: Liz Jose

Whose dedication and keen insight and support in refining the content and ensuring clarity and was monumental in the early stages of development of this book.

Contact: justin.liz.jose@gmail.com

Line Edit and Formatting Editor: George Verongos

Whose incredible eye for detail, precision and unparalleled writing skills made this book much more enjoyable to read.

Contact: www.LiteraryServices.net

Proof-Reading Editor: Mary Tice

Whose friendship, support and perceptiveness put the final touches on this great story. Thank you for being my dear friend in Christ.

Publisher

Published by Amazon Kindle Direct Publishing, enabling a wide and accessible distribution, reflecting the book's aim to reach and inspire a diverse audience.

ISBN

The International Standard Book Number for this edition is 979-8-218-26537-3.

The making of this book has been a journey of passion, dedication, and collaboration. More than anything it has been my surrender to God. Every element has been chosen to enhance the reader's experience and to faithfully convey the powerful message within.

www.ingramcontent.com/pod-product-compliance
Lightning Source LLC
Chambersburg PA
CBHW062321120626
46553CB00015B/120